The International Library of Sociology

STUDIES IN
ECONOMIC DEVELOPMENT

Founded by KARL MANNHEIM

The International Library of Sociology

ECONOMICS AND SOCIETY
In 11 Volumes

STUDIES IN ECONOMIC DEVELOPMENT

With special reference to Conditions
in the Underdeveloped Areas
of Western Asia and India

by
ALFRED BONNÉ

ROUTLEDGE

First published in 1957 by
Routledge

Reprinted in 1998 by
Routledge
2 Park Square, Milton Park, Abingdon, Oxon, OX14 4RN
or
270 Madison Avenue, New York, NY 10016

First issued in paperback 2010

British Library Cataloguing in Publication Data
A CIP catalogue record for this book
is available from the British Library

Studies in Economic Development
ISBN 978–0–415–17534–0 (hbk)
ISBN 978–0–415–60521–2 (pbk)
Economics and Society: 11 Volumes
ISBN 978–0–415–17819–8
The International Library of Sociology: 274 Volumes
ISBN 978–0–415–17838–9

Publisher's Note
The publisher has gone to great lengths to ensure the quality of this
reprint but points out that some imperfections in the original
may be apparent

CONTENTS

PART ONE

MEASURE AND CHALLENGE OF INEQUALITY

PART TWO

THE MOVE TOWARDS ADJUSTMENT

CONTENTS

APPENDICES

INTRODUCTION

SINCE the end of the First World War our ideas on the desirable political and economic relations between the nations and communities of the world have been deeply affected by the events on the social and political plane which, for three decades, stirred up the Old World in a nearly ceaseless sequel. Many established patterns of thought and behaviour in international affairs have not survived the test of this crucial period. Classification of the countries of the globe by political and social criteria as used a few decades ago has become out-dated.

The drive for the political liberation of subjugated peoples and nations, which gave direction and content to an important segment of international relations during the first half of this century, has been extended to a new area: rights to economic and social equality, or at least to adjustment of the profound differences between the various living standards of the human race, have been added to the older demands. Political equality only a short time ago highly coveted, means little, when the share in economic and social benefits which modern civilisation can offer remains as appallingly inequal as before.

Such a demand for the economic and social adjustment of nations and regions is a formidable goal. It implies a huge transformation of human and material conditions within national boundaries and beyond them. It requires a new orientation of national and international policies which will have to rely much more than before on the findings and recommendations of science and arts. It raises problems of a magnitude which defy all but the most determined attempts at solution.

The first industrial revolution came to a world which accepted the division of society and nations by political status and possessions as a dictum of fate. The new political credos which grew out of the turmoil of the first half of this century and were strengthened by the formidable potential of the second industrial revolution bear the marks of an activism which was absent in earlier periods; these credos direct pressure against the inequalities of human society and

vii

endeavour to make the benefits of modern civilisation available to all. The advance of underdeveloped societies throughout the world has thus become the central economic issue of the second half of this century.

The question arises: in what way can the social scientist cope with this subject? His task is twofold: he has first to survey conditions in underdeveloped countries, to become acquainted with existing facts and trends, to analyse them from the viewpoint of whether and how an improvement is possible. His second task is then to use his findings in the formulation of development policies. The elaboration of such findings and policies requires, as he will soon discover, an exceptional command of sources and methods which is much beyond the scope of an individual effort. Thus social scientists who work on these problems on a broader scale increasingly feel the inadequacy of any single-handed attempt made in this field. Nearly all recent surveys of existing conditions in given areas and their analysis have been the result of teamwork of specialists well supported by national and international agencies. Individual writers cannot compete with these group efforts. In addition, the material itself is frequently not available or freely accessible to the individual author; nor can he organise detailed investigations over a wide range of subjects, or organise joint discussions of the issues in the way teams are able to employ collective efforts. Still, many though the shortcomings may be in an individual contribution, it may also have certain advantages. An individual attempt is, as a rule, less hampered in the expression of views than the work of official or semi-official bodies. The treatment of a wider range of subjects increases—simultaneously with the danger of spreading over less familiar ground—the perspective, the absence of which is sometimes felt in the more specialised official studies. The opportunity which I have had over many years to learn about the problems of many underdeveloped countries on the spot and to obtain an immediate sense of the prevailing conditions has probably induced me to persist in an effort which for the reasons mentioned will be inadequate in other respects.

Over a long period, I have consistently expressed my belief in the development capacity of important underdeveloped regions, where such potentialities do exist largely as untapped human and material resources. I certainly maintain these views now when a more dynamic approach to these issues has become generally accepted. This adherence to an expansionist school is, I feel, compatible with a critical evaluation of the new experience and facts which are constantly added to our knowledge and of the sometimes exaggerated claims based on them.

The present treatise is basically an empirical study. The analysis

INTRODUCTION

of the new trends of thought on economic development at the end of this volume does not and cannot aim at a full discussion of its theoretical aspects: it is my hope to resume work on this subject when more data are available and permit an appraisal of results of major development activities in important countries.

The area dealt with in this book lies chiefly in Asia. The treatment leans heavily towards those regions in Asia with which the author has become more closely acquainted than with others—namely, the Middle East and India. Though this might appear to be a somewhat incidental motive of delimitation, it is not the case. The regions of the ancient Orient from the Eastern Mediterranean to the Ganges share important features in human and physical landscape: the impact of ancient and medieval civilisations on present-day society is felt here more than in other parts of the world. The dry climate creates the necessity of irrigated agriculture, which profoundly influences labour–land and capital–output ratios. Pace and rates of population growth show a similarity throughout the region which tempts the student towards generalisations. Though these marks point to the existence of certain patterns of development specific to the regions dealt with, it is hoped that the conclusions may be of relevance also to other underdeveloped areas.

I wish to express my gratitude to the colleagues and friends who readily offered advice for the improvement of the book.

In particular I owe thanks to Professors W. A. Lewis, H. S. Frankel, G. Myrdal, A. Lowe and H. Bloch, Dr. A. Morag and H. Smith for their readiness to go over the whole or part of the manuscript and to provide me with helpful suggestions. My thanks are also due to my former assistants Ephraim Ahiram and Elieser Sheffer for their help in the preparation of part of the statistical data. Needless to say that I am alone responsible for any mistakes and faults which may be found in the text.

I am much indebted to Mrs. Judith Shorr for her contribution to the readability of the style and to Mrs. Aliza Argov for her devoted work in the preparation of the typescript. Finally I wish to thank the Editors of *Annals of the American Academy of Political and Social Science*, and *Kyklos* respectively, for permitting the inclusion of the chapters 'The Role of the Incentive' and 'Towards a Theory of Implanted Economic Development in Underdeveloped Countries', published before in these periodicals.

ALFRED BONNÉ

The Eliezer Kaplan School of Economics and Social Sciences,
  The Hebrew University,
    Jerusalem, June 1956

LIST OF TABLES IN APPENDIX II

PART ONE
Measure and Challenge of Inequality

CHAPTER I

ECONOMIC DEVELOPMENT: AN AUTOMATIC OR INDUCED PROCESS?

THE currents of modern economic thought which are derived from a study of productivity trends have an optimistic ring. They are based on the concept of a universally applicable scientific technique which has before it a nearly limitless realm. Industrialisation and rationalised agriculture are so far the main fields of application for the scientific techniques which have become instrumental in the formation of a global society with higher standards of living.

At present the world is composed of wealthy countries, blessed with the riches of the earth and enjoying the fruits of a highly developed material culture, and of vast underdeveloped regions where the population is badly in need of food, housing and elementary provisions in the fields of public health, education and other social services. A gulf exists between these have-nots and the more fortunate lands with well-developed economies and resources utilisation. The experience of recent generations tends to show that the path of material civilisation since the industrial revolution is a continuous striding away from poor conditions of life, not infrequently even from starvation and destitution, towards more advanced stages of well-being and plenty.[1] Were it not for the high natural increase in most underdeveloped regions, the adjustment of their levels of living to those of economically advanced countries would have assumed a different pace. It is the belief in the feasibility of such a course, on the one hand, and in its necessity, on the other—assumptions encountered in numerous variants and degrees of both naïve and scientific thought—which lie at the root of modern trends and movements for the development of backward areas.

[1] It is true that the absolute size of the 'gap' may increase owing to the quicker pace of technological progress in highly advanced countries. Yet this does not contradict the improvement in former levels of living, factual and potential, which can be observed in underdeveloped countries.

MEASURE AND CHALLENGE OF INEQUALITY

Three lines of reasoning, in particular, have become significant for the emergence of modern thought in the field of economic and social development and its application to less advanced areas:

1 First is the belief in the self-propelled process and continuation of economic advance and in its spread from one area to another. Those who share this belief, relying primarily on the experience of recent generations, conceive economic progress as the spread of forms and rates of growth to all those places where no artificial obstacles arrest their advance.[1]

There are certain considerations which support this belief. The past one hundred years have seen the unparalleled growth of Western material achievement, a well-nigh unlimited fount of Western ingenuity in the utilisation and extension of the resources of mankind. These resources have been brought increasingly under the command of man, with the effect of far-reaching changes in population growth; a rise in levels of consumption, housing and transport; the spread of

---

[1] A notable version of this assumption is given by Colin Clark in his *Economics of 1960*, 1942. According to Clark the general rate of economic growth in different countries is scarcely affected by depressions or even wars. He produces a diagram showing the slow yet steady, and therefore nearly 'predictable', trend of economic growth in these countries and adds the following commentary:

'The effects on this diagram of the great depression of the early 1930's are almost invisible. This depression was a failure to employ the available working population, not a failure of productivity on the part of those who were employed. The widespread disorganisation of that period produced a slight temporary setback to the curve in the U.S., Britain and Germany, but this had been overcome and the old trend resumed in each case by 1935. In other countries not even a slight movement was noticeable.

'What is more surprising, and even more significant, is the comparatively slight and temporary effect of the war of 1914–18. These effects had all disappeared, and the pre-war trend been resumed by about 1922 in the U.S., Britain, France and Australia. In Sweden and Japan the disturbances were still slighter. In Germany the war was followed by the still worse disorganisation of the inflation which culminated in 1926. Even in Russia, where war, revolution, civil war and famine acting in combination had by 1921 reduced real production per capita to not much more than one-third of what it had been in 1913; where the so-called "Five-Year Plan" and compulsory collectivisation of agriculture between 1928 and 1933 had caused a further reduction in real income; even here the old trend of growth had been recovered by 1937.

'However, from these undifferentiated data of real income per worker we can draw one very important conclusion, namely, the tendency towards convergence. Countries which at present have a low income per capita show the most rapid rates of increase.'—Colin Clark, *op. cit.*, pp. 4–5.

The impressive data for the growth of output in Simon Kuznets, *National Product since 1869*, New York, 1946, lend themselves more than any other body of data to the acceptance of a trend of sustained economic growth over a protracted period.

Another confirmation of the persistence of long-term trends seems to be offered by the surprising recovery of Germany's economy. All indications point to a quick resumption of upward trends and rates of growth in the economic development of post-war Germany after a measure of destruction and disorganisation without precedent.

4

education and of knowledge of parts of the world hitherto unexplored or only partly known. However, the effective realisation of these achievements was until a short time ago limited to Western society. Here a unique coincidence of scientific and technical advance, of improvements in social and political conditions conducive to entre-preneural activities and a slowing down of population growth has indeed caused an unprecedented rise in national production and consumption and in the share of the individual in it. In the under-developed countries these factors have not yet operated in concert, and are not, in that specific combination, reproducible. The reasons for this situation will be discussed below, but it should already be made clear that any analogy derived from recent economic and social history in the West should be applied only with great caution to such regions where no similar combination has prevailed.

2 The thesis of the inevitability of economic progress in the orbit of political changes is another, scarcely less significant version of the belief in the self-realising force of such progress. The main reasoning of this approach derives from Marxian thought and its elaboration of the theory of historical progress. The phenomena of crises and underconsumption in Western countries, which were the primary object of study of early Marxism, are due to the supremacy of the property-owning class, which is threatened by economic advance.[1] This class tries to slow down economic development, detrimental to their interests, yet cannot stop the powerful, inevitable process of socio-political liberation, which in due course must also bring about a release of the arrested factors and blocked sources of economic progress. Since the process of political liberation has proceeded like an avalanche during recent decades, the way for economic advance, too, has according to this version been paved everywhere in the liberated areas. It should be noted that in early Marxist writings on the nature of the class struggle, emphasis is laid preponderantly on the issue of political liberation. There is no theoretical foundation, nor a blue-print for the *economic* reconstruction of colonial areas; just as early Marxism did not for a considerable time occupy itself with the planning of the future socialist society, which would follow after the elimination of the capitalist regime.

Discussions of the future of colonial areas are to be found in practically all neo-Marxist writings. The point of departure is nearly exclusively political, namely splitting of the national bourgeoisie

---

[1] 'Capitalism, at a certain stage of development, holds up the growth of pro-ductive forces.'—S. Lenin, *Works*, XV, p. 6, quoted after Carr, *The Soviet Impact on the Western World*, 1946, p. 29. There exists a multitude of formulations—not always identical—of this basic statement in Marxist literature. The important point, however, is that the arrest in the growth of production forces is a temporary phenomenon only.

into two camps: a revolutionary and a compromising party, the former continuing the revolutionary struggle and the latter entering into a bloc with imperialism. From the analysis of existing conditions in Oriental countries, three deductions are drawn, all of which point to the necessity of a change brought about by revolutionary force. These deductions are:

(*a*) The liberation of colonies and dependent countries from imperialism cannot be achieved without a victorious revolution: independence is not given gratis.

(*b*) The revolution cannot be advanced or the complete independence of capitalistically developed colonies and dependent countries achieved unless the compromising national bourgeoisie is isolated; unless the petty-bourgeois revolutionary masses are · freed from the influence of this bourgeoisie; unless the hegemony of the proletariat is established and unless the advanced elements of the working class are organised into an independent Communist Party.

(*c*) No lasting victory can be achieved in colonial and dependent countries unless a real bond is established between the movement for emancipation in these countries and the proletarian movement in the advanced countries of the West.[1]

Communist practice has indeed accepted these conclusions as important guide lines in global strategy as well as in the field of economic reforms to be executed after the political changes had taken place.

3 The third line of reasoning is different from the preceding ones and is based on two premises: the first—primarily a non-economic consideration—is that economic progress in underdeveloped areas is an urgent necessity in international relations, although there is no socio-economic law according to which it *must* really occur; the second premise is that such progress depends on a well-conceived and co-ordinated set of activities from within and without, which do not necessarily imply violent changes.

The roots of this view can be traced to considerations of economic welfare in the broadest sense of the word. If the desirability of economic progress has been fully accepted for Western countries, with their fairly advanced conditions of well-being, then it becomes a dictum of political expediency for regions lagging so far behind in economic and social levels as most Oriental countries.

---

[1] Joseph Stalin, 'Marxism and the National and Colonial Question, A Collection of Articles and Speeches', London, Martin Lawrence Ltd., (without year), p. 215.
This is, of course, a very different stand from that expressed formerly by Marx on the basis of a far-reaching scepticism as to the role of colonial peoples themselves in the process of capitalist production.

ECONOMIC DEVELOPMENT

The contrast between the incessant improvement of living conditions in advanced economies, and the simultaneous continuation of appalling conditions of human existence over wide areas of the globe, is indeed one of the central factors responsible for the growing momentum of policies towards economic and social development of backward areas.

We have not at this stage considered as a driving motive the effect of development activities in backward economies on the advanced economies themselves. The issue is familiar to students of contemporary economic affairs: conditions in countries with a mature economy call for opportunities to promote, through capital export, the development of less developed areas, since this process serves to maintain stability and growth at home. It is an important consideration which has had a powerful effect on capital export to underdeveloped areas, and it deserves a more detached treatment on the part of the capital receiving countries than that which was accorded to it.

The deductions elaborated in this book are not based on proposition number one of a self-propelling mechanism, an assured continuation and spread of Western economic advance into other regions; neither is the second approach accepted, which relies on the inevitability of violent political changes and the use of revolutionary techniques in order to achieve economic and social progress. Economic development is not simply inevitable; it must be actively promoted in order to come into being. The concept as used here is based on the recognition of the urgent necessity to generate economic progress by well-co-ordinated measures of national and international policies, without relying on 'infectious trends' of economic activities and without infringing upon the sovereignty of national governments.

This standpoint also implies a certain differentiation between the meaning of economic development and economic growth. Whereas economic growth comprises each kind of an economic expansion, including a self-induced process, the term economic development is used here in the first line to denote that kind of growth which needs conscious and active promotion. Such a process needs a measure of planning and control of the various activities envisaged in the phases of development. Economic development may thus be feasible in situations where pre-conditions for self-induced economic growth do not exist at all. In fact it is just such absence of economic growth for a prolonged period which has led to the emergence of modern policies of economic development. Many undeveloped areas, when left to the free play of economic forces, have produced the phenomenon of 'secular stagnation', though in a different sense from that established in modern economic writing. It is a stagnation caused not by an *embarras de richesse* which may affect the welfare of mature countries, but by a prolonged *embarras de pauvreté*. Underdeveloped countries have been by-passed by those factors of economic growth which basically changed levels of economic performance and consumption in economically advanced countries.

In view of the gaps which have now become so spectacular, it is evident that specific measures, i.e. an 'aggressive' policy of economic development, have to be conceived to overcome this secular stagnation. Yet before such a policy can be devised the question of the uniformity of the development goals and the influence of different social systems must be discussed.

INFLUENCE OF DIFFERENT SOCIAL AND ECONOMIC SYSTEMS ON
DEVELOPMENT POLICIES

The volume of recent literature which deals with the aims and objectives of economic development is impressive; its scope makes it nearly impossible to absorb it; furthermore, even a cursory perusal shows that there has been continuous refinement and specialisation in the contents of the various programmes. Not too long ago, official, semi-official and private statements concerning the aims of international bodies, of national governments and of schools of learning in the field of economic and social development were formulated mostly in general terms.

It is quite understandable that the original promoters of these policies and movements should have conceived their task in fairly broad generalisations. They looked at the world primarily from the viewpoint of its division into two very unequal parts: the majority of the world population living at sub-standard levels, and a minority enjoying moderate to generous living conditions. In the elaboration of goals and opportunities acceptable to all, many things were taken for granted. No particular attention was paid to the peculiarities of the social, national and geographical entities which make up the bulk of the underdeveloped populations. Formulas and economic simplifications were used on the assumption of potentially similar or uniform economic trends and structures in the various parts of the world, disregarding the danger of indiscriminate analogy and equation of processes and systems which, in fact, are frequently quite different from each other. A comparative appraisal of the resources—land, mineral or others—of two regions may, for instance, yield a clear numerical result; still, it is only one of the data of relevance for the judgment of development prospects in the two regions.

The development specialist should not lose sight of the fact that societies in the various undeveloped regions present a multitude of concrete social systems, each with its own conditions, tradition and structure.

There are many factors that make for a differentiation of economic societies, and consequently call for a different approach to their respective problems of development. In an economy with a fully developed monetary mechanism, for instance, the formation of commodity prices and exchange values proceeds on lines quite remote from those found in an economic system still largely dependent on barter. Though the extent of the latter in the present world is limited, there still exist primitive barter areas of remarkable size in backward economies. To apply to them methods of finance as used in monetary economies is obviously wrong.

Another dividing line is the way in which income is distributed in society. Differences in income distribution produce different economic and social effects. A relatively equitable sharing of income favours even trends and levels of consumption and a balanced yet rather moderate pace of socio-economic growth. An uneven distribution allowing a larger margin for capital accumulation affords greater possibilities for speedy expansion, yet is apt to create economic and political dissatisfaction and unrest.

A factor of very considerable influence is the nature of the regime or government. An economic system dominated by an authoritarian and strongly intervening government evidently presents a set of conditions for economic activities very different from those of a national economy controlled not at all or only loosely by a governing apparatus. Yet the significance of this factor is also reflected in a reverse direction. Agriculture in an arid climate which depends on artificial irrigation is a case in point, particularly before recent technical achievements are introduced.

A large-scale irrigation economy presupposes a distinct administrative regime with widely uniform devices of control deriving from the need for large-scale artificial irrigation. The observation of river rises and recesses, the regulation of water flow and distribution, the co-ordination of sowing and reaping in the watered areas—all these cause a high degree of mutual inter-dependence in irrigated agriculture. As against this, agricultural systems relying on rainfall function in quite a different way; they are much less dependent on community and governmental supervision and may exist quite comfortably in rudimentary stages of political organisation.

A primitive agrarian collectivism shows considerable shortcomings with regard to the degree of initiative and devotion to farming, as compared to a system of land tenure based on individual property rights and its effects on the relation of peasants to their land. The prevalence of absentee landownership in a certain region will require a development policy quite different from that to be applied in an underpopulated area with land in the hands of owner-cultivators. The planner, whether economist or social scientist, must consider all of these points carefully when dealing with problems of development and arrested and potential growth in national economies. Not always are these differences fully taken into account in the analysis of potentials and in the preparation of development schemes.

THE IMPACT OF CULTURAL HERITAGES AND TRADITIONS ON ECONOMIC ACTIVITIES

Classical economic thought, as conceived in the writings of Adam Smith and his immediate successors, implied an institutional framework which can be identified roughly with the early English liberal society. It was the economic world of the then-beginning Industrial Revolution, composed mainly of relatively small economic enterprises enjoying a fairly equal status vis-à-vis the government, a situation which has to this day left its imprint on the development of Western economic thinking.

The spiritual background of this society was a mixture of Christian and Middle Class values[1]—concepts which had a limited appeal and validity for the world at large, already then—as now—under the sway of richer and more varied traditions than the society in which Adam Smith lived. This larger world also showed, then as now, much greater inequality and almost throughout an absence of the rational approach to the phenomena of life which was such an established virtue in the world of the Scotch scholar. Compared with the multitude of values, social systems and attitudes in the non-European regions, the Western world of that period appears a rather monotonous place. Western capitalism, which has spread over the globe, was fed by a peculiar blend: puritan asceticism and worldliness, generating an urge of enterprise and the increasing rationalisation of conduct; all of which has led to the emergence of a new texture of life, where high rewards in wealth and status are offered to those following the urges of self-control, thrift and acquisitive enterprise.

Hardly any reasoning of this kind associated with corresponding social and economic outlooks was to be found at the time in the large Asian and African societies.[2] Prospects of gaining wealth in

[1] Cp. the stimulating paper by A. K. Davis, 'Sociological Elements in Veblen's Theory', *The Journal of Political Economy*, Vol. LIII, 1945, p. 134.
[2] Certain exceptions from this general attitude can be observed in smaller communities such as the Jains and Parsees in India, for instance.

these areas frequently do not, even now, release efforts comparable to the average endeavour of Western people actively engaged in earning their livelihood. Visitors to many Asian lands are impressed by the contented state of mind prevailing among certain creeds in a setting of extremely reduced living conditions. The followers of these creeds quite often prefer an austere way of life to one afforded by the possession of material riches. Their desire for well-being can apparently be fulfilled at a low level of material want. Their attitude towards facts of mass destitution is quite different from that of observers who measure these phenomena with the measuring rods of an advanced Western society.

Even the religious system of Islam, which has in certain periods evinced considerable activism, has favoured the virtues of contemplativeness and traditionalism. The compromising philosophy of life inculcated by the teachings of Islamic schools, together with the deterring influence of certain religious doctrines on economic practices, has in no small measure been responsible for the stationary features in the economic life of Moslem societies.[1]

Consequently, the problems of economic development as affected by the religious teachings of Asian peoples require an approach which must account for these religious characteristics. They point to the necessity of considering, beyond the questions of immediate economic relevance, other factors operative in the formation and transformation of these societies. At the same time they show the difficulties which lie in the way of bringing about an adjustment of depressed levels of living in underdeveloped regions to the living standards of an advanced and predominantly industrialised society.

Considering all these qualifications, one might ask whether it is possible to arrive at a generally recognised concept of 'underdevelopment' and, consequently, at a common programme of economic and social development goals for the regions under discussion. Can we find some common denominator for a group of countries so vastly different from each other as those areas termed 'underdeveloped'? It is evident that without the acceptance of certain common criteria of underdevelopment in respect of these countries we should have to face great difficulties in formulating generally acceptable development targets.

[1] Cp. the present author's *State and Economics in the Middle East*, Chapter XXXII 2nd. ed., 1955. The significance of institutional obstacles to economic advance is also discussed in the excursus added as Appendix I.

MEASURE AND CHALLENGE OF INEQUALITY

In the definition of underdeveloped countries, the common point of departure is frequently seen in the fact that income and consumption levels in underdeveloped areas are conspicuously substandard; the levels regarded as standard being those broadly representative for levels of income and consumption in Western countries. In the report, 'Measures for the Economic Development of Underdeveloped Countries', prepared by a group of experts for the U.N., the term 'underdeveloped area' is applied to countries in which 'per capita real income is low when compared with the per capita real incomes of the United States, Canada, Australia and Western Europe'. In this sense, an adequate synonym would, as the report says, be 'poor countries'.[1]

These and similar definitions which centre around the gap in real income or an inferiority in the level of economic performance do not convey the dynamic element implied in the term 'underdeveloped'. This term carries a connotation in the sense of leaving a margin for 'fuller' or normal development. Nor do the definitions indicate the factors responsible for underconsumption, even if the very fact of being poor could be seen as an explanation for the continuous state of being underdeveloped. It seems necessary to broaden the definition so as to include these omissions.

Professor J. Viner introduces the potential of unused resources by defining an underdeveloped country as 'a country which has good potential prospects for using more capital or more labour or more available natural resources, or all of these, to support its present population on a higher level of living, or, if its per capita income level is already fairly high, to support a larger population on a not lower level of living. This definition puts the primary emphasis where I would think it properly belongs, on per capita levels of living, on the issue of poverty, although it leaves room for secondary emphasis on quantity of population. . . . The basic criterion then becomes whether the country has good potential prospects of raising per capita incomes, or of maintaining an existing high level of per capita income for an increased population.'[2] This is certainly a desirable broadening of the definition although the criterion of 'good potential prospects for using more capital and more labour' may turn out to be less explicit than it seems. In an age of entirely unexpected changes in

---

[1] The wording of this definition is in part similar to that used in the memo. on Financing Economic Development, submitted by the International Bank and included in the U.N. Publication, *Measures of Financing Economic Development in Underdeveloped Countries, 1949.*

[2] J. Viner, *Lectures on the Theory of International Trade,* 1953, p. 98.

the resources potential of many countries an element of considerable uncertainty is thus unavoidable in the appraisal of development prospects of many underdeveloped regions.

Another aspect in the definition which needs more consideration is the capital factor. With all the importance of natural resources they can be substituted by capital. In the case of Switzerland or Holland, for instance, which have few natural resources of consequence, the high average level of income and economic performance in general is largely due to the high per capita rate of available capital resources.

Finally, it seems necessary to include in the definition a psychological factor involved, namely the measure of interest of the population in economic growth. Although this latter item is in part a 'non-economic' aspect, it is of outstanding significance to the process of economic development; the degree of its presence vitally affects the degree and prospects of development, and we should include it in our definition of an underdeveloped area, thus offering four criteria for the state of underdevelopment of a given area:

a Low real income per capita.
b Low rate of reproducible capital per capita and per unit of area.
c A favourable ratio of unused resources to population.
d A scarcity of entrepreneurial qualities in the population.

As already pointed out, our approach does not regard economic development as a process concerning only economic factors and activities; it is a more comprehensive phenomenon and includes numerous non-economic aspects and actions. Indeed for the determination of the targets of development a division of work is clearly necessary between the economist and various specialists in other social science disciplines. For the economist, the ends of development programmes should be clearly conceived in economic terms; which means that all ends not conceivable in this way are, for the present, not his concern. He aims at a rise in real income, composed of goods and services, and at their improved distribution. As his interests are in the field of economic reasoning and calculations, he is entitled to refute and oppose economically 'doubtful' and irrelevant habits if they prevent the attainment of welfare. Cases in point are the maintenance of millions of unproductive cows in India, prestige-securing excessive spending on tribal and family celebrations in many underdeveloped countries, and other satisfactions, which a sociologist may, perhaps, evaluate highly from a very different viewpoint. There will be disagreements between social scientists on the desirable ends; a clearing and delimitation of the areas of disagreement is vital, though not always simple.

There will be a number of border cases—ends of an economic as well as of a sociological character—which have to be included in the programmes of sociologists and economists as well. It may be taken for granted that the following general development targets will be widely accepted:

(I) rise of real income per capita to be used for the attainment of
  a decent levels of nutrition;[1]
  b decent levels of housing;
  c decent levels of education.
(II) improvements in the field of employment and income distribution.

As to the determination of the *means* to achieve the ends, economic as well as non-economic, there should be co-operation on the part of all social scientists concerned, since it will be necessary to consider 'non-economic' means as well in order to attain the ends. These 'non-economic' means and needs and the effect of their satisfaction on economic life have their place in our general strategy of development. Some of the means of the economist to achieve a higher real income may be ends for the sociologist, as for instance a decent level of education. At the same, time when an improvement in general education is possible only through a rise in real income, the end for the economist is a means for the sociologist. There is thus a clear mutual dependence. In this phase of our discussion we are primarily concerned with the definition of the economic goals which constitute the substance of economic advance in underdeveloped countries, and therefore disregard other problems. In a different context we shall also have to touch on various non-economic elements which play an important role in the promotion or arrest of economic development.

Before the conclusion of this chapter, a word should be added on the attempts occasionally made towards a wholesale deprecation of efforts for the improvement of backward areas through the introduction of modern devices of economic progress. This paves the way —thus runs the argument—for the unbridled spread of materialism. Quite frequently such negative evaluation of economic and social advance serves, under the pretext of protecting spiritual values, to perpetuate destitution and poverty. The message of the spirit has an appeal to those who have not been endowed with earthly goods. But poverty and asceticism have never become a cherished ideal for the masses. With the universal advance of material civilisation, it becomes more and more difficult to imagine any functioning society

[1] The term 'decent' in this context means *much improved* in comparison with the preceding levels of destitution.

ECONOMIC DEVELOPMENT

without some essential achievements of that civilisation. The maintenance of an order of values itself becomes dependent on the securing of a decent average standard of living; only those who can enjoy it will appreciate the need for an order of values and act upon it. Under present conditions, the majority of the population in under-developed countries undergo a desperate struggle merely to eke out a bare existence; their every thought is absorbed in obtaining a minimum ration of food, water, clothing and often shelter. Not until these elementary needs have been satisfied can the countless millions living in backward lands contribute their full share to the economic and spiritual welfare of the world.

Thus this book deals with the conditions and problems of *material* backwardness and *material* well-being in underdeveloped areas, and with the answer the economist can give to the question: how can these conditions be changed? It is the question of the present scope and levels of consumption and production in relation to the require-ments of a decent standard of living and the prospects to satisfy these requirements, which forms the main part of this treatise. This selection in no way implies that the other issues involved, dealt with here less elaborately or not at all, are irrelevant to our central subject. They will be touched upon as well, but not treated to the same extent as the economic issues.

OUTLINE OF TREATMENT

In order to develop the 'strategy' of economic development, we must first analyse existing conditions and trends. The great *im-portance of demographic problems* makes it necessary to start the First Part of the book with an exposition of trends and problems in the field of population growth. A high rate of population growth coincides with a low average life expectancy, and is thus responsible for a great waste in human and material values. The absence of a well-balanced age structure in which the productive ages are pre-dominant characterises most underdeveloped societies. Continuous high increase of population and low levels of output result in sub-marginal per capita levels of national income. A rigid occupational structure prevents rapid changes in income generation and distri-bution.

The first part of the book then goes on to show to what extent underdeveloped areas are affected by low levels of food consumption, limited demand for other consumer goods, and low levels of produc-tivity and industrial organisation. At the same time the close causal interrelationship of these conditions with the demographic situation will be elaborated.

15

MEASURE AND CHALLENGE OF INEQUALITY

The negative effect of low per capita income on the production potential of an underdeveloped economy is enhanced by inequalities in distribution, which favour habits of luxury consumption among the owners of production means, at the expense of tenants and workers.

The promotion of new policies in order to achieve higher standards of living in underdeveloped countries has a remarkable effect on demand trends, primarily for manufactured goods. These policies help to spread the phenomenon of 'contagious' consumption, which though up to a short time ago affected primarily the middle classes, extends now over growing numbers of people in all sections of society in underdeveloped areas. The new consumption habits have a twofold effect: they reduce the saving propensity of the population in underdeveloped countries, on the one hand, whilst they stimulate the formation of an acquisitive mentality, on the other.

The Second Part of the book is devoted to the discussion of prospects for a change, under the general head, 'The Move towards Adjustment'.

In this part, too, the treatment is based largely on empirical material from the regions under review. It starts with a fairly detailed discussion of motives for and obstacles to changes and the incentives needed to overcome at least part of these obstacles. The central theme of this part is the elaboration of the experience in improving real income by a rise in productivity and changes in the ratio of major occupations. A historical outline of industrial development in the areas surveyed is given from the viewpoint of its lesson as to the potential of higher productivity and the expansion of industrial production. For the first time the concept of 'industrialisation' as an induced process of change in methods of production can be applied to developments in a number of underdeveloped countries. Heavy industries such as iron, steel, other metals and cement have found their way to many of the countries under review. Generation and consumption of electric power for industrial purposes show an impressive relative rise. Indices for total industrial production in most underdeveloped areas all show remarkable expansion of output.

Certain aspects concerning the sequel and structure of industrialisation in underdeveloped countries are similar to those observed in recent economic history of advanced countries. Food and textiles head the list of products for the home market, yet new industries steadily diversify the industrial structure of the countries concerned.

The discussion of the various aspects of industrialisation is followed by that of the prospects of agricultural expansion. Agriculture, too, is in many ways affected by industrial progress: the application of new techniques in the preparation, enrichment and conservation

16

of soil; in crop rotation; in location, lifting and use of ground water for irrigation; and in the fight against plant and animal diseases has been made possible by the progress in industrialisation. The ever-increasing use of power-driven machinery in practically every phase of agricultural production and in marketing has basically changed the production potential of large regions, and transformed countries formerly dependent on food imports into export economies. The sustained international demand for food operates as a continuous impetus to programmes for the utilisation of natural resources in underdeveloped countries, such as land, water for irrigation and power, lakes and seas for fishing.

The last major subject treated in the book, finance, is closely connected with the analysis of development prospects. In the field of financing development grave problems arise as a result of the contradiction between traditional concepts and practices of fiscal administration maintained in most countries for generations and the new claims for acceleration and enlargement of economic develop-ment. Since the scope of savings in underdeveloped economies was and is small, financial means had been provided from abroad since the middle of the nineteenth century, mostly from private sources protected by the governments of the countries from which the capital flowed in. After the First World War the scope of private capital in-vestment abroad decreased to a fraction of its former volume. Infla-tionary devices such as credit expansion, and not infrequently even monetary transactions, were applied to solve problems of financing development.

A discussion of the more modern means of development finance follows, such as manipulation of terms of trade and others which have been introduced for fiscal purposes. All these devices have been used with varying success, but rarely has it been possible to avoid inflationary effects such as price rises, dwindling of exchange reserves and dislocations in the production and circulation of goods. The majority of these efforts can, however, contribute only to a limited extent to the solution of financial problems in underdeveloped countries if the development process there is to assume a substantial scope and pace. The magnitude of investment as required by the claim for rapid adjustment of production and consumption levels exceeds by far the financial potential available from traditional sources.

A new factor has thus become of cardinal importance for the execution of development programmes; large-scale capital transfer from developed countries, and in particular the increasing participa-tion of foreign public capital in such activities. Foreign capital resources, mainly of American origin, are supplied mainly as public capital, and used largely for the financing of schemes which, owing to their technical and economic character, are unsuitable for financing from traditional sources of private business.

The concluding part of the book is devoted to a comment on some of the recent evaluations of the development potential of Oriental countries, and to an attempt to develop a thesis of *development by implantation* as a contribution to the ever-growing efforts to build up a theory of development.

In the existing theories of economic development the entrepreneur has been given a key role in the process of economic development. But entrepreneurs have emerged so far only in Western countries as a factor of sufficient strength to shape economic history. Marxian development theory shares with Schumpeter's theory the same scene and objective, namely the capitalist process and its explanation; but neither theory includes the case of underdeveloped countries which now operate development policies towards higher levels of living and economic performance on lines different from those of mature capitalist countries.

This change is being brought about by a transfer of means and techniques of economic development from without through a process of implantation. Instead of the specific incentives which worked in the Western world, yet are not reproduced to the extent required to stimulate a comprehensive process of development in the immediate future, others will have to operate. Modern nationalism is one of the motive forces of economic development in underdeveloped countries. The acceptance of entrepreneurial functions by governmental agencies lies on the same plane.

The progress in transferability of modern techniques of production also has immensely facilitated the promotion of modern processes of production and distribution in underdeveloped countries. Finally, there is also a difference in the economic mechanism by which the various elements of the socio-economic process are geared together and kept in motion, at least for the period of initiation.

An appendix dealing with the subject of institutional resistances to economic development and a series of statistical tables relevant to the text complete the book.

CHAPTER II
THE DEMOGRAPHIC ASPECTS

A DISCUSSION of the causes of economic backwardness and the prospects of a rise in the levels of living over large areas of the world must start with an appraisal of the number of people involved. Most programmes for economic and social betterment are in the nature of middle- and long-term schemes; thus not only is the present size of a population an important datum, but also its future size and the changes in the rates of its growth which may occur during what is envisaged as the period for the implementation of a programme. Data on potential trends in the future are necessarily of a speculative character; the more so, the more deficient are the statistical series and services on which they rest. Yet no planning of economic and social development can forego population projections because they serve as points of departure for the calculation of development needs and magnitudes of human resources. However, let us first examine the existing demographic conditions now prevailing in underdeveloped areas.

GROWTH OF POPULATION BY REGIONS

The available data on recent population growth in underdeveloped countries point to the existence of trends no longer operative in other regions. Though these trends are not completely uniform, they have certain elements in common which justify the classification of most of these countries as areas of rapid population growth, differing widely in this respect from Western countries, where the pace of increase is slowed down or at least controlled by a successful application of family planning. The group usually termed as 'Western Countries' comprises—in addition to West and Central Europe—Canada, the United States, New Zealand and Australia. The countries of Southern Europe and Soviet Russia still show trends of rapid growth, largely due to the absence of birth control; although at the same time some of them show a declining rate of increase. The main areas of rapid growth are, however, India, Pakistan, the Middle Eastern countries, South East Asia and Latin America; but in some of these countries the rates of increase do show slight changes. Owing to deficiencies in the collection of basic data in these countries, there are still many gaps and inconsistencies in their demographic statistics; yet these hardly affect certain basic conclusions.

The available data show the classification of countries by groups according to rates of population increase during recent periods.[1] There are three main groups: countries where the population is stationary or growing slowly, with birth rates below 25% p.a.; countries with a 'transitional growth' with birth rates from 25 to 35%; and countries with a 'high growth potential' and birth rates over 35%.[2] Most underdeveloped countries belong to the second and third groups. Most countries with an advanced economy fall within the first category, marked by relatively low birth rates and low death rates. The rise in birth rates in certain developed countries after the Second World War is a new phenomenon and was originally attributed to the impact of the war on marriage conditions. It appears now to be of a more persistent nature.

In the second group, marked by 'transitional' growth, birth and death rates are falling. Since death rates are also falling, a process of rapid growth is maintained, though its continuation is doubtful. In some countries of this group there are indications for a slowing down of the present rate of growth. The areas in this group occupy a medium position as against the third group, countries with a 'high growth potential' where birth rates are still over 35%, yet where death rates are declining. Here the prospects are that rapid growth will continue for a considerable time.

TYPES OF POPULATION GROWTH AND LEVEL OF NATIONAL INCOME

Various attempts have been made to relate the classification of countries and groups by their potential of growth to levels of national income.

The National Advisory Council on International Monetary and Financial Problems presented to the American Senate in 1947 estimates showing the national per capita income in the last pre-war year, 1939, of 53 countries with 85% of the world's population. The results are summarised in the following table.

[1] See tables in Appendix II.
[2] This classification follows the schema used in 'Point Four', *Dept. of State Publication 1950*, Appendix C1, p. 114.

THE DEMOGRAPHIC ASPECTS

Country Groups According to Per Capita Income, 1939

	Income Groups		
	Upper (over $200) 15 countries	Middle ($101–200) 10 countries	Lower ($100 and below) 28 countries
Per capita income, 1939 (U.S. dollars per annum):			
Mean (weighted)	461	154	41
Median (unweighted)	389	149	53
Population Type:			
I. Low growth	14	5	—
II. Transitional growth	1	5	2
III. High growth potential	—	—	26

Among the 28 countries listed in the lower income group ($100 and below), all except two belong to the population type III marked by a high growth potential. The two exceptions, Yugoslavia and Poland, are European countries. Among the 10 countries with a medium per capita income, 5 belong to the 'low growth' type and 5 to the 'transitional growth' group. Of the 15 countries of the upper income level, 14 are in the 'low growth' and only one in the 'transitional growth' group.

A similar picture evolves if other indices of vital and social statistics are related to income groups.

Indicators of Pre-war Life Expectancy, Health and Education for Selected Countries*

Country Groups According to Per Capita Income, 1939

	Upper (over $200)	Middle ($101–200)	Lower ($100 and below)
1 Expectation of life at birth:			
Mean (unweighted)	63†	52†	40† (30)
Median (unweighted)	63	52	40
2 Tuberculosis death rates in 1939 (per 100,000 population):			
Mean (weighted)	64	143	333
Median (unweighted)	62	138	172
3 Percentage illiterate (population age 10 and over):			
Mean (weighted)	Below 5	20	78
Median (unweighted)	Below 5	20	64

* From 'Point Four', p. 105.
† Unweighted averages for countries with data. (Data were available for only 8 out of 28 of the lower-income countries.)
A weighted mean for the low-income group would approximate 30 years if China and Indonesia were assumed to have the same average expectation of life as India.

Higher income is thus associated with higher life expectancy, and also with lower birth rates and mortality rates. Quite evidently the percentage of illiteracy shrinks quickly with rising income.

It is important to note that the relationship between population growth and national income works in both directions. As true as it is that unrestricted growth of population must, in stagnant economies, lead to a reduction of per capita income, it seems no less true that increases in income through industrialisation, urbanisation and education have a negative effect on birth rates. It would, however, be difficult to identify the exact effect of each factor on the birth rate.

Stephen Raushenbush, on the basis of a series elaborated by L. Bean, W. S. Thompson and other sources, has compiled interesting tables on the relation of income increases and industrialisation to population growth.[1]

According to these data, the birth rate decreases by a little over 2·5 persons per 1,000 for every increase of $150 (1948 dollars) in per capita income. Raushenbush's figures cover 33 nations for the period 1935–9, which represents the end of the cycle of population change in the industrial nations, and a quite different point in the cycle in other countries.[2] It is an interesting attempt, although the qualifications implied in the insufficient period of observation and the deficient data should not be ignored.

No conclusive data are so far available on the impact of industrialisation on population growth in underdeveloped areas. There is hardly any doubt that this impact expresses itself in a decline of growth; though it would be difficult to indicate the exact magnitude of this influence. In an analysis of data relating to the number of children under 5 years of age per 1,000 women 15 to 49 years old, interesting results were obtained.[3] Without exception the rates of children to women in the childbearing ages are higher in rural than in urban areas in the countries selected.[4] According to the same source the unweighted averages of the 'fertility ratios' for both rural and urban areas show that the ratios are lowest in the industrialised countries and highest in the agricultural countries. On the other hand the average ratio for urban areas in agricultural countries is lower than for rural areas in industrial countries.

Writers on problems of population growth frequently assume that the experience in Western countries will repeat itself, and that a

[1] Stephen Raushenbush, *People, Food, Machines*, Washington, 1950, p. 67. For tables see Appendix II.
[2] Stephen Raushenbush, *op. cit.*, p. 25 and Appendix.
[3] The data referred to 21 countries arranged in three groups, roughly indicative of the degree of economic development measured by the percentage of males engaged in agriculture: 60% or more, 35% to 59% and less than 35%.
[4] *Demographic Yearbook*, 1952, U.N., New York, 1952, pp. 16–17.

decline in fertility will come everywhere only very gradually, and after a preceding decline in the death rate. They emphasise that the time-lag in the decline in fertility behind that in mortality in Europe continued for a period of approximately three hundred years and resulted in a sevenfold multiplication in the population of European extraction.[1] There are no cogent reasons for a repetition of this development, in particular for such a protracted period of adjust-ment, under conditions prevailing in the second half of this century. Many of the factors responsible at the time for the maintenance of high birth rates are now absent; others effective today did not operate then, especially those connected with the declining role of the family. The family is increasingly losing the function of ultimate judge and arbiter of the behaviour of its members. The dramatic events in Asia, dissension and fermentation in the great indigenous societies of the Old World are accelerating the disintegration of the value of systems and institutions which once determined habits of procreation and the size of the family.[2]

AGE DISTRIBUTION AND ITS ECONOMIC IMPACT

A demographic factor of considerable economic significance is the age distribution of the population. The available data indicate again striking differences in the age composition of various regional groups. Whereas in underdeveloped areas like India, Egypt, South America and the Middle East about 40% of the inhabitants belong to the first age group (0–14 years) and about two-thirds of the total population are below the age of 30, the position in Western countries is very different. Here two-thirds of the population belong to the three active age groups: 15–29, 30–44, 45–59 years. The inference is clear. The majority of the population in Western countries belongs to age classes within the productive age range. The impact of the situation on total output and per capita output is immense. An 'earner' in Western countries is easily able to repay to society the cost of his

[1] Cp. the discussion in *International Approaches to Problems of Underdeveloped Areas*, foreword, pp. 10, 11.

[2] A remarkable recent development is the officially supported drive for the introduction of birth control in India. In November 1952, the Third International Conference on Planned Parenthood took place in Bombay and found a warm reception for its ideas in leading Indian circles. Though of immense importance in its long-term effects, the immediate impact of the new drive should not be overrated. The results obtained hitherto were disappointing. Cp. *Final Report on Pilot Studies in Family Planning*, 2 vols., W.H.O. Regional Office for S.E. Asia, New Delhi, September 1954. On the other hand, the rate of increase in Japan's population has recently fallen. Instead of an estimated increase of one million per year, the increase in 1955 was actually 660,000. The slowing down of the rate is ascribed to widespread birth control. See *The Nippon Times*, Tokyo, February 25, 1956.

upbringing, training, etc., since he has a fair chance of reaching the end of his productive years and, therefore, of contributing his share for a period of about 40 active years or more.[1]

As against this, life expectancy in underdeveloped countries is from 30 to 50 years. The high percentage of persons belonging to the first age group in underdeveloped countries is a transitional feature. Since life expectancy is so much lower in underdeveloped countries, only a fraction of the first group reaches the higher age ranges. In pre-war India, only 54 out of 100 infants born would live to the age of 15 and only 15 out of 100 would attain the age of 60. In the United States, according to vital statistics tables of 1939–41, 92 out of 100 children born would reach the age of 15 and about 70% would reach the age of 60, thus contributing 40 years or more of productive adult life to the creation of goods and services. Economically speaking, the underdeveloped countries suffer a considerable loss of investment —material and immaterial—in upbringing and educational efforts in respect of a substantial number of young people who never reach the prime of life. Even if the amount invested per capita is below the equivalent of the cost of education, clothing and food customary in Western countries, the outlay lost in the aggregate is staggering.

POPULATION DISTRIBUTION IN TOWNS AND VILLAGES

The economic structure of a country and its development are closely affected by the way the population is distributed over towns and villages. The pattern of consumption of villagers is, with numerous variations, quite distinct from that of city dwellers. It is true that urban and rural consumption patterns in prosperous Western countries tend to adjust themselves to each other. But for the large underdeveloped regions the differences in urban and rural consumption levels and modes are still large. A villager spends a fraction of what the city dweller regards as a necessary standard of living.

The effect of a change in the ratio of urban to rural consumers can be explained schematically in the following way; let us assume three cases of different ratios of rural to urban population. In the first case, the percentage of village population is 80%; in the second, 70%; in the third, 60%; the respective proportion of urban population is 20%, 30% and 40%. Total consumption, in the first case, reaches $140y$, under the simplifying assumption that the total of the population is 100, that consumption per unit of the rural population is $1y$, and per

---

[1] H. W. Singer, of the U.N. Secretariat, has frequently elaborated this problem, particularly in his essay 'Some Demographic Factors in Economic Development' (mimeogr.) and his paper 'Population and Economic Development', presented to the U.N. World Conference on Population, Rome, 1954.

unit of urban population $3y$.[1] In the second case, total consumption amounts to $(70 + 90)$ $y = 160y$; in the third it reaches $(60 + 40 \times 3)$ $y = 180y$. In other words, even with a stable per capita consumption in both sectors, an increase in urban population raises total consumption, since most urban occupations in underdeveloped countries have a higher per capita real income than farming.

Let us now further assume an absolute rise in per capita consumption, more pronounced for the urban population, but not at all negligible for the rural sector either. This assumed rise would increase per capita consumption to $1 \cdot 5y$ for the rural sector and $4y$ for the urban sector in the second phase and to a level of $2y$ and $5y$, respectively, in the third phase. The following table shows the schema:

Phase	Rural population in %	Consumption per unit	Urban population in %	Consumption per unit	Total consumption
1	80	$1y$	20	$3y$	$80y + 60y = 140y$
2	70	$1 \cdot 5y$	30	$4y$	$105y + 120y = 225y$
3	60	$2y$	40	$5y$	$120y + 200y = 320y$

As the table shows, an increase in the ratio of the urban population from 20% to 40% and a simultaneous rise in both rural and urban per capita consumption mean a very substantial expansion of total consumption, although the majority of the inhabitants is still rural and no population increase has been assumed.

Of course, we ignore in this context all the economic problems implied in the rise of consumption, i.e. the sources from which the increased outlay for consumption has to be covered. Yet it should be already remarked that the same forces and inducements instrumental in the phenomenal growth of Western cities have become effective in the process of urbanisation of Eastern lands. Oriental urbanisation is promoted as in the West by the advantages a large market offers to industrialisation; large towns offer a varied supply of workers, skilled and semi-skilled; they possess research and management facilities and transport arrangements which in the course of time become more and more vital for industrial progress.

The hectic growth of Oriental towns has quite frequently produced the appalling phenomena of Oriental slums. The decay and ugliness to be found here even exceeds similar features in Western urban growth. It is also true that moving into and settling in a city is expensive for the villager, who frequently finds on this occasion that he must allocate considerable means for his housing needs.

[1] This ratio is hypothetical yet it reflects conditions in many regions.

For the first time yet, it seems that even marginal conditions of urban life appear more satisfactory to him than the existence of a partly occupied worker in a backward village society.

Contemporary economic history has shown that the process of urbanisation is practically bound up with the process of economic development throughout the world; in particular urbanisation is inseparable from industrialisation. Although the percentages of urban population for large underdeveloped countries are still far behind the corresponding figures for Western countries, the growth of towns in recent decades has become a conspicuous demographic feature in underdeveloped continents. The following two tables show conditions prevailing in some developed and underdeveloped countries. The first table points to the trend of concentration of the population in large urban centres, where economic opportunities attract the fluid population from rural areas. The percentages of this concentration are still smaller than in Western countries, and considerably below 50%. But its pace now exceeds that of the growth of urban population in most Western countries, which decades ago reached a high degree of urbanisation.

The second table shows how in two important underdeveloped countries the main urban centres owe their growth to a large extent to the influx of persons born in rural areas.

I. Increase in the Percentage of Urban Population in Selected Countries

Egypt	1907	13·8	England and	1901	77
	1937	25·1	Wales	1921	79·3
	1947	30·1		1951	80·7
Algeria	1906	16·6	New Zealand	1901	43·1
	1931	21·1		1921	53·9
	1948	23·6		1951	61·3
Ceylon	1901	11·7	Canada	1901	37·5
	1921	14·2		1921	49·5
	1946	15·4		1951	57·4
Puerto Rico	1899	14·6	Finland	1900	10·9
	1920	21·8		1930	18·9
	1950	40·5		1950	32·3
Japan	1920	18·1	France	1921	46·4
	1935	32·9		1936	52·4
	1950	37·5		1946	52·9

Source: *Demographic Yearbook*, 1952, U.N., New York, 1952, p. 14.

THE DEMOGRAPHIC ASPECTS

II. India, Egypt: Percentage of Population Out-born in Cities

City	Percentage out-born	City	Percentage out-born
(a) *India—1931*		(b) *Egypt—1937*	
Bombay	75·4	Cairo	38·1
Cawnpore	41·4	Alexandria	31·6
Baroda City	38·2	Suez	45·5
Madras District	34·8		
Hyderabad City	30·4		
Lucknow	29·6		
Agra	22·4		
All cities, average	37·3		

Sources: (a) K. Davis, *The Population of India and Pakistan*, Princeton, 1951, p. 134.
(b) Census of Egypt, 1937, p. 64.

OCCUPATIONAL STRUCTURE

The occupational structure of a population is to a large extent connected with its geographical distribution. An urban population by matter of definition gains its livelihood from urban occupations which in most underdeveloped countries offer a higher level of satisfaction of material needs. The occupational structure is thus a datum of primary importance in the analysis of the economic conditions of backward areas, and a point of departure in every practical scheme for the promotion of economic progress in such areas. The close interrelation between changes in the occupational structure and national income has been referred to and will be discussed again; but it is not only this nexus which is relevant to the discussion here.

Many underdeveloped countries show over a period of decades a nearly rigid and even uniform occupational structure. The majority of earners remain employed in agriculture and related occupations. Available statistics indicate only slight and slow changes in the occupational pattern, though these changes may affect the numerical ratio between rural and urban population. The lack of mobility which marks such predominantly agricultural societies retards the process of increasing specialisation and industrialisation so characteristic of economic development in advanced economies. The figures of the table point in some cases even to an increase of people engaged in primary occupations, a fact which can be explained by the higher fertility rate of rural populations as compared to urban rates. For most Oriental countries, however, the data are approximations only.[1] In addition, the comparability of data for tertiary industries is limited, owing to the absence of a uniform definition of individual

[1] See Appendix II, Table No. 7.

27

service occupations in the various countries. This deficiency is probably responsible for certain contradictory features in the data of the table though the increase in the absolute number of earners in secondary industries is above doubt.

MAIN ASPECTS OF POPULATION GROWTH IN UNDERDEVELOPED REGIONS OF THE WORLD

During the first half of this century the average rate of increase of world population rose from 0·75 per cent to one per cent per annum, i.e. to over 20 million persons yearly. The disquieting feature is not, however, the size of the increase, but its distribution. Since the share of underdeveloped areas in world population amounts to two-thirds of the total, at least a similar proportion of the annual addition to the world population accrues to the population of underdeveloped regions. The relative growth in many of these areas is higher than in the economically developed countries, and is still on the increase in some of the areas concerned. Urbanisation and the new national and international measures for the prevention of epidemics will result in a reduction of mortality in underdeveloped countries, before birth control will effectively spread.

World population today is already very much larger than in 1939; yet if the birth rates now prevailing in underdeveloped regions remain constant their population will in the not distant future reach a staggering numerical supremacy. Though some of the present conditions of population growth in underdeveloped countries might prove to be only temporary, prospects of a continuous upsurge of population in underdeveloped Asia, Africa and Latin America imply formidable issues for the peace and well-being of the world. An improvement of levels of living of the existing population would constitute a tremendous issue even without the constant increase of numbers in underdeveloped regions. The continuation of this growth must widen the gap and make the inequality of nations and societies in economic status, achievements and capabilities a primary cause of international tension and disequilibrium, and a foremost issue in international politics. Yet the problem is not incapable of solution. We shall see later how recent developments in some of the countries under review justify a more hopeful appraisal of the prospects facing them. In this stage of our discussion we wish to sum up the main economic aspects of demographic conditions in underdeveloped areas as follows:

1 Regions where birth control is practised are largely identical with economically advanced countries enjoying improved levels of living.

28

THE DEMOGRAPHIC ASPECTS

The absence of birth control in underdeveloped countries coupled with the absence of energetic development policies creates zones of heavy population pressure which are potential danger spots of the first order.

2 While most underdeveloped areas are still areas of rapid population growth, a few of these regions have already reached the stage of transitory growth, i.e. a stage of falling birth and death rates. The attempts to introduce birth control, though theoretically admitted over large regions, are restricted for the time being to urban districts; they do not yet, at this stage, affect substantially the majority of the population concerned.

3 The work span of adults in underdeveloped countries is considerably shorter than in economically advanced societies, with the result that the economic performance of the average earner in underdeveloped countries is far below that of his colleague in advanced countries.

4 Owing to the low life expectancy (or the high mortality rate among younger people), a large part of the efforts and means invested in the upbringing and education of children in underdeveloped countries must be regarded as a total loss to the community.

5 The scope of adequate capital supply, one of the cardinal problems of economic growth in underdeveloped countries, is vitally affected by the waste of resources implied in high mortality up to working age and the reduced contribution to capital formation which results from the relatively short active period of those who reach maturity.

6 Lines and levels of consumption patterns in underdeveloped countries are largely determined by the habits and purchasing power of a low-earning rural population. The shift towards urbanisation is in its more advanced stages apt to improve conditions of living, but will in its first phases create great difficulties of adjustment, economic and social.

7 The weight of world population gravitates today towards underdeveloped areas. For a long period major political decisions in world affairs were largely made in the capitals of Western countries; the dynamics of population growth in underdeveloped countries will tend to shift the location of power in the world towards other centres.

For the economist the crucial issue deriving from these considerations is the ratio of population growth to economic growth. One of the major devices of economic policy influencing this ratio is the increase of productive capital, either from current income saved or

29

from other sources. To obtain a clearer picture of the potential of growth we have to study levels and composition of national income in underdeveloped countries and to compare them with corresponding data for advanced economies. This will help us also to become acquainted with concrete conditions of per capita consumption of goods and services and of productivity levels, a necessary prerequisite for the elaboration of development plans.

CHAPTER III

LEVELS AND COMPOSITION OF NATIONAL INCOME

THE gulf which separates the standards of living, housing, health and education of peoples in developed and backward economies may, in terms of a broad generalisation, be described as the contrast between the way of life of the industrialised nations of the West and of the as yet predominantly agrarian peoples of the East.[1] The discrepancy assumes many forms and aspects. Per capita computations reveal large differences in the consumption of food and industrial goods, in the outlay for health and education, in the scope and density of communication services on the one hand, and in power supply, productivity levels and many other fields of economic and social development, on the other.

We propose for the purpose of this study to consider mainly the data for the Middle East and India. Other parts of the world will occasionally be referred to when the data offer relevant information. The material is frequently scanty or deficient, and the quality of many figures even for the main territories under discussion unsatisfactory. None the less, we feel justified in regarding these areas and the available data on them as sufficiently representative of conditions in the underdeveloped regions of the Old World. Almost all of these countries depend largely on primitive agriculture. Generally, they belong to the areas which 'lag behind', that is, which, in comparison with economically advanced areas, show striking deficiencies in their productivity—in the performance of fundamental economic services, in the occupational structure of their populations, in cultural and health levels and in political organisation. These deficiencies are in themselves enough to invest the material world of the peoples concerned with a stamp of inferiority; seen from the West, this material inferiority might form their single common

[1] This crude classification does certainly not take into account the position of Latin America and of some less advanced countries in the West. Yet for the schematic confrontation needed here it is adequate.

31

feature, against the background of a great diversity in cultural and ethnological patterns. India, for instance, with her multifarious cultural forms, surprises the observer by the uniformly depressed economic conditions in the different parts of the vast sub-continent. The same was and is still widely true in respect of South East Asia, and, to a lesser extent, of the Middle Eastern regions.

NATIONAL INCOME AS A MEASURING ROD OF ECONOMIC WELL-BEING

The most frequently used over-all measure for the economic activity of a country is the national income estimate.[1] If these estimates are reliable, sufficiently detailed and prepared along the same lines, they can convey a true picture of the economic structure and contribution of a given region as compared to those of another; if these estimates are available over a period they show us the direction of changes in

[1] For the purpose of this discussion we take this as the sum of all goods and services produced during a year, after deduction of all those commodities consumed in producing, including depreciation and those already in the production account.

The modern methods of calculating the national income of a given economy are based on three principles or approaches usually combined in an income-output-expenditure tabulation. The three principles of construction are confronted in three columns, the totals of which, when complete, balance out.

Net National Income	Net National Output	Net National Expenditure
By factors of production	By industries	
Wages and salaries	Agriculture	Expenditure on goods and
Profits	Mining	services for current con-
Interest	Manufacture	sumption
Rent	Distribution and transport	Net investment
	Government	
	Other goods and services	
Total National Income	Total National Output	Total National Expenditure

The second column of the table, showing the net national output, is essentially a re-arrangement by industries of the data contained in the first column. The third column shows how the incomes earned in the first column were used. Thus by definition, each of the three methods should, when all data are included, produce the same total. (Cp. P. Deane, *Colonial Social Accounting*, Cambridge, 1953, p. 13.)

It is evident that a computation which is based on the data available for an advanced economy and intended to serve the policy needs of such an economy differs in construction and aim from that concerning an underdeveloped economy. The concepts by which national income is calculated from rents, profits, interest, wages and salaries are hardly applicable to an economy consisting mainly of peasants. For the time being the elaboration of conceptual tools for under-developed economies has remained far behind those developed for advanced economies. In addition there is, of course, a radical difference in the scope and refinement of basic data available in each case. Perhaps the most important problem for the time being is the comparability of real incomes, if the earners are in one case wage earners and in the other producers living on subsistence crops in villages. Part of the difficulties involved has been referred to in the text.

these data over a period of years. As Professor Kuznets has pointed out, they enable the economist to perceive the economy of the nation as a whole and in its particular aspects, to 'distinguish its major components—groups of economic agents and types of economic activities, and to find a basis upon which both the parts and the whole can be measured to secure comparable magnitudes.'[1]

The use of national income data for the analysis of problems of economic development and in particular for the comparison of conditions in underdeveloped and developed countries pre-supposes an agreement on the general meaning and commensurability of such data. No serious student of problems of underdeveloped countries can therefore afford to neglect the arguments Professor Frankel advanced in his important essay on 'Concepts of Income and Welfare and the Intercomparability of National Income Aggregates' against the common practice of such comparisons.[2] Professor Frankel's intentions go in fact much beyond the question of the comparability of certain income concepts. His doubts start from the basic difference in the objectives and ideals which consciously and unconsciously dominate the communities whose individual and social economic activities are being compared. According to him historical and traditional factors and not merely the state of technique and organisation are the basic causes of differences in the nature and form of the income produced by these activities.

For Professor Frankel it is clear that at all times the attempt by the individual to obtain what we call income is an attempt to achieve a social purpose and is not an isolated activity. He also refers to the remarkable experience of colonial administrators in observing how individual Africans who returned from successful training activities in a modern environment to their own tribal community, broke off contact with the market economy and abstained in general from applying what they had learnt.[3] He sees in this behaviour a renunciation of the objectives and ideals which dominate or are assumed to dominate advanced societies and of the accounting symbolism on which the European economy in the West is generally based.[4]

If this experience would be generally applicable to the economic and social processes occurring in underdeveloped countries today it could rightly serve as a verdict on an immense amount of thinking and policies which guide developments in these countries. But it

---

[1] Introduction to the Bibliography, *Income and Wealth*, Vol. I, 1951, published by Bowes & Bowes for the International Association for Research in Income and Wealth.

[2] S. Herbert Frankel, *The Economic Impact on Underdeveloped Societies*, Oxford, 1953.

[3] *Op. cit.*, p. 31.   [4] *Ibid.*

seems to me that we have to be very careful before generalising on this kind of experience and that we should not be unduly influenced by the experience in specific societies at a time when very different forms of behaviour can be observed in other areas.

Professor Frankel places too much emphasis on the difference in sets of values in the societies whose income-producing activities are being compared. An identical or similar orientation in the economic sphere concerning business goals and directions can be fully compatible with far-reaching differences which exist between different societies in respect of religious matters and beliefs. Unique mental processes which are released by specific systems of moral and ethical incentives operating in different societies must not exclude the use of identical symbols in the sphere of commercial transactions and of income-producing activities, particularly if the objective is a comparison of measurable quantitative results.

Another important aspect not fully taken into account by Professor Frankel is the pace with which members of less advanced communities nowadays acquire modern economic mentality as well as new methods of production and habits of consumption. The pace and preparedness of adjustment may differ by regions and communities but there can be no doubt that the Turks, for instance, certain Indian and Arab communities and numerous other societies in the Old and New World show many indications of their susceptibility to the impact of what we may term in a general way 'westernisation'. This receptivity includes the acceptance of methods for raising productivity in agriculture, for industrialisation, introduction of modern social services, the establishment of modern communications, etc. Perhaps it is the influence of his African experience which has been responsible for the sceptical approach of Professor Frankel to the problems of economic acculturation and commensurability. Numerous examples can be adduced in order to prove that new orientations and urges concerning the economic behaviour of the people in the economically less advanced countries are now spreading at varying speed.[1]

Professor Frankel refers to the situation of Robinson Crusoe in support of his thesis that income creation is not a solo act of a marooned islander but conditioned by the influences of a society to which the income producer belongs. Robinson Crusoe 'brought with

[1] There is abundant literature available on which to draw for supporting these lines of argument. Only a few sources shall be mentioned which deal with the practical and theoretical sides of these problems and their frequently contradictory aspects: *Hands Across Frontiers, Case Studies in Technical Cooperation*, Cornell University Press, 1955; Wilbert E. Moore, *Industrialization and Labour*, Cornell University Press 1951; A. Bonné, *The Adjustment of Oriental Immigrants to Industrial Employment in Israel*, Unesco, International Social Science Bulletin No. 1, 1956.

him from the society to which he belonged not only a stock of goods but, far more important, a set of values, ideals and objectives'. This description characterises exactly what is going on today in many economically underdeveloped societies. There are numerous Robinson Crusoes inserted into these societies from without and implanting, as a rule, 'streamlined' sets of values and objectives which strike root, here gropingly and there more rapidly. It is this process of change through implantation which works towards the increasing comparability of data relating to income-producing activities.

Although this is an extremely cursory treatment of an important problem of economic and social theory, it should suffice to justify the use of the income data and their analysis made in the following sections.

For our immediate purpose we are primarily interested in interspatial comparisons of national income data: whether there exist essential differences in the composition of the national income of underdeveloped areas as compared to that of advanced economies; whether there are differences in the pace of its growth between both categories; whether there are differences in the rate of saving and capital formation; or whether there are any other relevant characteristics. Needless to say the value of such deductions will depend on the availability of reliable and detailed data.

Detailed national income estimates for underdeveloped areas are not only scanty, but reveal numerous imperfections in the basic data, such as size and composition of the earning population, evaluation of subsistence production, internal distribution of income. Our claims on the quality of national income data have become increasingly more severe with the progress in refining the technique of national income computation. For this reason interspatial comparisons of monetary data, which are perhaps the most desirable series to be elaborated, require particular caution. Such comparisons can scarcely take account of factors and circumstances such as diet habits and housing conditions; many of these conditions which considerably affect human welfare, evade a precise monetary definition.

One of the most important points in this context is the evaluation of local production. Home consumption is frequently not inserted into the evaluation of production. But even where it is, the same product is sometimes given quite different values in national income accounting because of differences in the relative price structure of the local market. Comparisons of the value of food production may even be meaningless when in one country agricultural production for home consumption will be estimated at 'factor cost' and in another at market prices.

The treatment of social services is another point: some unpaid

35

social services provided by local communities are, as a rule, not included in national income accounting, whereas governmental social services are included.

An interesting problem also results from the presence and exploitation of outstanding national resources for national income computation. In some Oriental countries the income deriving, for example, from oil production reaches staggering heights, and has raised national per capita income figures much above their former level. But the practical meaning of this revenue for the individual citizen and the population as a whole has in one or several cases been limited, because of the irresponsible waste of this income by the rulers.

Yet even with these limitations—part of which can be accounted for, we are able to make certain generalisations. Differences in level and structure of income of various countries can be usefully interpreted and conclusions as to the possibility of changes in national production and consumption can be supported by the results of comparisons. Deductions of this kind are also important for the analysis of recent development processes from the viewpoint of their real contribution to national production and for the appraisal of the potential of finance from domestic sources.

The following table gives per capita figures for the national income in dollars of 1939, and of 1949 purchasing power. These data are not comparable, but indicate the order of magnitude existing at both dates. The figures for many underdeveloped countries are crude estimates; those for other countries, official or semi-official estimates. According to the data there do not appear to have been striking changes in the order of the individual areas by size of per capita income during the 1939–49 period. The two countries with the largest population in the world are China and India. The level of per capita national income in both of them was in 1949, as before, less than 10% of that for the United States and United Kingdom.

	Per Capita National Income in 1939 $	in 1949 $
South and East India		
India	34	57
China	29	27
Ceylon	63	67
Indonesia	22	25
Philippines	32	44
Middle East		
Palestine	81	
Israel		389
Egypt	74	100

LEVELS OF NATIONAL INCOME

	Per Capita National Income in 1939 $	in 1949 $
Middle East		
Turkey		125
Syria		100
Lebanon	60	125
Iraq	50	85
Iran		85
Western Countries		
United States	554	1453
United Kingdom	468	773
Canada	389	870
Australia	403	679

Sources:
For 1939: 'Point Four', Dept. of State, January 1950, p. 114; Palestine, Egypt, Syria and Lebanon and Iraq, own crude computations and estimates.
For 1949: Statistical Office of the U.N.: *National and Per Capita Incomes of Seventy Countries in 1949*, New York, October 1950, pp. 14–16.

A picture of immense disparities evolves also from the data on national and per capita income classified by continental divisions.[1] In 1949 the majority of the world population, 61·3% of which live in Asia and Africa, still fell within the two lowest income brackets, $50 and $75 per capita. The somewhat higher per capita income of the Middle Eastern countries cannot change the continental average, since their share in the population of the two continents is so small.

Approximate National and Per Capita Incomes of Continental Divisions and the World, 1949

	Amount in billions of $	Percentage of World Income	Population	Per capita income ($) All countries
Asia	58·0	10·5	53·0	50
Africa	14·0	2·6	8·3	75
South America	18·0	3·5	4·5	170
U.S.S.R.*	59·5	11·0	8·1	310
Europe	148·5	27·3	16·6	380
Oceania	7·0	1·5	0·5	560
North America	237·0	43·6	9·0	1100
	542·0	100·0	100·0	230

* 1946.

[1] *Volume and Distribution of National Income in Underdeveloped Countries*, U.N., E.C.O.S.O.C., E 2041, June 1951, pp. 4–5.

MEASURE AND CHALLENGE OF INEQUALITY

RELATIVE SHARES OF MAIN INDUSTRIES IN NATIONAL INCOME

The comparison of absolute levels of per capita income conveys a summary notion of the large gaps between the volume of goods and services produced in the different regions.

A break-up of the net domestic product by industrial origin shows that for many underdeveloped countries the percentage share of agriculture is frequently of the same order of magnitude. In frequent cases this refers also to the share of manufacturing. Underdeveloped countries with a low average income level are marked by the concentration of income-producing activities in agriculture. In Egypt, Turkey, India, the Philippines and in Latin American countries agriculture produces as a rule about 40% of the net domestic product. As against this, in high income countries, mostly identical with industrialised regions, only a low percentage of income—frequently less than 20%—is derived from agriculture; this may even apply to some of the high income countries which export farm products. Manufacturing participates, as a rule, with a third and more in the generation of income.

Although the share of the major industries in the individual countries may vary, the general proportion of the shares of agriculture and the other sectors is not much affected by these variations.

The data in the tables given in the appendix outline these differences.

It should be noted, however, that all the data used in the tables refer to conditions prevailing during recent periods of limited length only. Thus they do not allow us to arrive at conclusions concerning a sustained trend of economic growth. For most underdeveloped countries computations of national income were started only a short time ago and are, as stated above, far from being satisfactory.

THE RATE OF SAVING AND CAPITAL FORMATION

Though the potential of capital formation in underdeveloped regions seems considerable when judged by the high share of output retained by the landowner, actual capital formation goes on at low rates. Oriental landlords have been known for generations for their high propensity towards 'unproductive' use of accumulated revenues. Even if the money is not spent in travelling abroad, it is invested largely in hoards of cash, jewellery and gold. On the other hand, the majority of the tenants and land workers are scarcely able to save and re-invest their earnings. Certainly, there exists a great contrast between the rate of capital formation effective in advanced economies and in underdeveloped countries.

LEVELS OF NATIONAL INCOME

Against a rate—net capital formation—of 9 to 12% of the national income in advanced countries, net capital formation in most under-developed countries reaches hardly 5%; in many of these countries the savings have only been sufficient to keep up with population growth. The United Nations Reports on related problems contain data on the scope of domestic savings in underdeveloped countries; according to one source it amounted in 1949 in the Middle East to 6%, and for other Asian and African countries to 4·4% of the national income.[1]

Gross and Net Capital Formation in Certain Western Countries*

	Gross Capital Formation (CF) as percentage of Gross National Product			Net Capital Formation (CF) as percentage of Net National Income		
	Gross domestic CF	Foreign invest- ments	Total G.C.F.	Net domestic CF	Foreign invest- ments	Total Net CF
U.S.A. 1909–48	20·8	1·4	22·2	8·3	1·6	9·9
Canada 1941–50	16·9	1·9	18·7	9·9	2	11·9
Sweden 1891–30	18·5	− 0·6	18	11·7	− 0·6	11·1

* S. Kuznets, 'Towards a Theory of Economic Growth' (mimeogr. paper), 1954, Appendix, Table 8.

With a prevailing capital–output ratio of 4 to 1, the re-invested savings would suffice to produce just enough in order to maintain a population increase of close to 1·3% on the same income level. But it is evident that a rise in levels of living would demand a much higher amount of savings and foreign investment.

Is such a rise in the rate of saving in underdeveloped countries feasible? A more detailed treatment of this question will be found in the sections on financing economic development. At this stage we will only refer to the experience in Western countries where a rapid growth of population did not prevent capital formation from taking place at fairly high levels over a long period, owing to the simultaneous growth of per capita income.

THE RATE OF GROWTH OF PER CAPITA INCOME

Professor Kuznets has calculated the percentage growth of per capita income for Western countries and compared it with the rates of population growth.[2] The data indicate the occurrence of various combinations: a high rate of national income growth coincides with a low rate of population growth; it coincides in other cases with a high rate of population growth. A low rate of per capita income

[1] *Measures for the Economic Development of Underdeveloped Countries*, U.N., May 1951, pp. 35, 76.
[2] S. Kuznets, *op. cit.*, Appendix (mimeogr.), Table 5.

growth may be combined with a low rate of population growth. In the following table Japan stands out as the country with the highest per capita rate of income growth though it had a high population increase during the period of comparison.

Percentage Rates of Growth per Decade—Selected Countries

(*constant prices*)

		Percentage growth of total income	Percentage growth of population	Percentage growth of per capita income
United Kingdom	1860–1939	20·7	9·0	10·7
France	1840–1938	14·5	1·7	12·6
Italy	1861–1938	17·9	6·8	10·4
Switzerland	1890–1951	22·7	17·6	14·1
Norway	1900–1950	32·7	7·9	23·0
Sweden	1861–1944	29·4	6·5	21·6
U.S.A.	1869–1948	37·7	18·0	16·8
Australia	1901–1951	31·3	16·4	12·8
Japan	1878–1937 (Ohkawa)	52·6	12·4	35·8

OTHER CHARACTERISTIC DIFFERENCES

A distinct feature of underdeveloped countries is the high share of unearned income accruing to landowners in the form of land rent. National income estimates do not, as a rule, specify the total amount paid to landowners in the form of land rent. Until recent times land rent was generally remitted to the landowner in kind, and was thus included in the calculation of the real income from agriculture. However, the huge extent of rented agricultural land and the political position of landowners in numerous Oriental countries lend this source of income a special importance. It would be fully justified to accord to 'land rent' a separate account in national income break-ups. The picture of national income for underdeveloped countries would gain an important characteristic from this addition.

In Egypt, for example, the share of rent, according to Anis, amounted to no less than 52% of the output value of agriculture in 1939–40, and no less than a fifth of total national income.[1] This high proportion decreased somewhat during the war years, since prices of agricultural commodities rose quicker than rental rates. Still, even after this decrease, total revenue from agricultural rent exceeded a third of the value of total net output, and reveals socio-economic conditions which must be appalling to observers not familiar with this pattern of exploitation.

[1] Mahmoud Anis, *National Income of Egypt*, Cairo, 1950, p. 752.

LEVELS OF NATIONAL INCOME

Data from other contemporary Middle Eastern countries and from countries in Southern and South Eastern Asia convey a similar picture. The variations concern forms of payment (produce, cash and labour) and the size of rent. From all the data available for the areas under review, it appears that a rather similar level of land rent has established itself for most of these areas: rent claims, by and large, a share of between one-third and one-half of the gross output of non-irrigated land, and approximately one-third of irrigated crops. Since rented land is frequently a very substantial part of the total cultivated area, and since agriculture is the main source of revenue in these underdeveloped regions, the amounts involved are very considerable indeed.[1] The allotment of such high shares to landowners must be regarded as out of proportion to the total income of the industry and out of all proportion to the value of the landowners' service. As the social consciousness of the population towards the issue of absentee ownership and unearned income from land rent becomes more developed, the stability of the existing tenant-landowner relationship weakens and vistas open for different methods of income distribution.

We wish now to recapitulate:

1 The size of per capita income in underdeveloped countries is a fraction of per capita income in advanced Western economies. Even considering all the qualifications affecting the comparability of national income data of countries with different social structures, the meaning of the large discrepancies between the national income figures is clear and simple. The majority of the population over large areas of the globe cannot afford more than a fraction of the amenities which the inhabitants of high income countries enjoy.

2 Agriculture accounts for the preponderant part of total national revenue in underdeveloped countries, although the proportion of agricultural income in total income is lower than the share of agricultural earners in the economically active population. In most high income countries the active population employed in primary occupations is a small percentage of the total and produces a much smaller share of the national income than the earners in manufacturing and even in transportation or government services.

---

[1] A high level of land rent is not a novel feature in Oriental and Asian agriculture. Sources from ancient China indicate that rates of land rent approaching half of the crop were common during olden times (cp. K. A. Wittfogel and Feng Cha-Sheng, *History of Chinese Society*, New York, 1949, p. 124). According to available data, land rent in ancient Egypt amounted to one-third of the gross product; in times of a decreasing pressure of population these rates decreased somewhat, but not so much as to change the situation substantially (cp. Colin Clark, *op. cit.*, p. 563).

3 Owing to the low level of national income the margin for new capital formation out of savings is very small. Considering the significance of a substantial degree of capital formation for the increase in production, the prospects of underdeveloped countries for economic expansion out of local sources are at least for part of them very limited. Yet it should be stressed that the proportions of the current income which can be used for investment, also depends on the rate of economic development and not only on the rate of savings.

4 Progress in the rise of per capita income through increase of output and improved distribution has been slowed down in underdeveloped countries by the rapid growth of population, institutional and other obstacles. But it would be wrong to regard population growth as the major cause for the lack of economic progress. Numerous sparsely populated underdeveloped countries show a low rate of growth of per capita income, whilst a more rapid pace of growth is frequently found in densely populated countries.

5 A significant feature in low income countries is the high level of land rent and of fees collected by landowners and rural intermediaries. In nearly all of these countries a high share of agricultural revenue accrues to landowners in the form of land rent. It is supported by a socio-economic structure which has long ceased to exist in Western countries, and is now under increasing pressure from new social forces, emerging in the East as well.

6 The gainfully employed population in underdeveloped countries shows a high percentage of earners in services largely unspecified, whereas the proportion of earners in manufacturing, mining and construction combined is nearly everywhere relatively limited. Considering the rudimentary stage of social services and the limited scope of entertainment trades, a low share of total income for the large number of earners in service occupations would be natural. However, the scanty data available point to a different situation, i.e. to a high percentage of income deriving from tertiary occupations, with varying proportions for trade, transport and public services.

The discussion of the structure and level of per capita national income has shown the deficiencies in the size of income in underdeveloped countries as expressed in terms of monetary income. We are now interested to learn more of the concrete conditions of living in underdeveloped countries, in particular through comparing consumption levels in the main fields of consumption goods.

CHAPTER IV

CONSUMPTION LEVELS IN UNDERDEVELOPED COUNTRIES

RELATIVE SHARES OF MAIN ITEMS OF CONSUMPTION IN TOTAL SPENDING

STRIKING differences in respect of level, composition and growth of national income are only one aspect of the 'backward' character of underdeveloped countries. There are also significant differences in the way in which income is *spent*: most of these countries show a percentage distribution of expenses in which food takes pride of place. Inquiries into the distribution of Oriental household expenditure cover, as a rule, only limited numbers of the population, mostly farmers and workers. The results of these inquiries suffer frequently from their technical shortcomings, yet they are in line with the established findings of economic theory: since the low income groups form the vast majority of the population in underdeveloped regions, and certainly rank with the lowest groups of the globe on an international scale—food expenses claim a high share among the various items of expenditure. From the viewpoint of the urgency of requirements or, to use the customary term, income elasticity of food, the share of food exceeds considerably the percentage to be found in industrialised high income countries.

THE SHARE OF FOOD

Any investigation of food consumption levels, and certainly an interspatial comparison of these levels, has to face considerable statistical difficulties. A very substantial part of the food consumed in underdeveloped countries is produced by the farmers on their own farms, and is not fully accounted for in crop estimates. In addition there are food items such as game, fish and berries which do improve nutrition to a fair degree, yet they too escape exact

43

MEASURE AND CHALLENGE OF INEQUALITY

Main Groups of Expenditure in Certain Economically Developed and Underdeveloped Countries*

Country	Year	Food	Percentage spent for: Housing	Clothing	Misc.	Total
Food expenses below 50%:						
Sweden	1948	37·9	21·3	16·3	24·5	100
U.S.A.	1944	36·0	27·7	16·4	21·9	100
Israel	1950	37·7	14·6	11·2	36·5	100
Norway	1945	38·0	26·0	14·7	21·3	100
Germany (British Zone)	1946	40·7	18·5	18·7	22·1	100
Netherlands (Amsterdam)	1946–7	41·3	18·9	12·2	27·6	100
Switzerland	1945	42·0	23·2	10·1	24·7	100
Britain	1948	45·4	17·6	9·0	28·0	100
Germany (American Zone)	1947	46·6	17·0	6·4	30·0	100
Food expenses above 50%:						
Hungary	1947	50·6	19·7	9·1	20·6	100
Egypt	1950	56·0	5·4	—	38·6	100
Japan	1947	65·8	8·9	10·1	15·2	100
China	1941–2	74·7	13·6	4·4	7·3	100
Turkey	1938–9	57·9	19·9	11·5	10·7	100
Pakistan	1944–5	69·3	10·2	9·0	11·5	100
India	1940–1	63·9	6·4	13·2	16·5	100

* Figures according to *Yearbook of Labour Statistics*, 1949–50, except for India (Desai) and Egypt (Anis).

measurement. Food consumption in underdeveloped countries might thus be somewhat higher than the aggregate figures indicate. On the other hand, consumption figures in highly developed wealthy societies probably present somewhat inflated data because they disregard the considerable waste of food which is a common occurrence there. Large quantities of food thrown away in the United States, for instance, must be deducted from actual food consumption. But even with these modifications, the picture which emerges reveals a wide gap between food standards regarded as necessary and supplies available for the population in underdeveloped countries.

Further, there are remarkable differences in the food habits of the various regions. Wealthy Western countries, which head the list in respect of total per capita consumption, consume far less cereals per head of the population than China or the Middle Eastern countries. The same holds good for pulses. On the other hand, consumption in Western countries of fruits, meat, milk, fats and sugar exceeds by far the average intake of these foodstuffs in the Far and Middle East.

Pre-war Food Supplies in Certain Countries*

(retail indices per head per year)

Country	Total	Cereals	Roots and tubers	Sugar	Fats	Pulse	Fruits and veg.	Meat	Milk
U.S.A.: (in kg.)	718	90	66	48	20	9	203	88	194
(indices)	100	100	100	100	100	100	100	100	100
U.K. (indices)	84	107	121	104	105	67	56	98	80
South and East Asia:									
Japan	54	180	94	31	10	167	46	38	5
China	42	184	64	2	25	300	21	16	—
India	41	153	12	31	15	256	18	9	33
Middle East:									
Turkey	70	189	14	10	15	333	56	23	80
Palestine	73	197	24	38	60	100	89	28	46
Syria and Lebanon	77	161	14	31	20	111	98	13	82
Egypt	44	190	5	17	30	267	29	14	17
Iran	48	154	—	13	5	111	46	19	41
Iraq	47	143	0·750	19	5	78	47	20	38
Trans-Jordan	54	149	—	21	5	100	74	22	33

* From *World Food Survey*, F.A.O., Washington, 1946.

Indices of Calorie and Protein Intake from Pre-war Food Supplies in Certain Countries

*(per head per day at the retail level)**

Country	Calories									Grams of Proteins		
	Total	Cereals	Roots and tubers	Sugar†	Fats‡	Pulse	Fruits and veg.	Meat§	Milk‖	Total	Animal	Veg.
U.S.A.												
(absolute figures)	3,249	887	139	515	502	105	210	524	367	88	50	38
(indices)	100	100	100	100	100	100	100	100	100	100	100	100
U.K. (indices)	92	101	89	90	101	64	41	111	73	91	86	97
South and East Asia:												
Japan	70	176	113	32	8	140	40	20	3	76	24	145
China	68	175	81	3	26	248	17	18	—	77	10	166
India	62	147	27	32	14	200	20	7	43	64	18	124
Middle East:												
Turkey	80	181	12	10	17	253	77	20	90	115	52	197
Palestine	79	182	22	39	59	71	62	18	37	84	32	153
Syria and Lebanon	74	154	12	32	20	73	115	11	102	88	52	134
Egypt	68	179	4	17	28	188	20	11	21	78	16	160
Iran	60	148	—	13	7	84	90	16	51	75	34	129
Iraq	60	137	0·7	19	6	55	136	19	46	69	32	118
Trans-Jordan	59	141	—	21	7	95	83	16	41	73	30	129

* From *World Food Survey*, F.A.O., Washington, 1946.
† Refined sugar equivalent.
§ Fresh equivalent.
‡ Pure fat equivalent.
‖ Fluid milk equivalent.

CONSUMPTION LEVELS

The underdeveloped countries are far behind in respect of protein intake, in particular animal protein; in the supply of calories the deficiency is still quite appreciable and diets contain from 20 to 40% less calories than in well-fed Western countries. There is, it is true, a larger consumption of cereals and pulses than in these countries, but the under-consumption of sugar, meat, milk and fruits is not compensated for by it.

The preceding tables contain details on pre-war food supplies in the individual countries of the regions under review. The figures given are average figures, and as such do not reflect deviations towards the extremes. In every country there are many who obtain food greatly above the average, and many more who have to be content with a food intake far below it. Yet the averages in the tables should be representative for the bulk of the population in under-developed countries which belong to the low earning classes. Computations in the 'Point Four' pamphlet point expressly to a correlation between national income per person and per capita calorie intake. All the countries in which the average supply of calories per head was 2,150 a day were countries with an average per capita income of less than $100 a year. At the other end of the scale, where the average supply of calories amounted to 3,040 per person per day, stood the countries in which the average annual income exceeded $200 per person. An average daily food supply of 3,000 calories in the top income group is about 1,200 calories above the commonly accepted life-sustaining minimum of 1,800 calories. As against this an average food supply of 2,150 calories meant a margin of only about 350 calories over this minimum. Since there are frequently seasonal or regional fluctuations in food production, many consumers in underdeveloped countries with an average intake of 2,150 calories were dangerously near or even below the minimum intake.[1]

The emphasis frequently laid on the grave effects of permanent malnutrition has led to an interesting discussion of the assumption usually made in global comparisons, namely that diet requirements are equal throughout the world. Dr. M. K. Bennett, of the Food Research Institute of Stanford University, contests the universal applicability of international nutrition standards.[2] The population of Oriental countries includes a larger proportion of babies and very young children than that of Western countries. In addition, normal adults in Oriental countries weigh about 30% less than the adults of some Occidental populations; further, climatic conditions in the warmer regions in which most Oriental populations live, reduce

[1] 'Point Four', pp. 107–8.
[2] M. K. Bennett, 'International Disparities in Consumption Levels', *American Economic Review*, Vol. XLI, No. 4, September 1951.

physical effort and the need for calorie intake alike. When differences among the nations in the consumption of food calories are related to the body weight of the consumers, to climate, physical activity and economy in the use of food, they are, according to Dr. Bennett, much smaller than the differences indicated by the calorie consumption estimates of the Food and Agricultural Organisation. The generalisations usually made in this field indeed frequently leave numerous questions open. In some countries where there exists a state of deficient nutrition, if measured by international standards, mass symptoms of grave nutritional deficiencies are absent. There must, therefore, be other criteria as well in order to determine a state of actual malnutrition. Modern nutrition science is not yet developed enough to provide us with standard patterns of nutritional requirements adjusted to conditions of various regions, such as climate, physical constitution of the inhabitants and their average energy output.

But whatever our judgment would be as to the refined nutritional aspects, it appears that people who subsist on a low level of calorie and protein intake will show the impact of this condition. They are to a certain extent under the influence of a vicious circle. Because of poor diet, their physical and energy output is reduced, and because their output capacity is reduced, they cannot easily achieve the production of a fully satisfactory diet. Thus while the adjustment of a population to a reduced nutrition level might attain a remarkable degree, that population would at the same time become less active and less eager to exert themselves in efforts to improve their lot.[1]

Changes in world consumption over the last decade have formed the subject of a paper by Chatfield, Scott and Mayer in the *Milbank Memorial Fund Quarterly*, April 1950. The main conclusions of this investigation are as follows:

First is that the decade during which the Second World War took place was marked by an aggregate increase in the supply of calories and protein of 1 to 2 per cent, an increase in population of 8% and therefore a resultant decrease in per capita supply for the world at large of about 6 to 7%. That period, it had been noted, was characterised by widespread destruction of agricultural facilities, as well as by an increase in world population of 200,000,000. Second, the effect was felt very unequally according to regions. Generally speaking, regions with a low consumption status sank even lower, while

---

[1] But low productivity is, of course, the outcome not only of poverty, i.e. of reduced nutrition conditions and a correspondent low physique. There are other factors at work as well: absence of modern equipment and implements; lack of understanding of, and training in, progressive methods of work; effects of political and social regimes which have left their marks on the peasants. We shall deal with some of these handicaps in their proper context.

countries where the food situation was good maintained themselves or improved.

These conclusions seem, however, to underrate the degree to which some of the low consumption regions succeeded in raising their status through increase in food production. Towards the end of the forties there was a decided improvement in per capita food production as compared to the immediate postwar years. The per capita production of food crops on a regional basis, as well as comparison of the per capita world output of the same crops, shows an interesting increase which persisted in certain regions also after the year 1950. The index of per capita food production reached a level of 102 in 1953–4, as against 91 in 1946–7 and 100 in 1934–8, a result of a simultaneous increase in population and food production.

Index Number of Total and Per Capita Food Production*
(1934–8 average ≡ 100)

Region	Total Food Production: 1948–9 1950–1 average	1952–3	1953–4 prelim- inary	Per Capita Production: 1948–9 1950–1 average	1952–3	1953–4 prelim- inary
Western Europe	103	114	121	94	102	107
North America	138	152	150	118	123	119
Latin America	128	136	138	98	97	96
Africa	123	134	134	102	106	105
Near East	114	133	140	95	104	108
Far East (excl. China)	99	105	109	84	85	87
Oceania	111	117	120	96	93	93
All above regions	115	126	128	98	102	103
World†	109	117	120	97	101	102

Source: F.A.O., *The State of Food and Agriculture*, 1954, p. 19.

* The following commodities are included in the index: grains, starchy roots, sugar, pulses, oil crops, nuts, fruits, vegetables, wine, livestock and livestock products, fibres, rubber, beverage crops, tobacco.
† Including rough estimates of U.S.S.R., Eastern Europe and China.

The large share of food in household expenditures in under-developed countries finds a counterpart in the low relative shares of housing and clothing. But whereas the food position as a whole is a relatively inelastic item, the amounts spent on housing and clothing vary considerably. This variation is in part connected with the different climatic conditions prevailing in underdeveloped countries and allowing for a certain elasticity of this expenditure. In warmer regions a modest or even poor outlay for housing and clothing does not cause the degree of inconvenience which poor care for these needs would produce in northern regions.

MEASURE AND CHALLENGE OF INEQUALITY

CONSUMPTION OF INDUSTRIAL GOODS

It stands to reason that populations subsisting on a low level of food consumption show poor standards of consumption also in respect of other commodities and services. A suitable measuring rod is the per capita supply of industrial goods and electricity. Such figures make it clear that Western man has proved himself a nearly insatiable consumer of industrial goods, absorbing many times what the average inhabitant of economically underdeveloped communities consumes. In fact, it is the former's wide demand for manufactured goods and services, such as textiles, household utensils, furniture, motor vehicles, books and newspapers, radios, films, pharmaceutical products, recreation and travel facilities, etc., which invest Western society with its peculiar mark of diversity and abundance.

Comparisons of growth and composition of per capita consumption of industrial goods and services are thus a meaningful expression of differences in wealth and consumption power between the various regions of the world. They point to a fundamental discrepancy in the consuming capacity of the various countries which is primarily related to the difference in the production levels of these areas.

The following figures, taken from *Industrialisation and Foreign Trade*, refer to the period 1926 to 1929; yet as we shall presently see, no substantial changes took place until the Second World War, according to figures available for 1939.[1]

For the period 1926 to 1929, the United States, with an annual per capita supply of $254 worth of finished factory products, ranked first, followed by four British Dominions, the United Kingdom, Germany and minor industrial countries which used factory goods valued at between $164 and $100; then came the less industrialised countries, with amounts varying below $100 per capita. Japan's per capita figure was no more than $28, but exceeded by far that of China and India, where the supply of manufactured commodities amounted to barely $3 per head of the population. In the Middle East the Jewish population of Palestine had a per capita supply of $100 worth of finished factory products, as against about $18 for the Arab sector. Arab countries showed an even lower level. Turkey, which at the time severely restricted the import of manufactured goods, had an average supply of $10 per head.

An interesting computation from the data given by Colin Clark in *Conditions of Economic Progress* enables us to learn about the levels of per capita demand for net production of manufacturing on the eve of the First and Second World Wars, respectively. These data, which

[1] *Industrialisation and Foreign Trade*, League of Nations, 1945, p. 22.

CONSUMPTION LEVELS

Per Capita Consumption of Selected Commodities

Quantities in Kg. where not otherwise stated	U.S.A.	Egypt	Turkey	Israel	India
Cement, 1950 or 1948	220	39·3	17	300	7·3
Cotton fabrics ⎫					
Woollen ⎬ pre-war	14·8‡	2·7‡	2·2§	6·7‡	2†
Silk and rayon goods ⎭					
Major apparel fibres,* 1951	18	3·3	3·6		1·6
Energy consumed in terms of coal (m.t.), 1950	7·74	0·22	0·26	0·80	0·10
Radios—number licensed or estimated in use per 1,000 inhabitants:					
1938	300	4	2		0·2
1950	600	9	10	126	0·9
Passenger cars in use per 1,000 inhabitants:					
1928	170	1	0·2		0·01
1937	197	1	0·2 (1949) 5·4		0·02
1950	260	2	0·4 (1953) 8·4		0·02

Where no other sources stated, quantities were calculated from production and import-export figures, various U.N. periodicals.
* From F.A.O. Commodity Series Bulletin No. 21, December 1951, including Cotton, Wool, Rayon.
† Calculated from 'Point Four', U.S. Dept. of State, 1950, p. 118.
‡ From *Survey of Palestine*, Vol. II, 1946, pp. 846–7.
§ Computed from British Overseas Economic Survey, Turkey, 1947, p. 88.

are included in the table on p. 52, refer however to total demand for industrial products, measured in I.U., as against the preceding data, which were gross output figures excluding foodstuffs, expressed in dollars.

On the eve of the First World War the demand for industrial goods in advanced Western countries was far above that of low income countries in Europe and Asia. About 25 years later, on the eve of the Second World War we find that per capita demand has nearly everywhere risen very much. Yet the inter-regional gaps are apparently the same; for certain commodities they are even larger as the comparison of basic consumption goods shows. Altogether we are impressed by the absence of marked changes in the order of the countries when arranged by the size of per capita demand. On the other hand, the percentage increase of demand in England is conspicuous. Within the group with low levels of industrial consumption Japan's advance is quite remarkable.

MEASURE AND CHALLENGE OF INEQUALITY

Analysis of Demand for Net Product of Manufacturing, 1913
and 1936–8

	1913			1936–8		
Country	Population (in millions)	Total demand (millions of I.U.)	Per capita demand	Population (in millions)	Total demand (millions of I.U.)	Per capita demand
U.S.A.	92	10,551	114	128·8	17,587	136
Canada	7·5	805	110	11	1,237	112
United Kingdom	45·2	2,665	60	47·2	5,390	114
Germany	65	4,046	62	67·8	5,341	79
Hungary	8·1	196	24	9·1	243	26
Poland*	27·5	368	13	34·4	442	13
Roumania*	17·3	184	10	19·5	234	12
India	315	485	1·5	370·3	830	2·2
Japan	50·5	348	6·9	70·9	1,768	25

* The figures refer to 1926–9.
Compiled on the basis of figures from Colin Clark, *The Conditions of Economic Progress*, 2nd ed., 1951, pp. 356 ff.

THE LEVEL OF HOUSING CONDITIONS

(a) *Middle East*

Housing occupies a central position in human wants' satisfaction. In view of its significance a short survey of housing conditions in the countries concerned is given; it will focus one of the crucial differences in living levels between advanced and underdeveloped countries.

Housing conditions in underdeveloped Oriental countries vary considerably from region to region, and even from town to town. In the cities we find throughout the beginnings of well-planned modern residential quarters, which are attainable, however, only by the well-to-do. Cheaper living quarters, built some decades ago, especially for the poor classes, bear today the features of slum quarters: congestion of building space and excessive density in the interior, unclean streets and courtyards, deficient water supply, sanitation or sewage. Still, some of the new industrial enterprises have made provisions for improved workers' quarters and given increased attention to modern views on housing requirements.

Conditions in the countryside are, in a way, more satisfactory, since the beneficial effect of the open air on man and beast cannot easily be counteracted. Yet even so the peasant houses frequently offer appalling settings, though they seem well adapted to their physical environment from the viewpoint of the material used, the technique applied in their erection and the shape of the dwellings themselves. In regions where the main building material is mud, the floors form an excellent breeding ground for diseases, as man and beast frequently dwell together in one room. There are only slight differences in the housing standards offered by the earth hovels in the interior of the Anatolian steppes and in the river valleys and plains of Syria and Egypt, the reed huts of lower Iraq and the stone huts and houses in the mountains of Palestine and the Lebanon. With increasing distance to the towns the level of housing comfort— equipment and hygiene—decreases. The absence of ventilation, the lack of furniture and conveniences, the muddy and dusty courtyards considerably affect the well-being and health of the rural population.[1]

(b) India
The housing problem seems to have reached its most acute state in India, especially in the urban areas. Whereas in rural areas the problem of congestion is of lesser importance than deficiencies in building technique, hygiene and comfort, the reverse situation pre-vails in the towns, where congestion is problem number one. The numerous urban centres have grown incessantly during recent dec-ades, and building has not kept pace with the influx of newcomers attracted by better living conditions in the towns. The result is congestion beyond description. A few references from official docu-ments, selected at random, illustrate the situation which prevailed 10 to 20 years ago. Owing to the increase in urban population it seems hardly possible that a substantial improvement could have changed the basic situation as existing then.

The descriptions in the *Main Report*, Labour Investigation Com-mittee, Government of India, 1946, pp. 297–310, 320–4, give a vivid picture of conditions in various regions of the sub-continent:

'*Bombay:* An inquiry by the Bombay Labour Office into housing conditions in privately-owned buildings in 1938 shows that 91% of the families lived in one-roomed tenements, with an average of 3·84 persons in each unit. 55% of the families living in these buildings paid from 18–23·5% of their income for rent, the overall percentage being 17·1%. Housing provided by government or industry resembled the foregoing. If rooms were larger, the number of persons per room increased, running as high as ten persons per room in some instances (two children being counted as equivalent to one adult).'

Ahmedabad. According to the Census Report of 1941, there were about 64,000 tenements in the suburbs of Ahmedabad, 75% of these one-roomed tenements. According to a 1938 inquiry, the average number of persons per room was 4·1. According to the Assistant Director of Public Health the average number of persons per room

---

[1] According to a letter report published by the Middle East Institute, Washing-ton, in *Middle East Report*, Vol. VII, No. 8, 1954, it is estimated that there are 5,500 mud hut flats in Bagdad; about 31,000 people live in these huts.

in 1944 was three adults and four children. In some cases the total number of inhabitants went up to 10–14 in a room generally measuring 12 ft. by 10 ft., with in some cases a verandah 6 ft. by 10 ft. It was not uncommon to find more than one family living in one room. The structures were pucca, and most floors were of mud. Rooms were dark and ill-ventilated. 15% of these buildings had water tap connections, and the rest depended on surface wells, most of which were unsanitary and polluted. A recent investigation showed that there were only 223 bathrooms for 57,516 rooms. At least 20% of the rooms had no latrine facilities, and where such were provided, they were in a most unsanitary condition. Tenements built by the municipality and by various industries in Ahmedabad seemed to be slightly better than the above-mentioned privately-built ones, but they were exceedingly few in number.

Calcutta. The majority of workers lived in mud huts without clean water facilities of any kind, and without drainage or ventilation. The size of the rooms, including a so-called verandah, was about 80 sq. ft. and providing accommodation for about nine persons. Housing supplied by employers in Calcutta was slightly better than the *bustees* described above, though sanitary arrangements and ventilation were still wholly inadequate. The jute mills apparently supplied a large proportion of the industrial housing, with 22,000 rooms under their control. Almost 60% of these rooms provided from 75 to 85 sq. ft. per family, and in 94% of the cases the floor space available to a worker and his family was less than 100 sq. ft.

There have been some recent attempts to introduce changes in housing conditions for industrial workers. Mention should be made, in the first place, of the schemes which the Tata Iron and Steel Company at Tatangar has designed and in part executed for its workers. The company has introduced a number of interesting improvements and innovations which take into consideration the specific conditions of the location, the climate, etc. The experience was not in all cases satisfactory. Housing is a crucial part of the culture of a society and a major change like that of moving into altogether different habitats involves considerable adjustment.

Housing of Plantation Workers
That the problem is not limited to the Indian urban population is shown by the following quotations from the same source describing housing conditions of the plantations mentioned below, according to a 1944 survey.

Tea Plantation in Assam. Rooms generally 15 ft. by 12 ft. per family (defined as up to six persons). Water from wells. No latrines in houses or in vicinity.

CONSUMPTION LEVELS

Tea Plantation in Bengal. Rooms approximately 15 ft. by 15 ft. per family, with iron or bamboo frames. Walls of bamboo matting plastered with mud, and thatched roofs. No reliable water supply and no latrines.

Tea Plantations in Punjab and United Provinces: Rooms 14 ft. by 14 ft. and windowless with four or five persons per room. Water for drinking and washing from springs or streams. No latrines.

Tea Plantations in South India. Many houses have kitchen and verandah, but if so, one family occupies the kitchen, a second the main room and a third the verandah. Rooms approximately 8 ft. by 12 ft. Many houses have water taps, and latrines are provided for each block of houses. *Coffee Plantations:* Rooms are generally 10 ft. by 10 ft., with mud walls. No windows, ventilation, latrines or running water. *Rubber Plantations:* Six to eight persons occupy rooms of 10 ft. by 10 ft. or 10 ft. by 12 ft. Only one of the rubber plantations supplies latrines. Water is from wells or streams.

Housing conditions present one of the gravest social economic problems in India by the sheer magnitude of numbers involved. They are less pressing though a no less serious issue in most Middle Eastern countries, in the villages no less than in the rapidly growing towns.

New Trends in Consumption Habits

For a number of years slight but persistent changes in habits of living can be discerned in numerous underdeveloped countries. Such new habits appear quickly where levels of real income are improving; yet the urge to alleviate severe living conditions by spending part of scarce income for 'non-essentials' operates even in low income areas, without notable changes in income level. The movies, radio, cheap magazines—even modern housing accessories—invade, surprisingly rapidly, countries where the average national income per capita is at a subsistence level. The considerable latent propensity of consumption for such non-essentials stimulates the development of service occupations which provide many of these amenities, and of industries producing non-essential consumer goods. It appears that one of the effects of the spread of Western consumption habits in underdeveloped countries is to shift part of the earning population in the towns and larger villages to those secondary and service occupations which produce the above commodities and services, and at the same time divert part of the national income into these new channels of outlay.

Recent investigations in a number of Oriental countries have made it clear that even in impoverished countries such as India and the Middle Eastern areas, rises in non-essential consumption could take place without a marked effect on the nutritional situation.

For India, reference is made to the comprehensive investigation by R. C. Desai, published in the *Journal of the Royal Statistical Society*, Part 4, 1948. Desai gives a detailed break-up of the consumer expenditure for India for the years 1931-2 to 1941-2, and expresses all figures in 1938-9 prices. In addition to the prices he also gives variations in consumer expenditure in percentages of 1931-2 levels. The results are very interesting. There was, first, a very low total per capita expenditure of under fifty rupees, remaining the same for all ten years. The share of food (excluding alcoholic drinks) remained nearly constant throughout the decade, and claimed approximately 60% of total expenditure. Two features stand out quite clearly:

(*a*) In spite of a slight rise in total consumer expenditure, the per capita outlay for food decreased consistently. The explanation given by Desai points to the rapid growth of population, which outstripped food production.

(*b*) There was a rapid increase in the outlay for many manufactured consumer goods, such as household goods, clothing and motor vehicles, and in private expenditure on education. This rise supports the conclusion that simultaneously with deterioration in the food supply there must have been either an increase in the demand for consumer goods other than food by the higher income sections, or a more general, though limited, rise in the standard of living following new income opportunities.

An illuminating case is offered by recent developments in Turkey. Prosperity caused by the remarkable yield of cereal crops has led to a wave of spending on non-essentials. Observers who recently toured Turkish villages report large-scale improvements in housing conditions in Turkish villages, and the quick spread of radios and bicycles, which were scarcely known before in these parts of rural Turkey.[1] Economic surveys made by U.N. agencies confirm these impressions.[2]

In the State of Israel, where a considerable influx of capital has carried with it a substantial increase of purchasing power among wide sections of the population, the standard of living has grown by nearly 100% for a considerable share of the total population.[3] The acquisition of industrial consumer goods such as refrigerators,

---

[1] Cp. H. A. Reed, 'A New Force at Work in Democratic Turkey', *The Middle East Journal*, Winter, 1953, pp. 37 ff.

[2] U.N., *Economic Survey of Europe in 1953*, Geneva, 1954, pp. 90 to 93.

[3] A. Bonné, 'Recent Changes in Levels of Living in the Middle East', *Middle Eastern Affairs*, October 1954, pp. 309 ff.

modern kitchen utensils and household conveniences has become a general feature. Similar experiences are reported in Lebanese and Egyptian cities.

Phenomena similar to those described above have been studied and commented upon in economically advanced countries as the 'demonstration effect',[1] and formed a focal point in studies of spending habits in the United States and other Western countries. These studies revealed that it is not the absolute but the relative level of real income that determines the propensity to save. In the United States, higher income groups save a larger proportion of their income than do low income strata. 75% of American families, according to Duesenberry, save virtually nothing, whereas the remaining upper income groups, comprising about 25% of the population, apparently account for all the personal saving in the country. In wealthy countries like the United States there is no harm in this trend. The savings derived from 25% of the families will compensate for the absence of savings by the other 75%. The problem is different in underdeveloped countries, where the same psychological stimulation operates without the supporting material potential. The reaction of low income groups who come into contact with 'superior' goods or patterns of refined consumption for the first time appears to be the same as that of the more well-to-do, if not even more reckless. Their desires are stimulated sometimes violently, their consumption propensities shifted upwards. The implications of these tendencies will be described below.

The available data on family budgets, trends in total expenditure and the proportion of food and manufactured goods in total spending of underdeveloped economies all seem to be in line with the familiar generalisations of modern theories on consumer behaviour; though there are important differences in percentages in underdeveloped countries. Consumption of primary produce relative to total expenditure is largely a function of the size of income; obviously other factors affect it as well. In low income countries food consumption reaches about half or more of the total national income, and may even claim 70% or more in areas with a large majority of agricultural population. In view of the large number of farmers who consume their own food, the mode of calculation of the value of food is of some importance: it can be computed at retail or at farm prices. The composition of total national consumption at representative income levels has been calculated by Colin Clark for a number of countries, as shown by the following table presenting a range of income levels from 138 to 2,222 I.U. per year and person at work.

---

[1] J. S. Duesenberry developed this concept first in his *Income, Saving and the Theory of Consumer Behavior*, Cambridge, U.S.A., 1949, pp. 39 ff.

According to his data, the consumption of food by farm families, if income is computed at retail price levels, reaches 59% of the national income in the case of China, and 56% in the case of India. To this has to be added the consumption of farm products at wholesale prices; thus percentages of 78 and 70 relative to the produced national income in India and China are arrived at. The consumption of products of large-scale manufactures in both cases does not exceed a few per cent; the demand for services and small-scale manufactures is between 20 and 30% of income.

	Income level, I.U. per person at work about 1935		*Consumption as percentage of national income*			
			Imputation of income from valuation of food consumption by farm families at retail prices	Consumption of farm products at wholesale value	Consumption* of products of large-scale manufacture	Consumption of services and small-scale manufactures
	per hour	per year				
China	0·03	138	59	19	1	21
India	0·08	223	46	24	3	27
Italy	0·18	395	9	21	21	49
Netherlands	0·44	1,054	2	15	20	63
Australia	0·64	1,421	—	13	16	71
U.S.A. (1941)	1·00	2,222	1	10	22	67

Colin Clark, *The Conditions of Economic Progress*, 1951, 2nd ed., p. 366.

* Including goods representing new investment. Excluding depreciation and replacement of manufacturing equipment, and excluding value of raw materials and of tertiary services incorporated in manufactured goods.

As against this, in high income countries the demand for farm products falls to 11% of national income. Large-scale manufactured goods claim about 20–25% of national income, while services, including building, handicrafts and small-scale manufacture, rise to 70% or more of national income.

The data in the second table show the ratio of demand for manufactured goods to total real income for a number of countries for two periods prior to the Second World War and point to a substantial increase in the consumption of manufactured goods for countries undergoing industrialisation.

For Russia and Canada the increase rates were surprisingly high and indicate the pace of industrialisation of their economies. Relative and absolute consumption of secondary products was low, however, in countries like India and China.

In countries with a rapid population growth a sustained rise in

CONSUMPTION LEVELS

Demand for Net Product of Manufacturing in Relation to Total Real Incomes*

Low income countries			High income countries		
Japan	1906–10	0·100	U.S.A.	1871–5	0·170
	1936–8	0·127		1936–8	0·195
Spain	1913	0·075	Canada	1901–5	0·126
	1931–5	0·059		1936–8	0·205
India	1901–5	0·024	Belgium	1913	0·258
	1936–8	0·034		1936–8	0·228
Russia	1881–5	0·022	United	1871–5	0·151
	1936–8	0·137	Kingdom	1936–8	0·189

* C. Clark, *The Conditions of Economic Progress*, 1951, 2nd ed., pp. 356–60.

per capita consumption of manufactured goods cannot occur without a very substantial increase in production. If, for instance, population growth over a period of 10 years amounts to 10 or 15%, production must rise during this time by at least a similar amount to keep per capita consumption at the *same level*; but must expand by a multiple of it to allow for a substantial *rise* in per capita consumption.

Yet while such a large sustained increase in production and consumption is very rare in low income countries, partial developments may change the level of consumption even here for certain segments of the economy and for certain categories of goods. In the history of industrialisation it has become apparent that the increase in industrial consumption did not take place at the same pace for each group of consumption goods. Available data point to a 'differential' between the rates of increase in the consumption of various groups of industrial consumer goods. The largest increase did not take place with respect to essentials like cloth and other soft goods, but in hard and metal goods. Per capita consumption of soft goods in high income countries, in particular textiles, is considerably higher, often many times higher than in low income countries. But levels of textile consumption for both groups are still much nearer to each other than consumption levels for hard goods, especially those with an iron and steel content. Per capita consumption of metal and steel can in fact be regarded a criterion of the level of development of a given country: it follows quite closely the indices for per capita income.

Contemporary Western civilisation has been characterised as a civilisation 'on the move'. The conquest of space, on land, on sea and in the air, is a conquest by vehicles built largely from hard and metallic materials. Automobiles, airplanes, steamships, railway cars and railroads consume tremendous quantities of iron and other metals.

Another feature of contemporary living is the change in methods of domestic work by the introduction to our homes of modern accessories. Mass production of electric stoves, refrigerators, steel furniture, modern lighting, heating and air-conditioning systems, washing machines, plumbing, as well as the construction of buildings itself are making great inroads on available quantities of iron and other metals. High income as well as low income countries show a steep rise in the consumption of these basic materials. In low income countries the absolute volume of such consumption is so far only a fraction of that in advanced countries; yet its relative growth is phenomenal since it starts from zero or close to it.

In spite of these trends, however, the bulk of the population is not yet able to afford most of these goods, but continues to live at an extremely austere level. Thus the size of the market remains extremely limited. Consumption data on a per capita basis as a rule indicate very limited use of the new goods, as indeed even cursory acquaintance with living conditions in Oriental countries conveys.[1]

LIMITS AND PROSPECTS OF INDUSTRIAL MASS CONSUMPTION

Thus the situation is indeed complex. The new urges for a higher income level deriving from social pressures and the example of new consumption habits in the advanced countries, presented by the wealthier classes, tend to expand the demand. Yet this demand is largely ineffective. The restricted purchasing power keeps the effective demand in close limits; it can be enlarged only in the following ways:

1 By raising real wages and the share of tenant farmers in farm revenue, i.e. by a change in distribution of income;
2 By cheapening prices of industrial consumer goods;
3 By an increase in employment in existing enterprises or through new plants, leading to an increase in effective demand;
4 By infusion of purchasing power transferred from without on account of non-economic considerations.

It is not our intention, in this context, to elaborate these lines of reasoning for a full analysis of the prerequisites for a rapid expansion of the market of industrial mass commodities. Suffice it to say that the common element of the devices listed under (2) and (3) is the application of new capital. By the introduction of more efficient means of production the prices of goods would be reduced and thereby the real income of the consumers increased. Additional funds would make possible the addition of workers and thus increase earn-

[1] See also table on p. 51.

ings and demand. Large-scale production in underdeveloped countries faces the obstacle of inadequate means for the acquisition and operation of the expensive capital equipment necessary for mass production. The only readily available factor of production in most underdeveloped countries is labour, usually unskilled, which can be drawn from the reserves of disguised unemployment. A better use of this resource may contribute to the expansion of production by substituting for part of the necessary capital, but certainly not change the basic fact of paucity of productive capital which must thus be regarded as point of departure for policies aiming at the raising of levels.

CONSUMER BEHAVIOUR AS CRUCIAL FACTOR

In our discussion of the impact of new consumption habits on the mentality of the low income population in underdeveloped countries we assumed the preparedness of the consumer to yield, without any other limit than that of his income, to the inducement of new consumer goods. This is, however, an assumption which is correct only if individuals organise the spending of their income on the basis of free consumer choice for the purpose of maximum satisfaction. In this case, to follow a formulation given by Professor Bowen, it is necessary:

(a) That they behave rationally;
(b) That they possess adequate knowledge of the alternatives open to them;
(c) That they choose within an appropriate cultural setting.

Unless these three conditions are attained, free consumer choice can not be depended upon to make for maximum satisfaction.[1]

These assumptions are frequently not fulfilled even in countries with fully developed modern market systems and they are certainly much less applicable in underdeveloped countries with rudimentary elements of modern economic organisation.

As to the first criterion, it can safely be said that in strongly traditional societies the consumer's chance for a 'rational' choice in the sense in which this term is used in modern economic thought is limited. Traditional habits of consumption determine to a very large extent the character of material wants. This would not contradict the possibility that the individuals in an Oriental society obtain maximum satisfaction or approach rationality in terms of their own way of life; but it is evident that the predominance of traditional behaviour, so different from the 'Western' urge for the acquisition of new

[1] H. R. Bowen, *Toward Social Economy*, New York, 1948, p. 212.

61

consumer goods, would never result in the enormous spurring of demand and consumption which has marked recent Western economic history. In large segments of the society in underdeveloped countries the range of consumer choice as developed in Western countries has hardly ever been relevant to the man in the street.

The second condition for the attainment of maximum satisfaction under free consumer choice is that each individual have ready access to reliable information in order to be fully aware of all possible alternatives open to him. The complexity of this point is readily admitted in discussions which concern the availability of the necessary information in literate societies. Under conditions of backward societies, with their low degree of literacy and very rudimentary general knowledge of the economic mechanism, the possibility of attaining maximum satisfaction, which depends on the free availability of knowledge, seems extremely doubtful.

The third precondition for the achievement of maximum satisfaction under free consumer choice is that the actual choice of goods be in line with the general notion of maximum satisfaction implied in the prevailing cultural setting. This condition, which seems obvious in literate societies, becomes less so in a situation typical for contemporary underdeveloped countries, where a change occurs in the cultural set-up and causes shifting and ambivalent consumer outlooks and wants.

Perhaps the most important precondition for the spending of real income on new industrial goods is that this real income be really available for spending. This, too, sounds obvious, yet it is less so in underdeveloped countries where produced income is frequently a multiple of available income, and the demand for industrial consumer goods is determined by the level of available real income, rather than by produced income. In underdeveloped countries a substantial part of the produced income, as we have seen above, is not available to the producers, but transferred to the owners of land; the latter, who are only a small fraction of those employed in primary production, cannot stir up a mass demand for industrial products.

Thus one of the main obstacles to a quick spread of mass consumption of industrial goods lies in the prevailing inequality of income distribution in underdeveloped agrarian economies. The accumulation of agricultural revenue in the hands of large property owners is not the only form of inequality. Relatively large incomes were and are still drawn by government functionaries, traders, religious dignitaries, etc. These incomes stimulate demand for selected, high-priced goods, whereas the low incomes accruing to the masses scarcely suffice to cover primary essentials such as food, housing and clothing. With progressing equalisation the size of the market for mass goods is increasing in such countries. The incentives which will operate towards such a broadening of the market therefore have to include changes in the distribution of income.

The problems of consumer behaviour in underdeveloped countries are of the greatest significance for their development policies. So far only few studies are available to guide the development economist in this area. Problems of consumer habits share one very important aspect with the problems of how to raise production, namely the institutional resistances against economic changes.

The subject has been dealt with in an excursus—Appendix I—in view of its predominantly sociological character. The reader will bear its close connection with the problems discussed in the following chapters well in mind.

PART TWO
The Move towards Adjustment

CHAPTER V

THE ROLE OF THE INCENTIVE

I

THE role of the incentive in inaugurating processes of economic development has become a significant subject of modern economic and historical research. This incentive is no abstract notion; it is an effective attitude of mind inseparable from its carrier, usually the 'entrepreneur', whose activities are fraught with such important consequences for modern economic history. For the greater part of the period since the industrial revolution, this entrepreneur has been recognised as the driving force in the formation of Western industrial society. The entrepreneur might have been an industrialist with novel ideas on production; he might have been a merchant or an engineer with new business designs; he might have worked singly or as a member of a group. The motives which have driven him in his activities may have varied widely. In any event, it is he who was primarily responsible for the economic and technical advance of Western society.

The analysis of the various types, functions and achievements of the capitalist entrepreneur has been decidedly advanced by Schumpeter and modern schools of economic historians and sociologists. The qualifications which made entrepreneurs have been for many years a subject of research and discussion. An important point in these discussions is that the type of entrepreneur who is largely responsible for the growth of modern capitalism is not a capitalist who is looking for a maximal realisation of profits, but a pioneering type who invests, in addition to his means, considerable personal effort and initiative in order to achieve a combination of the factors of production which would otherwise not be brought together. The criterion of the specific performance of the entrepreneur was thus quite frequently not the material gains but the successful execution of a project based on the use of new methods of production or marketing.

THE MOVE TOWARDS ADJUSTMENT

Schumpeter considered development to consist of the carrying out of new combinations, a concept which covers five different cases of specific economic operations: (1) The introduction of a new good—that is, one with which consumers are not yet familiar—or of a new quality of a good. (2) The introduction of a new method of production, that is, one not yet tested by experience in the branch of manufacture concerned, which need by no means be founded upon a discovery scientifically new, and can also be a new way of handling a commodity commercially. (3) The opening of a new market, that is, a market into which the particular branch of manufacture of the country in question has not previously entered, whether or not this market has existed before. (4) The conquest of a new source of supply of raw materials or half-manufactured goods again irrespective of whether this source already exists or whether it has first to be created. (5) The carrying out of the new organisation of any industry, like the creation of a monopoly position (for example through trustification) or the breaking up of a monopoly position.[1]

Now it stands to reason that these cases occur in particular in a society which is favourably disposed towards innovation. This susceptibility to changes could derive either from widely spread individual urges towards continuous activity, generating a move for material or spiritual progress or ascertainment, or it could follow historical political events like the conquest of new lands and the opening of new trade routes which encourage the introduction of new forms of production and habits of consumption.

The urges towards intensive secular activities which were fed from mundane philosophies as well as from religious currents in European countries since the beginning of the reformation and the advance of science since the eighteenth century encouraged indeed an expansion of production to an extent never experienced before. Competition flourished in regard of the invention of new devices and innovations of all kinds for the making of goods, and their application created ever-widening fields of production and circulation.

These new activities frequently originated from a specific type of industrial and commercial leaders who happened to be quite often Puritans, Quakers and, on the Continent, Protestants. Their share in the growth of numerous industries of national and international importance exceeds by far their numerical proportion; the startling development of big shipping concerns, the story of large banking houses and numerous new industrial enterprises belong here. Without the impetus given by these entrepreneurs and their ability to combine foresight and knowledge, to calculate in advance economic

[1] F. A. Schumpeter, *The Theory of Economic Development*, Harvard University Press, 1949, p. 66.

prospects and to conduct their affairs in a rational, business-like fashion, the Western world would be a different place from what it is today.

II

The changes in the functions of government which can be observed for the last two to three decades could not but vitally affect the role of the entrepreneur. Though this role is still very prominent in the United States and a few other areas, it appears that in Europe the increasing influence of the State on economic matters has already modified the significance and position of the entrepreneur. This has not at all affected the scope of production in these countries, since the State has become as production-minded as the entrepreneur. To conduct and expand production, modern thought and practice have developed new devices and forms which have proved workable instruments for the execution of the new functions of government.

There now exist ramified official and semi-official agencies providing for and maintaining co-operation between the population and government in vital economic functions covering the fields of production, distribution and marketing.[1] The main difference, as compared with the past, lies in the following: in addition to the operation of the entrepreneurial incentives which induce the private industrialist or merchant to conceive and realise his economic plans, powerful public bodies have acquired key positions not only in the provision of services, but also quite frequently in the domain of nationally important industries. If these new agencies fulfil efficiently the economic functions present-day society has entrusted to them, the expansion of state activities is well justified. Western society has, indeed, profited from the new patterns of public initiative and enterprise. Perhaps it is too early to judge the potentialities of the new government policies in the West in view of the short span of time which has passed. Yet many of the new official bodies have given ample proof that they can perform their new tasks with honesty and ability.

[1] Professor F. Kenneth Galbraith describes the impact of Keynes on the American free-enterprise system in the following pertinent way: 'The Keynesian System, though it implied a decidedly non-revolutionary change in the relation of the government to the economy, implied nonetheless an important one. For a doctrine that excluded government it substituted one that made government indispensable. . . . Where in economic life people had previously looked upon business decisions as the ones that had shaped their destiny, now they would have regard for government decisions as well. Those of an Assistant Secretary of the Treasury on interest rates were now of more importance than those of any banker. Those of a regional administrator of public works on investment attained a significance greater than those of a corporation president. . . . The Keynesian system also . . . opened the way for a large expansion of government services and activities.' F. K. Galbraith, *American Capitalism*, Boston, 1952, pp. 84–5.

69

THE MOVE TOWARDS ADJUSTMENT

The situation is very different in large parts of the world which have up to now not had an economic history similar to that of the Western world. These underdeveloped areas are not yet able to draw on human resources of their own for the establishment of the economic and social framework to the extent that will enable them to stand up to the demands of the modern world. Yet they are eager to take their place in the family of nations, not as underprivileged paupers but as full-fledged members equal in spirit and in productive capacity.

But here the problem only begins. The high standard of living and the material conditions, all that which lends to the modern forms of life in the Western world their characteristic note, is the outcome of a protracted development. It owes its existence no less to the social heritage of the last two centuries than to recent technical achievements. The underdeveloped areas cannot rely on such a heritage. They have not got a steady supply of able organisers, engineers and public administrators. Yet the need for them in order to make up the difference in economic and social levels and attaining the potentialities and amenities of the modern world is increasingly felt.

Thus arises the question: Can the unique contribution which the entrepreneur personalities made in the West be repeated in backward areas, and in what way? To answer this question we must look at conditions in backward societies.

The situation in many underdeveloped areas was during the last 150 years, and still is, marked quite frequently by the co-existence of an advanced economic sector, limited in extent, but important in influence and output, which was under foreign control, together with the indigenous economy comprising the activities of the vast majority of the local population. Economic advance was usually initiated by foreigners, who were either employees of foreign companies or themselves entrepreneurs. In both cases they were the vanguard of an economic penetration which transferred capital and skill from more developed and technically advanced regions. These foreigners were moved primarily by massive profit interests, though political motives and adventurers' expectations also played a part.

Corresponding to the general expansion of economic activities in the metropolitan areas, foreign influences in underdeveloped countries too grew in importance. At the same time, resentment against and opposition to the continued existence of conditions encouraging the hold of foreigners developed. The wave of economic nationalism quickly reached the former dependent areas, and led in certain cases even to a liquidation of the economic and social position they had obtained. The outcome was, and quite often still is, a vacuum which has not yet been filled. True, a number of local entrepreneurs occu-

70

pied the vacant places or tried to secure the services of the foreigners by offering them secondary positions as advisers, technical managers, etc., but it seems doubtful whether this replacement would be sufficient to maintain and guide the process of industrialisation and reconstruction in the necessary dimensions.

Is this scepticism justified in the light of the significant economic performance of local business leaders, bankers and industrialists? Have not names like Tata, Sassoon and Birla in India become by-words for locally-grown-up large-scale enterprises, and groups like the Parsees, Marwaris and Jains, and quite a few others in Middle Eastern countries, been known since long as communities widely recognised for their commercial capabilities?

Yet the real issue is that of the numbers involved, i.e. whether efforts as indicated by these names can form a sufficient basis for the process of a swift economic reconstruction and adjustment to conditions in the Western world, industrial, rural, transport? The answer is definitely in the negative. Even if it were certain that the number of locally-developed large-scale enterprises and their employees would multiply in the course of the next generation or two, it would add only a small percentage to those at present employed in secondary or tertiary occupations. The solution to the problem of introducing economic change in underdeveloped areas cannot, therefore, be found by relying solely on the initiative of individuals; it must be sought in different directions: by conferring upon the State, as a temporary measure, the incentive function, and, simultaneously, in the purposeful generation of a new conscientiousness and sense of economic and social progress among the population.

The first method, the separation of the incentive from the principal bearer, the private entrepreneur, and its transfer to the State, has been attempted in the past in Oriental countries. We might call the approach the development 'from above' method.

As early as the nineteenth century, outstanding reformers with a deep insight into the nature of Oriental society were proceeding along the lines of a development policy enforced from above. This was not a policy introduced from *without* by a foreign power or their agents, political and commercial, but it was an imposed policy all the same, i.e. imposed from above through state initiative and state management. The chief objectives of this early planning were: to provide a substitute for capitalist incentive, to procure financial resources without loss of political independence, and to regenerate the social body. The methods were clearly not what we call today 'democratic planning', i.e. to carry out by democratic leadership, by persuasion, in an atmosphere of free discussion and co-operation, bold plans for social and economic changes. But failing these qualities there remains only compulsion from above and even that not as a safe method.

There is, perhaps, no better lesson than that afforded by the experiments of Mohammed Ali in Egypt more than a hundred years ago. In view of the general stagnation and the improbability that the Egyptians would of their own accord make profitable use of the ideas infiltrating from Europe, the conviction grew in Mohammed Ali that active and compulsory policies in the sphere of industry and education were imperative. The mentality of the Oriental at that time did not hold out much hope that he would be able to overcome all the difficulties confronting the revival of industrial initiative, let alone the introduction of European production methods of his own account. This could be achieved only by a dominant body invested with extensive powers. Thus, the State itself, i.e. its ruler, Mohammed Ali, embarked in grand style on an ambitious programme of economic and socio-political activities, and assumed a number of national-economic functions. His plan to transplant the Industrial Revolution to Egypt came to nothing, however, because the Egyptian population was not interested in it and the State administration of his time failed to grasp the importance of Mohammed Ali's daring ideas and to sense their potential effect. Similar attempts made in the Ottoman Empire achieved no more than ephemeral success.

Since that period the contact of the Oriental world with the West has been considerably intensified. Yet difficulties of a similar kind occurred again, every time the attempt was renewed to change the existing economic structure by a preconceived, imposed, long-term policy. In most recent times similar experiences have been had in the implementation of the Five- or Four-Year Plans in certain countries. The main obstacle has been the close association of the main government bodies, or the departments responsible for carrying out the plan, with 'vested interests'. These vested interests are in the nature of things concerned about changes in the sphere of production and distribution because these changes would imply a modification of the network of economic and social relations which is now entirely adjusted to their ideas of a convenient distribution of income. The attitudes shown at the various levels are however not equal and vary even between the regions of a single country. Genuine identification with the development programmes can be found side by side with indifference or even opposition to them.

The officials charged with the execution of the plans on the spot frequently lack the education, the skill and the honesty required to direct and supervise development projects which offer so many opportunities for personal enrichment. Government planning is entirely dependent on the existence of a comprehensive and loyal bureaucracy.

THE ROLE OF THE INCENTIVE

The administrative staffs in backward countries have not yet fully developed those qualities of loyalty and devotion, deriving from their identification with the aims of the State, which are regarded in most Western communities as the prerequisite for the exercise of any official function. To withstand the practically unlimited opportunities for personal enrichment, and hence for defeating the purpose of public service as such, requires a mentality which is not yet common in many underdeveloped countries. Hence planning and developing of government projects in underdeveloped regions are likely to be moderately successful only if they do not involve any excessive demands on the personal loyalty and conscientiousness of the officials who execute them. The more time that will be available to imbue all the parties concerned, through a broadly conceived educational effort, with new concepts of devotion and identification with the cause of the State and its development policies, the more promising will be the prospects for success. Here, however, lies the dilemma for the evolutionary approach to the problem. It is no use telling millions of people who are conscious of their destitution and misery that they should wait for many years, develop their educational systems and work for the improvement of the instruments and attitudes of their governments until projects of economic betterment can be executed with fair prospects of a beneficial effect on the life of everyone.

This is a challenge which also exists in other parts of the world, but it presents itself with particular force in underdeveloped areas. It is for this reason that a development policy from above must be accompanied and complemented by educational activities which could be termed 'development from within'. Definite progress can be assured only by an all-out educational drive at all levels of the population toward identification of its majority with the aims of this programme. That is no easy matter. In many countries it is still not understood that a general rise in the standards can be obtained only when an informed community is actively participating in the various undertakings and obligations implied in the drive for betterment.

Yet this process itself might be speeded up. The Russians went perhaps to the utmost limit to obtain the maximum integration of the inhabitants of an underdeveloped country in the efforts induced from above. The incentives for the reconstruction of their economic and social system were fed from and carried on through a new social and national ideology imbued in a sufficiently large cadre of men who acted as a disciplined and utterly devoted group for its fulfilment. Certainly it would be wrong to belittle the important role which even in Soviet Russia personal incentives like monetary rewards for increased output or a higher grading for organising efficiency played in the process of economic reconstruction. But it would likewise be wrong to think 'that the lure of high income and a better apartment, fear of dismissal and punishment, seductions of power, have by themselves been sufficient to make the machinery go round and grow so rapidly. When the Soviet manager must achieve higher labour effort or produce a new technical process, he does not merely give orders. He must explain and justify the innovation, campaign for it, appeal above all to the public interest. One must not forget the tense atmosphere in which industrial work has been done in Russia, the fighting spirit necessary in the Civil War and later to prepare for foreign war. The humblest worker has been made to feel that he is defending an important, dangerous position. Every engineer and director is running a "battle" section, feels himself a "commander in the production front". The plant manager, in fact, must satisfy requirements rather similar to those expected of military commanders. This quasi-military frame of mind accounts for many shortcomings of Soviet industrial management, so often over-impulsive and unmethodical. Instead of systematic, regular work, there are often periods of strain alternating with relaxation; frequent failures called "front-breaks" are followed by spasmodic drives called "attacks". But could the task of rapid industrialisation and preparation for a modern war set by Russian political leaders have been fulfilled without this fever of combat and self-sacrifice?' [1]

Among the attempts to develop new forms of economic and social life the Zionist efforts in Israel also deserve mention. Society in the new State of Israel is not modelled on homogeneous layers. European, Oriental and, recently, American influences are at work to create a multi-faceted structure showing a mosaic of economic and social patterns from many countries and societies. But if the question is asked how the remarkable growth and power of resistance of this small community against innumerable odds and obstacles can be explained, then the strong spiritual forces operating within it must be mentioned; the urge towards new improved social forms of living and production on the one hand, and the driving power of a national movement aiming at the regeneration of the people on the soil of its homeland on the other. Without these two incentives the transformation of the country and, in particular, its economic development would not have been possible. Without it the new entrepreneurial patterns, in particular the collective and public entrepreneurs, would not have come into being and would not have been able to contribute so spectacularly to the growth of the economy.

The vital question which poses itself in this context is whether lessons learned in one country can be applied elsewhere. The answer

[1] From Bienstock, Schwarz and Yugow, *Management in Russian Industry and Agriculture*, Oxford University Press, 1944, p. 103.

is that important as these lessons may be, they cannot be transferred lock, stock and barrel to other areas because they are too much the outcome of specific and non-recurrent local circumstances; the considerable amount of coercion which prevails in the Russian, and in any 'totalitarian' approach where the incentive is created and imbued from 'above', forms likewise a specific feature which will not be feasible everywhere. There is so far, therefore, no ready recipe for the inauguration of processes of economic development in areas where both the entrepreneur and a reliable government apparatus for economic promotion are lacking. A considerable measure of trial and error on the spot is necessary to find out the most suitable new approaches.

The need for such new approaches has already produced interesting attempts to transfer organisational skill and capitalist incentive to foreign countries along the lines of a new concept: 'joint enterprise'. Here the basic idea is a partnership where the manpower, resources and, as much as available also, the capital of underdeveloped countries shall be pooled with the capital resources and the technical and business experience of advanced nations. Under this slogan of 'joint enterprise', or 'partnership capitalism', co-operation is established between two partners each of whom desires the services of the other. From the viewpoint of finance, the difference from the former types of direct capitalist investment in foreign countries may be rather small; the financial outlay must in the first instance be supplied by the financially strong partner. But there are important modifications in the way of working and organisation of such joint enterprises. The local interests have been allotted a share in the personnel for technical and managerial posts. The determination of the lines of business follows the need for lines of development promotion, i.e. the investment does not limit itself to mining, transport and public services, but goes into food production, fish supply improvement, hog production and various other agricultural lines. The main area of these activities is Latin America; the International Basic Economy Corporation (I.B.E.C.) founded by Nelson Rockefeller and his brothers is the leading, though not the only, venture operating in this field. The Rockefeller programme of joint enterprise is enlarged by the activities of a non-profit membership corporation, the A.I.A.—American International Association for Economic and Social Development. Its purpose is to advance living standards and opportunities for self-improvement by devising plans with funds matched by the local governments concerned. These examples do not exhaust the list of the new approaches and techniques to tackle the problem of promotion in underdeveloped areas. Certain activities have recently been inaugurated by the United

Nations agencies—especially created to promote the social and economic development of backward areas; their investigations into conditions of living, health and education which have been undertaken to provide the basic data for the development programmes have proved invaluable to all interested in these problems.[1]

Opinions may differ as to the motives, experience and results of all these efforts. In a sense it can be said that the underdeveloped regions exist because incentives which started to change the Western world some two hundred years ago did not operate in them. The focusing of the world's attention on them gives reason to expect that in the not too distant future we shall be able to operate devices of promotion and development which will either fulfil or complete the function of effective entrepreneurial incentives.

[1] For an account of the diversified practical activities along these lines see H. M. Teaf, Junr., and P. G. Franck (ed.) *Hands Across Frontiers,* Case Studies in Technical Co-operation, Ithaca, 1955. The book is a highly instructive collection of papers describing the experience made in various fields of technical assistance to underdeveloped countries by way of international co-operation.

CHAPTER VI

RISE IN REAL INCOME THROUGH HIGHER PRODUCTIVITY

IN the preceding part of this treatise we have placed the issue of an increased per capita output of goods and services at the centre of our general problem. A sustained rise of average living standards in a given country is dependent on the rise of the average real income, and the latter again on the rise in real net output of that country. This is the central relationship which cannot be decisively affected by qualifying factors such as inequality in the distribution of national income, or by temporary diversions in its flow, in times of emergency, towards purposes of national defence.

The attainment of a high level of net output per capita and its maintenance require certain concrete pre-conditions of an economic nature, which will employ us in this chapter. Though there are clearly many general conditions of relevance for a high output level, we shall discuss here only the more specific factors having close and direct bearing on this issue.

The high level of net output in developed Western countries is usually interrelated with the simultaneous presence of several factors:

1 A high rate of capital investment (productive equipment) per worker;
2 An adequate level of physical fitness of the workers;
3 The spread of elementary education, as a rule by the introduction of compulsory school attendance;
4 A high standard of scientific research and knowledge and the ability of entrepreneurs and managers to turn them to good account;
5 A system of incentives directed at releasing optimum efforts on the part of the workers.

Abundant natural resources are most conducive to the attainment of high productivity levels, but are not essential to them.

THE MOVE TOWARDS ADJUSTMENT

The degree of skill and productivity of labour, a result of educational efforts and capital outlay, takes a prominent place among causes determining the scope of income and wealth. Figures showing the rise in output per worker and in per capita consumption in the United States are illuminating for a rise in efficiency and productivity unparalleled elsewhere, and for the close relation between a high level of income and of productivity. In the course of the last seventy years (1880–1950), output per man-hour has risen from $0·36 to $1·44 (1944 prices).[1] During the period 1869–1948 the per capita volume of commodities and services purchased annually by ultimate consumers has risen from $185 to $728, or almost four times, measured in 1929 prices.[2] The upward trend is still continuing. At the same time average weekly hours for workers have been reduced from 65 to 41.

These data are thus instructive in two directions: (a) they show that great improvements are possible under favourable conditions; (b) they tend to underline the close connection of a rise in labour productivity with the general improvement in national wealth and prosperity of a country. At the same time differences in output level may go far to explain gaps in real per capita income of various national economies.

COMPARISONS OF PRODUCTIVITY

The appraisal of productivity trends is thus an important element in the judgment of development prospects in underdeveloped areas.

Yet international comparisons of output values per unit of labour (or unit of cost) are hampered by difficulties in using a common measuring rod for widely differing conditions of production in the various countries. These difficulties are increased by the unsatisfactory quality of statistical data in underdeveloped areas; the hectic character of economic development, marked by a frequent sequence of expansion and contraction affecting the output level; and the influence of non-measurable factors in such regions—all of which limit the possibility of exact comparison. Notwithstanding these obstacles, the data used here can be regarded as reasonably adequate for the purpose of broad comparisons.

Remarkable attempts have been made by Colin Clark to overcome the difficulties in obtaining internationally comparable figures for net income or net productivity of many and widely differing countries. These attempts are based on the so-called 'International Unit',

---

[1] *America's Needs and Resources*, The Twentieth Century Fund, p. 26a.
[2] S. Kuznets and R. Goldsmith, *Income and Wealth of the United States*, Trends and Structures, Income and Wealth Series II, Cambridge, 1952, p. 59.

a real measure expressing the amount of goods and services which a dollar could buy over the period 1925–34 in the United States. Net production or services rendered in the main economic branches is calculated by deducting from the total volume of production the quantities consumed in the course of production; the remaining net output is valued at the same international standard prices. The resulting data afford an interspatial comparison and are more representative for agricultural productivity than for that in manufacturing and services. Agricultural production is less varied in scope, and measurable in volume and quality throughout, whereas the output of many industrial products and certainly of services cannot be compared by physical measurement.

AGRICULTURAL PRODUCTIVITY

The following figures convey the values for net agricultural production per male earner in international units based on the standard year 1934–5. The present author has computed a series of data for Middle Eastern countries by the same method in his *Economic Development of the Middle East*, and compared them with corresponding data for Western countries. In the 1950 edition of his *Conditions of Economic Progress* Mr. Clark has slightly amended these computations; for the sake of comparability with the non-Oriental countries the new figures are inserted in the table.[1]

Net Productivity per Male Earner Occupied in Agriculture on the Basis of 1934–5 Crops

Western Countries	I.U.*	Underdeveloped Countries	I.U.*	Bonné†
New Zealand	2,006	Palestine	232	(252)
Australia	1,329	Cyprus	159	(143)
Argentine	1,115	Turkey	119	(109)
U.S.A.	623	Syria and Lebanon	165	(98)
Holland	489	Iraq	108	(93)
Germany	416	Egypt	92	(90)
Great Britain	531	British India (excl.		
France	414	Native States)	83	
Poland	189	Philippines	83	

* Colin Clark, *Conditions of Economic Progress*, 1951, p. 201.
† *Economic Development of the Middle East*, 1945, p. 47.

The figures of the table show clearly the glaring discrepancy between the net agricultural output of Western and underdeveloped

[1] In the meantime a new unit of measurement has been compiled by Mr. Clark, the 'Oriental Unit' (O.U.).

countries. The figures refer, it is true, to the thirties; yet it can be assumed that there has been, with few exceptions, no substantial general rise in per capita productivity since then. To maintain existing consumption levels in underdeveloped countries requires a sustained increase in productivity, owing to the continuous growth of population; to raise these levels would mean a considerable expansion of all production factors involved in the output. On the other hand, the increase of productivity in Western countries is apparently quite uneven. For England, the available evidence is rather against the assumption of such a rise. According to a paper on the productivity of labour in agriculture by Mr. F. G. Hurrock, little trace can be found of increase of labour productivity since 1939.[1] As against this, figures for the United States points to a continuation of trends towards an impressive improvement of productivity, when calculated in terms of man-hours used to produce an acre of wheat, etc., for the period 1880 to 1940.

Estimated Man-hours Used to Produce an Acre of Wheat, Corn and Cotton[2]

	Yearly average for		
	1880	1920	1940
Wheat			
Man-hours per acre before harvest	8	5·5	3·7
Harvest	12	6·5	3·8
Yield per acre in bushels*	13·2	13·8	15·9
Man-hours per 100 bushel	152	87	47
Corn for grain			
Man-hours per acre before harvest	28	19	15
Harvest	18	13	10
Yield per acre in bushels*	25·6	28·4	30·3
Man-hours per 100 bushels	180	113	83
Cotton			
Man-hours per acre before harvest	67	55	46
Harvest	52	35	52
Yield of gross lint per acre in pounds*	196	160	257
Man-hours per bale	304	281	191

* Yields are 5-year averages of published data centred on year shown.

Whereas the requirements in man-hour per unit of land and crop show a conspicuous decrease over the last 60 years, the yield per acre during the same period reveals a substantial increase per unit. Part of the explanation may be seen in the use of machinery, in

[1] Proceedings of Agricultural Economics Society, 1950, p. 15.
[2] M. R. Cooper and assoc., *Progress of Farm Mechanization*, U.S. Department of Agriculture, October 1947, p. 3.

particular tractors, on an ever-increasing scale. The following table shows the development in this sphere:

Trends in Tractor Numbers, 1930–1949[1]

	Estimated tractor inventories[2] (thousand units)			Percentage of: World tractors 1948–9 (per cent)	World arable land[3] (per cent)
	1930	1938–9	1948–9		
North America	1,020	1,597	3,700	70·8	17·2
United Kingdom	20	60	285	⎰ 15·0	⎰ 12·2
Europe (excl. U.K.)	110	205	501	⎱	⎱
U.S.S.R.	72	523	500	9·6	18·4
Latin America	20	35	70	1·3	9·3
Near and Middle East	2	5	13	0·2	6·1
Far East	1	3	13	0·2	22·9
Africa	10	17	52	1·0	12·4
Oceania	32	53	101	1·9	1·5
	1,287	2,498	5,235	100·0	100·0

The table offers a picture of remarkable inequality in the use of mechanical equipment. Whereas the areas including most under-developed countries—the Near and Middle East, the Far East, Latin America and Africa—comprise half of the world's arable land, their share in tractor inventories in 1948–9 was only 2·5% of the total. It is true that tractor numbers alone do not indicate the extent of large mechanical power employed on farms. The rate of utilisation, too, is important and varies from country to country. In the U.S.S.R., for instance, it seems to be extraordinarily high according to available information. In 1936, tractors on collective farms worked from 800–1,600 hours p.a., and in 1940, 1,100 hours, from machine tractor stations. As against this, in Western Europe and North America individual tractor units are utilised much less. The figures for Switzerland and the U.K. are 600 and 800 hours respectively, whereas data for the U.S. indicate a utilisation of 500–600 hours per annum.

Another relevant aspect in the appraisal of these figures is tractor density. In the United States, the United Kingdom, New Zealand and Germany there were less than 150 hectares of arable land per tractor. In France, Italy, Egypt and Hungary one tractor had, on the

[1] *Progress and Economic Problems in Farm Mechanization*, F.A.O., Washington, September 1950, p. 5.
[2] As far as possible, the figures given here refer to agricultural tractors; but in some cases a distinction between horticultural types and tractors used for non-agricultural purposes can be made. In the fifties the number of tractors rose everywhere greatly.
[3] Includes temporary fallow, temporary meadows and pastures, garden land, orchards and fruit-bearing shrubs.

average, to serve 150–500 hectares. Where the area of arable lands per tractor amounts to more than 500 hectares, we can well assume that the country is 'underdeveloped'. In fact, in the large under-developed expanses in Asia arable land per tractor covers 1,500 hectares and more.

LAND RENT AND PRODUCTIVITY OF LAND

Rising productivity which results from increase in capital investment has an influence on the level and relative share of land rent. The higher yield in this case is clearly not due to the initial properties of the land, but to the larger input of other means of production. Having in mind the continuous and accelerating demand for food resulting from the phenomenal increase in population during the last 150 years, one should have expected a corresponding trend in the evaluation of land, a major agent in the combination of food-producing factors. Strangely enough, however, we find quite an opposite trend: in many Western countries the land factor has shown itself to be of decreasing importance within the aggregate of inputs necessary to food production. If this trend is measured by the price paid for land in the form of agricultural land rent, as T. W. Schultz has recently shown, the results point to a marked reduction in the relative share of such rent in national as well as agricultural income.[1]

Not only an increase of capital or labour input can change the productivity of land. An inestimable amount of 'mental' capital has been invested over many years in efforts to improve farming results. Applied research in soil chemistry, new methods of fighting plant diseases, genetic improvement of food plants and the introduction of mechanical power have led to an amazing increase of productivity in modern agriculture—an increase expressing itself in the rise of output per unit of land and per unit of worker. It is this remarkable increase in the production potential per unit which explains, on the background of an unparalleled expansion of industries and services, the paradox of increased production of food in the face of agriculture's decreasing share in national output.

PRODUCTIVITY IN INDUSTRY

Industrial productivity shows a revolutionary rise in output levels for all countries undergoing industrialisation. The fundamental change which the transition from handicrafts to machine production

[1] T. W. Schultz, 'The Declining Economic Importance of Agricultural Land', *Economic Journal*, 1951, pp. 725 ff.

has brought about can hardly be better demonstrated than by comparison of data per man-hour and worker over a protracted period. The following table from Colin Clark's *Review of Economic Progress*, August 1949, offers an interesting historical comparison of output data for manufacturing in the United States, Great Britain and France. It shows not only the superiority of American productivity since the second half of the last century, but the general rise of productivity per worker in each country.

Output Data in Manufacturing in the United States, Great Britain and France

Year	Numbers employed (million)	Net income produced (million I.U.)	Net income per head (I.U.)	Average hours in manufacture per year	Average product per man-hour (I.U.)
		UNITED STATES			
1869	1·95	(1,300)	667	3,200	0·209
1900	5·25	5,540	1,055	3,078	0·343
1930	8·63	14,980	1,737	2,266	0·765
1938	8·34	15,410	1,849	1,736	1·065
		GREAT BRITAIN			
1836–45	2·90	578	199	(3,200)	0·062
1870–76	4·60	1,638	356	3,000	0·119
1911–13	5·81	3,144	541	2,780	0·195
1938	6·53	5,670	870	2,440	0·356
		FRANCE			
1840–45	1·49	146	98	3,600	0·027
1861–65	2·0	410	205	3,600	0·057
1938	3·83	2,408	630	1,977	0·319

Output data for Oriental countries in the past are scarce; yet the few available indicate that there was probably a much closer resemblance between Western and Oriental 'efficiencies' before the mechanisation of production than there is today.

The former French Consul in Alep, Henry Guys, a prominent member of the Statistical Society of Marseilles, compiled interesting data on the structure of industries in the Syrian town of Alep in 1844.[1] They apply to one location only, it is true, but they support the view of the increasing gap since the introduction of the machine in the West.

[1] *Statistique de Pachalik d'Alep*, Marseilles, 1853, pp. 102. According to Guys, the gross output of 4,484 workers in 1844, employed in 337 manufacturing establishments and artisan shops, amounted to Frs. 4,477,065, i.e. Frs. 998 per worker. As the tabulation of Guys also contains an analysis of the raw material used and the cost of production, we are able to estimate the 'added value' as total value minus raw material, and thus arrive at a per capita figure of Frs. 362 (incl. the profits of the owners). If only the wage bill is taken into account, the 'added

THE MOVE TOWARDS ADJUSTMENT

In recent years more data have become available on the development of industrial production in underdeveloped countries which allow some qualified conclusions on the quantitative aspects involved.

PRODUCTIVITY LEVELS IN EGYPT

Recent enumerations and inquiries on industrial establishments in Egypt usually comprise only part of the industries of the country. The scanty data provided by these censuses do not include data on productivity; although certain output figures offer a meagre basis for attempts to obtain productivity trends.

Thus, for example, a partial inquiry arranged by the Egyptian Federation of Industries in 1948[1] makes possible the calculation of a few output data. The inquiry relates to 126 major industrial enterprises employing 85,534 workers, with a gross production of £E.83 million; indicating through simple division a gross output of £E.970 per worker, an average salary of £E.152 per employed, and a value of production of £E.665,000 per plant. These figures obviously refer to large-size establishments. The industrial census of 1944 counted 129,000 establishments, employing 500,000 workers and producing goods to the value of £E.167 million. If we calculate output data for these 129,000 enterprises, we obtain an average gross output of £E.334 per worker, against £E.970 for the 126 enterprises mentioned above; and an average gross output of £E.1,294 per establishment, against an output value per plant of £E.665,000 in the partial inquiry of 1948. Even if we concede some change in the value of the pound between 1944 and 1948 and an understatement in output evaluation for the majority of enterprises in the census of 1944, we shall have to recognise the average value of less than £E.1,300 for the gross output per establishment as an indication of the very small size of the large majority of the 129,000 establishments. Thus these average output data have only a very limited meaning.

A more differentiating approach is included in the break-up for 22,200 establishments in the 1944 census, giving gross and net output figures for the main industrial branches. This material has served as the basis of an elaborate compilation of productivity data, details of which are given in the following section.

A slightly more comprehensive enumeration dated 1948, counts 26,743 productive industrial establishments employing 367,336 workers, with a gross value of production of £E.197,384,000. This would value' is revised to Frs. 259 per worker, or approximately 70 centimes on a daily basis. These figures denote an extremely low level of output and earning, but this appears less so if we consider the low cost of living, which has been estimated by Guys at 30 centimes per day in the case of the poorer classes, and at 50–75 centimes per capita per day in the case of the middle and wealthy classes.

[1] See *L'Egypte Industrielle*, March–April 1949, pp. 29–30.

mean an output value of £E.510 per worker, which though somewhat higher than the corresponding figure for 1944, is still a low figure for the productive performance of an industrial worker and is largely explained by the small size of the majority of enterprises enumerated.[1]

But it is not only the small-scale character of most of these establishments which affects the level of productivity in Egyptian industry. The productivity of larger plants, too, is much inferior to average output levels in the same industrial branches in Western countries.

In a paper on the productivity of Egyptian industry, the author, Dr. Gamal Eldin Said, calculated net output figures per head and for each industry on the basis of the figures of the Industrial Census of Egypt, 1944.[2] It is quite clear that his figures, like those from other sources, should only be used with caution. The value of these data lies in the possibility they afford to compare output values per worker in Egypt with those of Western countries in a very general way. According to his calculations, the average output per operative in Egypt reached only 21, as against 100 in the United Kingdom, 111 in Germany and 225 in the U.S. Notwithstanding the reservations against the international comparability of output figures, the result can be regarded as characteristic of the very considerable inferiority of industrial productivity in Egypt in general.

The author of the study enumerates the reasons which explain the low output of Egyptian labour. He mentions ill-health, deficient nutrition and the general state of poverty, which affect the working capacity of the Egyptian operative. Additional factors are illiteracy, which prevailed in 1944 among more than three-quarters of the population; the abundance of cheap labour, which is inconducive to efforts to raise productivity and efficiency; the lack of technical ability and knowledge, a deficiency due either to the shortage of foremen and charge-hands or to difficulties in quickly imparting the necessary instructions; the high rate of absenteeism, a most disturbing element in industrial relations in Oriental countries; and finally, the low degree of utilisation of available production capacity in many Egyptian industries. The figures given by the author for ten Egyptian industries indicate that only from 21 to 70% of their capacity is utilised.

This inferior degree of productivity can be determined with a greater measure of accuracy for a specific industrial branch, usually in one of two ways: either by comparing the number of operatives needed for operating an equal unit of equipment, or by measuring the

---

[1] The most important industry, by number of workers and value of production, is textiles, with 82,419 workers and £E.62·6 million.
[2] See *L'Egypte Contemporaine*, Cairo, May–June 1950.

output for the same unit of working time (man-hour or man-day). Comparative data for Egypt's textile industry are more abundant than for other Oriental countries. Yet though these data may show some improvement over time, the gaps between the Egyptian productivity performances and of that of the United Kingdom and the United States have not substantially altered.

The numbers of workers per 1,000 spindles employed in Egypt was very much higher than that in Western countries. For 1941 it was estimated at 15–18 workers per thousand spindles,[1] as against 3·4 workers in the U.S. (1934), 4 in England, 6 in Japan, 9 in China, and 15 in British India.[2]

The report on the British Cotton Industry also compares the cost of labour for various countries. As the figures show, the cost of labour per thousand spindles per week was then very much lower in China and Japan, and even in Egypt, than in the United States and the United Kingdom. More recent investigations into productivity in the English and Egyptian spinning industries again reveal a discrepancy in the cost of labour per machinery unit. Yet owing to the higher productivity of the British worker, his higher wages do not prevent lower *labour costs* per machinery unit.[3]

Weekly Wages and Wage Costs per Machinery Unit in Egypt and the
United Kingdom, 1949 (in piastres)

| Occupation | Weekly wages per workman: | | Wage costs per machinery unit: | |
	Egypt	United Kingdom	Egypt	United Kingdom
Carding	316	558	39·5	13·3
Tending draw frames	253	412	109·7	34·3
Tending speed frames	315	419	5·2	1·7
Spinning	140	400	1·1	1·2
Weaving	492	658	123·0	65·8

The following table contains data for total output, number of looms and operatives, and average output per unit of work and per loom. The figures again reveal a great superiority of output per operative in England, and more so in the United States; it should be noted, however, that the figures for the latter countries referring to the year 1944 comprise only part of the English and American weaving industry.

[1] A. Eman, *L'Industrie du Cotton en Egypte*, Cairo, 1943, p. 77.
[2] See *Report of British Cotton Industry*, P.E.P., London, 1937, p. 80.
[3] R. Gasche, 'Pay and Productivity of Textile Workers in Egypt, Europe and the United States', *Egyptian Cotton Gazette*, September 1949; quoted in National Bank of Egypt, Economic Bulletin (Cairo), Vol. II, No. 4 (1949), p. 188.

RISE IN INCOME AND PRODUCTIVITY

Yearly Productivity in Cotton Weaving

		Total output (in 1,000 sq. metres)	No. of power looms	No. of opera- tives	Output per operative (in sq. metres)	Output per loom (in sq. metres)	Looms per individual operative
Egypt (2 shifts)	1941	150,000	8,400	20,000	7,500	—	—
Egypt (on 1-shift basis)	1941	150,000	17,000	—	—	8,900	0·8
U.K. (full-time)*	1937	3,790,000	420,000	206,000	18,400	9,020	2·0
U.K.	1942*	1,900,000	315,000	104,000	18,300	6,050	3·0

* Report of the Cotton Board Committee, January 1944; for the purpose of this table, square yards in the said Report have been converted into square metres.

The large percentage of hand-looms in the weaving industry had a considerable effect on its average productivity. In 1941–2 there were 35,000 hand-looms employing approximately 45,000 workers, as against 8,400 mechanical looms with approximately 20,000 operatives. However, hand-looms produced in Egypt nearly one-third or 70 million sq. metres of the total output for that year.

The great advantage which higher scale and superior capital equipment afford is also seen from a comparison between output figures in Palestine, England and America, though the industrial sector of Palestine is of comparatively recent origin. According to the figures of the table, production per man-hour in various textile processes amounted in Palestine only to a fraction of American production, and to 50% of English production in some processes. American mills used automatic high-speed spoolers, and even British mills obtained a better output per man-hour; though their winding machines are more backward in output than those found in the Palestine mill, the reason being that more spindles were handled by an operator abroad than in Palestine.[1]

Productivity in English and Egyptian Spinning*

		Number of spindles (mule spindles)	Quantity of yarn spun (tons)	No. of persons employed	No. of persons per 1,000 spindles	Yarn spun per person (kg.)	Yarn spun per spindle (kg.)
U.K.	1937	39,000,000	618,750	186,000	4·8	3,326	16
	1942	24,000,000	375,000	108,000	4·0	3,506	18·7
Egypt	1942	550,000	36,000	15,500	17·0	2,323	26·2

* The data for England were taken from the Report of the Cotton Board Committee of January 1944. They refer to mule spindles and to one shift. The data for Egypt were originally in respect of ring spindles and 2½ shifts, but have for the purpose of this table been converted into mule spindles and one shift, respectively (1 ring spindle = 1½ mule spindles).

[1] Bulletin of the Economic Research Institute of the Jewish Agency, Jerusalem, 1948, p. 34.

THE MOVE TOWARDS ADJUSTMENT

The greater productivity per worker in England, as compared to Egypt, is accounted for by the skill of English spinners. On the other hand, the lower productivity per spindle is attributed partly to the use of obsolete spinning machinery in England, which has meanwhile probably been largely replaced. The bulk of English spindles are mule spindles, which from the point of view of output are known to be inferior to the ring-type. One ring spindle corresponds to $1\frac{1}{2}$ mule spindles. A ring spindle produces 200 grams of cotton yarn during a 10-hour working day, while a mule spindle (heavy going) spins only 130 grams.

PRODUCTIVITY LEVELS IN INDIA

Since Western capital started large-scale industries in the empires of South and Eastern Asia, interest in the results of their activities as compared to those of the factories at home was keenly felt. The problem of productivity in particular became one of the central issues of industrial expansion in these areas, owing to the fact that the economic yields of the new factory production frequently did not come up to expectations which had been based on the low wage level. Hand weaving in India, for instance, still showed a remarkable prevalence in the thirties and forties: in 1935–6 the output of hand-looms amounted to 1,660 million yards, i.e. nearly a third of the total output of 5,160 million, hand-looms producing 1·8 billion yards of cloth.[1]

On the problem of comparing data for such diversified conditions as prevail in Indian industry, the following quotations from the Report of the Royal Commission on Labour in India seem appropriate:

'. . . So far as efficiency is concerned, comparisons are available of the number of workers required in India and in other countries, Western and Eastern, to produce certain quantities of material in a given time, and some of these will be found in the evidence. We do not quote them here, because apart from their limited scope, it is impossible to say that such quantitative measurements have taken account of all the other factors involved, such as difference in machinery, organisation, etc. But it must be admitted that the Indian industrial worker produces less per unit than the worker in any other country claiming to rank as a leading industrial nation. The causes of this low efficiency are complex. Some are to be found in the climate of India and other factors; but a powerful influence is exercised everywhere by the low standard of living. Inefficiency is attributable to lack of both physical energy and mental vigour. These are to

[1] According to *Foreign Commerce Weekly*, September 4, 1943.

a large extent different aspects of the same defect, for physical weakness cuts at the root of ambition, initiative and desire. . . . These hardships and conditions are mainly the result of inability to afford anything better, and this in turn arises from low efficiency. Thus poverty leads to bad conditions, bad conditions to inefficiency and inefficiency to poverty . . . The range of efficiency on the part of employers in India is very wide. There are enterprises that will stand comparison with any outside India; there are others whose inefficiency is obvious even to the casual observer. We are anxious not to enter on a field which lies outside our proper functions; but we have been struck by the contrasts presented in industrial and commercial organisation. We also found many employers unaware of the successful experiments of others in the labour field.'[1]

The material submitted by Indian industrialists in connection with the visit of the Royal Commission on Labour contains many data referring to the problem of industrial productivity. These data too lack the refinement which is offered in modern analyses of productivity problems. Yet even so, the available figures show considerable fluctuations in volume of output: they are lower for the end of the twenties than for the eve of the Second World War. Figures after the war still show the impact of war events.

Tons of Coal Produced per Annum per Person Employed

	Year	Tons	Year	Tons	Year	Tons
India	1928	131	1938	141	1948	92
Japan	1926	132	1938	170	1948	74
Great Britain	1928	250	1938	289	1948	297
United States	1926	780	1938	796	1948	1,240
Germany	1925	234	1936	402 (Dec.)	1947	170 (Bizonia)

The post-war figures for India show a recession following the general slackening down of productivity in that country after the war.

Another investigation refers to certain kinds of work in a locomotive workshop, which require 4·4 persons in England on the L.M.S. Railway, as against 20·5 persons in India.[2]

Interesting experience is available from the famous Tata steel works, the existence of which is in itself a remarkable contribution to the practice of industrial growth in underdeveloped countries. According to the evidence before the Royal Commission on Labour,

[1] Report of the Royal Commission on Labour in India, London, 1931, pp. 208–9.
[2] Evidence of the Chief Inspector of Mines in India, Royal Commission on Labour, Vol. II, Part I, p. 234, according to Lokanathan, p. 360.
Interesting data on pre-war conditions in Chinese industries are available from an article in the *Economic Journal*, September 1946. Output levels are not too different from those in the new Indian industries. There is, first, the immense lag

the Tata steel plant employs a far greater number of employees in relation to output than a similar plant would in Western countries. But at the same time certain lines such as tin plate manufacture show decided progress in the efficiency of skilled workers, though the levels reached do not yet equal those of American or European workers.

PSYCHOLOGICAL FACTORS AND PRODUCTIVITY

The data on productivity levels in Oriental regions have one feature in common: they are all below and in part very much below corresponding levels in Western countries. Owing to the crucial significance of this problem, it has become recently the subject of numerous reports which try to analyse the cause for the gap and to suggest measures for improvement.

In two reports brought out recently on problems of labour productivity in various countries, interesting conclusions are drawn concerning the causes of low productivity in the industries investigated. In a United Nations report[1] on 'Labour Productivity of the Cotton Textile Industry in Five Latin-American Countries', it is pointed out that the Latin-American textile industry is affected not only by the lack of technical progress as regards equipment, but also by defects in management. These two deficiencies are, however, not to be found to the same degree in all the countries investigated. Moreover, there are also numerous mills without administrative

in net output per head for all factory operatives. The authors of the article, Pao-San Ou and Foh-Shen Wang, give the following table:

Value of Net Output per head of Factory Operative in China, Germany, U.K. and U.S.

	China 1936	Germany 1936	U.K. 1935	U.S.A. 1935
£	31	294	264	595
Index Numbers	100	948	852	1,929

From 'Industrial Production and Employment in Pre-War China', *Economic Journal*, September 1946, p. 433.

The authors rightly remark that the astonishing differences in output per factory worker will be even more spectacular when comparison is made between the Chinese handicraft worker and the American worker. One day's work of an American worker will be found equivalent to fifty days' work of a Chinese handicraft worker.

The infant stage which marked China's industry in the thirties is shown in another table given by the Chinese economists in the same article. According to their figures, the volume of net output in the United States in 1935 was 162 times greater than that in China in 1933; compared with Germany the ratio was 1 : 64 and with the United Kingdom, 1 : 50, notwithstanding the much larger population of China.

[1] Published by the Economic Department, United Nations, New York, 1951.

defects. Thus the prospects for an improvement in productivity may be regarded as fairly good.

The shortcomings of the Latin-American textile industry in so far as equipment is concerned are ascribed mainly to the fact that, from the period of outstanding progress early in the century until the present, manufacturers have had little incentive to modernise their machinery. Four different circumstances could offer such encouragement:

1 A more spectacular increase of production per unit of equipment (spindle or loom), or, in a general way, per unit of capital invested;
2 Considerable savings in labour, per unit of finished goods;
3 A marked increase of quality in the textile goods per unit of capital invested; or
4 The compelling need to replace machinery because of physical deterioration.

The report then discusses the potential effects of these incentives and the meaning of their absence. The stimulus to modernise machinery offered by a reduction in the amount of labour required per unit of equipment has been extremely weak in Latin America, owing principally to the relative unimportance of the average wage level in industry as compared with the average price of textile goods. If the price of a popular fabric in each country is assumed to be 100, then the cost per man-hour would be 60 in Brazil, 82 in Chile, 36 in Ecuador, 86 in Mexico and 57 in Peru. Against this the cost per man-hour in the United States, where the price of labour is a weighty factor in production cost, would be 355.

The common inference that a low wage level for industrial workers is of vital interest to employers in underdeveloped countries is not generally shared. When visiting large-scale factories in the Middle East and India, the present writer was frequently told by owners or managers that they would willingly raise the wage if this would assure a rise in output per worker. But higher wages in their opinion were not always expedient to improving the low output; they contributed rather to a slackening down of the workers' interest in the maintenance of their scope of employment. The problem thus has two aspects: the effect of a change in wage level on the worker and its effect on the employer or firm.

In general the findings of the U.N. report on labour productivity relating to employers' and labourers' attitudes in Latin America can be applied also to conditions in other underdeveloped countries: the first conclusion, as mentioned above, attributes the lack of incentive to modernise organisation and equipment principally to the relatively low cost of labour. The manufacturer is thus induced to assign only very few units of equipment per worker. This ensures a high output from the machinery and reduces the inherent problems of maintenance of strict controls, training, readjustment or displacement of labour, etc.

The second conclusion concerns labour attitudes, in particular the resistance of labour to any change which may involve its displacement. This resistance, finding expression also in the rigidity of certain labour attitudes, restricts the possibility of administrative improvements, which would demand a higher degree of mobility of labour. In places where there has been no preceding industrial employment at all, the resistance of labour towards change expresses itself in more primitive forms.

The importance of labour attitudes is emphasised from a different angle in the 'Productivity Report on Conditions in the Steel Founding Industry', published by the Anglo-American Council on Productivity.[1] A comparison is made here, it is true, between two highly developed industrial economies, one of which has a clear lead in equipment. Yet it is exceedingly instructive to find the explanation of much higher American productivity in steel founding not in superior technical equipment, but in the attitude of labour. The authors stress time and time again the fact that the productivity consciousness found in American industry is primarily responsible for its achievements of high productivity. Every employee is fully aware of the advantages accruing to him and his fellow workers from high productivity. At all levels labour incentives are in evidence, and monetary incentives are truly effective for an additional reason: taxation is not so severe as to nullify the extra reward for extra effort. Incentives include not only the prospect of a high standard of living and pressure exerted upon the wage earner, but also the compulsion of fear. In the absence of unemployment benefits comparable with British practices, the consequences of the loss of a job can be disastrous to a wage earner.

The significance of such a fundamental difference in approach and attitude towards productivity problems to the actual level of performance itself could hardly be better elucidated than in this report which compares two industrial economies. In countries where these labour incentives play a much smaller role than in England, productivity levels must of necessity be extremely low. Yet it should be noted that there exists in underdeveloped countries a growing sense of the importance of improvements in workers' output levels. There are sufficient data to justify belief in a slow but sure increase in productivity in the underdeveloped regions. The problem clearly

[1] Published in London, September 1949.

exists on two levels: on the factory level, as a problem in industrial management and efficiency; and on a national level, as a problem of concerted measures towards the increase of national real income through increased and/or technically superior capital equipment. The data in the following tables offer an illustration of the points just discussed; one table compares machinery per head to real income per head for groups of countries, and the second relates output per worker to capital investment in the cotton industry in India.

As the table shows, there is a close nexus between the size of capital invested and the real income produced per head of the working population. If we limit the comparison to the amount of machinery in use instead of the total of real capital, we also obtain a confirmation of the close relationship between real income and machine investment. Professor E. Staley has compiled an index of machinery in use per head for most countries of the world; the United States heads the list and appears correspondingly with the highest real income per head of occupied population in the income schedule. On the other side, with a very low value for machinery in use, are the Balkan countries, Egypt, India and China, the latter with less than one four-hundredth of U.S. equipment.

Amount of Machinery in Use per Head and Pre-war Real Income

Countries	Index of machinery per head*	Real income per head of occupied population† (I.U.)
1 United States	403	1,381
2 Canada	296	1,337
3 United Kingdom, Switzerland, Australia, Germany, New Zealand	200–100	1,000 (average)
4 Belgium, Netherlands, Sweden, Denmark	100–50	700 (average)
5 Austria, Argentina, France, Norway, Czechoslovakia, Union of South Africa, Chile, Italy, Finland, Hungary, Latvia, Eire	50–25	430 (average)
6 Japan, Estonia, Spain, Poland, U.S.S.R.	25–10	385 (average)
7 Egypt, Brazil, Portugal, Lithuania, Bulgaria, Greece, Yugoslavia, Rumania	10–5	320 (average)
8 British India	5–1	200
9 China	1–0	100–120

* E. Staley, *World Economy in Transition*, 1939, p. 70.
† For real income estimates see Colin Clark, *The Conditions of Economic Progress*, 1951, pp. 46 ff.

The conclusions to be derived from this rough correlation have, however, only a very general meaning. Factors such as the abundance of natural resources, the attitude of labour, and the level of management have significant effects on the physical equipment—income ratio.

The following figures from an article in the *Eastern Economist*, July 23, 1943, by Dr. P. S. Lokanathan, are apt to show the complex character of the relationship. They demonstrate first of all the dependence of output on the degree of capital equipment. According to the table, output per worker is 15 times higher in modern mills than in hand-loom cottage industries.[1]

Capital Investment and Output in Cotton Weaving in India

Type of equipment	Capital investment per worker (rupees)	Output per worker (rupees)	Ratio of capital to output	Amount of labour employed per unit of capital (Unit of Capital = 1,200 Rs.)
Modern Mill (large-scale industry)	1,200	650	1·9	1
Power Loom (small-scale industry)	300	200	1·5	4
Automatic Loom (cottage industry)	90	80	1·1	13
Hand-Loom (cottage industry)	35	45	0·8	34

But it is not only the rise in output due to increasing capital investment which the table reveals; it shows another interesting feature, namely the larger absorptive capacity of the less capital-intensive types. Small-scale enterprises with power-driven looms employ four times as many workers per unit of capital as large-scale establishments, whilst the output per worker is only 31% of that in the latter.

CONCLUSIONS

1 The picture which evolves from the above data is one of a broadly uniform low level of per capita productivity in the major industries

[1] If we regard industrialisation as a main lever to a higher standard of income, we do not claim that it must proceed only by way of a rapidly increasing investment in mechanical power and equipment. True, growth of production is usually connected with an increase in investment per unit of worker. But these increases tend also to substitute capital for labour, and the immediate effect is increased unemployment, and thus destitution, in areas which are already under the impact of population pressures. It is definitely more promising and healthier to proceed gradually with a view to taking advantage of the plentiful supply of labour for the first stages of industrialisation. This has the double advantage of spreading benefits accruing from the more remunerative industrial occupations more equally over the whole population; at the same time it will educate and prepare the workers for the requirements of more advanced mechanised production processes. In the later stages the capacity of the market to absorb the increased output will become larger, as meanwhile the average income level will already have risen. For further discussion see also Chapter VII.

of underdeveloped countries. At the lowest level stands agriculture. It is followed by handicraft and transport; but even here, as soon as the use of motor power and mechanical contrivances spreads, productivity data in individual units show a move towards higher levels. In general, however, the inferiority of agricultural as well as manufacturing production is still so considerable that output data per worker amount to only a fraction of output in fully industrialised Western countries.

2 Frequently poor performance in output levels, industrial techniques and organisation of production can be observed to persist for a considerable time, although knowledge is available as to how to improve it. General experience confirms time and time again that strong incentives are required for substantial changes in productivity levels. Among these incentives competition ranks high. When cheap, machine-made imports compete with local products, the first effect is frequently, it is true, disastrous for local manufacture. But quite frequently also, the competitive urge leads to a revival of economic activity by introducing changes in technique of production. A distinction must be made here, however, in accordance with the character of the production. In all cases where, owing to the character of the work, the share of manual handwork cannot be reduced, the traditional patterns and levels of production show a capacity for survival. This holds good for quite a number of once famous trades of Oriental workmanship—such as carpet weaving, pottery, jewellery and the like. Yet wherever machine production competes with hand-made goods, the machine-made goods spread rapidly.

3 There is a fair measure of correlation between per capita data for real national income, on the one hand, and higher productivity, on the other. Recent developments in underdeveloped countries offer a good illustration of this relationship. With the increase in capital equipment, a rise of output occurs; though there always exist a number of individual industries which do not show an immediate and full effect of capital investment on their productivity.

4 Capital must be regarded as one major component in the aggregate of factors of production which is able to create a new order of magnitude in output levels. The nexus is evident in all cases where handwork is replaced by machine production with skilled labourers fully familiar with modern production techniques. The recognition of the predominant role of modern capital equipment shifts the problem of developing backward economies largely to the issue of obtaining financial means for the acquisition of capital goods—a major issue in present-day national and international economic policies. This

emphasis on the importance of capital is not meant to deny the immense potential of the development process itself for the creation of capital.

5 With the emphasis on the role of capital equipment, the other determinant, namely the attitude of the workers themselves, should not be minimised. The lessons from comparisons of the productivity of American and English industries are very pertinent to this subject. The Report of the Anglo-American Council on Productivity on the steel founding industry in the United States arrives at the conclusion that the principal cause of American high productivity is not superior technical equipment, but widespread productivity consciousness. This is a psychological factor dependent on the human element in production. American productivity programmes now give primary attention to means for output improvements per man; the total output per plant is considered largely the result of individual productivity. This productivity consciousness, which has to be regarded as a significant precondition for high productivity achievements, is to be found among all grades of employees, from executives to unskilled labourers. The application to underdeveloped countries seems clear: in order to produce a rise in living levels it is crucial to increase output. Owing to capital scarcity, the direct approach of introducing capital-intensive lines of production does not recommend itself everywhere. This leaves room for the use of numerous other devices to bring about higher output: promotion of capital-extensive lines of production in agriculture and industry, development of old-established promising handicrafts, and education of the worker. In more advanced stages of economic development higher targets of productivity can be established and realised by the use of capital-intensive equipment.

CHAPTER VII

INDUSTRIALISATION IN UNDERDEVELOPED COUNTRIES

THE IMPLANTATION OF NEW PRODUCTION PROCESSES

A RISE in productivity is one, if not the most important, pre-condition for the improvement of levels of living in under-developed areas. But it is only part of a complex network of measures which has many aspects, economic and non-economic. The most important event towards the attainment of a general rise in living conditions was, in the West, the introduction of the machine, or to use the conventional term, the process of industrialisation. The East, too, has been drawn into this process, though much later and much slower. An appraisal of certain general aspects of the indus-trialisation which started about 100 years ago in Oriental countries will contribute to our understanding of the requirements which have to be met to secure economic progress in contemporary backward economies.

When the Industrial Revolution of the West started, about two centuries ago, it touched altogether no more than a small fringe of the earth's surface, and drew only a fraction of its inhabitants into its orbit. Even as late as a hundred years ago it was restricted to the countries usually conceived as the Western World. Now, the process has spread over the huge underdeveloped continents of the Old and New Worlds and affects the fate of nearly two billion human beings. No one can foretell its outcome a few generations from now.

Moreover, industrialisation is no repetition of preceding modes of goods production; entirely new technical methods are used, replacing the old ones or narrowing the field formerly claimed by them. New consumption habits reshape patterns of diet, housing and transport, modes of pastime and holidays. New social concepts change the

97

mentality of entrepreneurs and workers. Different interpretations and reasonings as to the position and functions of governments influence and even determine the approach, direction and scope of industrial production, again a new and meaningful departure from former patterns of the economic process. The absolute figures for the new industrial expansion in underdeveloped areas remain for the time being modest, if compared to those relating to industrial growth in the West and in the Soviet Union; yet the process even in its limited scope means a fundamental change in the socio-economic history of the underdeveloped world.

The following survey outlines the characteristic features of this development on an empirical level. It will show some striking differences as compared with the development of Western industrialised society. At the same time it will become clear that important differences in industrial development exist also between the various underdeveloped countries themselves. In spite of its summary character the survey will, it is hoped, enable us to arrive at certain conclusions as to the course of industrialisation and its prospects in the areas under review. In particular we are interested in the clarification of the following questions:

1 What was and is the direction and scope of industrial production;
2 Who were the main agents of industrialisation?
3 What were the per capita rates of growth of industrial production;
4 How was industrial development financed?

DIRECTION AND SCOPE
OF INDUSTRIAL PRODUCTION

Power-driven machinery had been introduced in the production processes of many underdeveloped countries already as far back as the middle of the nineteenth century. Yet industrial production remained until a short time ago a very limited segment of these countries' total economic activities; furthermore, in many underdeveloped areas such production has been for a considerable period a domain of foreign interests, thus exposing still more its somewhat isolated position within the local society.

The two major conflicts in the first half of the present century contributed much to change these conditions: industrialisation has become a major goal in the economic and national policies of underdeveloped countries. In numbers of employed and in scope of production, manufacturing today vastly exceeds its proportions on the eve of the First World War. Three main reasons can be adduced to explain this new world-wide drive towards industrialisation:

a The lesson of dislocation and shortages caused by the war-time interruption of supply channels between countries providing goods and the lands dependent on them;
b The trend towards political independence, implying a maximum degree of economic autarchy in the orbit of the great movements for obtaining national and political freedom;
c The view that industrialisation is a foremost avenue towards a rise in levels of living.

It is remarkable that during the emergency periods in recent decades the erstwhile suppliers frequently and actively assisted the oversea areas to achieve a higher degree of self-support in the field of industrial commodities; many of these areas have thus been able to establish a fairly varied system of industrial production. The older industrial countries might have wished that the new offspring have only a rather temporary existence. But the seed they sowed grew. Supported by new concepts as to the needs of a balanced national economy and the roles of government in economic affairs, industrialisation has become a target of the first order in the policies of countries which have only recently achieved their independence.

The official reasoning behind the policy of industrial promotion is not always uniform. Quite frequently this policy is explained as being the main device to strengthen the nation's defence potential, which is primarily an industrial potential. More recently it has been emphasised that the improvement of living standards and the general economic development of a country are better secured by a shifting of resources—raw material and manpower—to industrial production.

But whatever the reasoning may be in each case, the motive power behind industrialisation in many underdeveloped areas today is profoundly different from that effective in earlier stages of industrial development in Western countries. It is fed largely by incentives arising from national movements. The entrepreneurs of the eighteenth and nineteenth centuries were not guided in this way by considerations of national interest or the necessity for social improvements. They had a different order of economic and social priorities in mind when conceiving the development of their enterprises.[1]

For these and other reasons—amongst the latter the revolutionary changes in uses of raw material and techniques of production—the

---

[1] The treatment of European and American entrepreneurs as one group versus industrial promoters in modern Oriental countries ignores, of course, differences existing between the Western groups. Yet this generalisation seems permissible for the purpose of this broad comparison.

direction and scope of industrial growth within the national economies are very different today from the early phases of industrial development. Let us first see to what extent the available data offer useful guidance for the interpretation of these trends in the underdeveloped world. We shall start with an appraisal of the data relating to the scope of industrial employment.[1]

Enumerations and estimates of the percentage value of production and the share of the main occupation in the active population show in respect of many countries a decline in the former predominance of agriculture. We have dwelt on the connection between increasing industrialisation and the rise of per capita national income in preceding sections of this book. Pre-industrial countries have, as a rule, from two-thirds to four-fifths of their population in agricultural professions; though it must be assumed that where a percentage of 80 or more is given for earners in farming, service occupations in rural areas are included in these high figures. For obvious reasons the accuracy of statistics of earners occupied in farming leaves much to be desired. But it seems that the spectacular predominance of farm occupations decreases as soon as industrialisation starts on a massive scale. Changes in the terms of trade for farm produce may raise the demand for farm labour, yet it can be satisfied from the large reserves of partially employed in the rural areas.

But if the proportion of those employed in primary production proper is on the decrease also in many underdeveloped countries, the percentage of earners employed in secondary industries, including handicrafts, has remained remarkably low: it scarcely goes beyond fifteen per cent even in the case of the countries where industrialisation has made some strides; the share of factory workers proper remains, as a rule, below five per cent, and thus, in any case, below the percentage of semi-industrialised countries in the West. Part of the increase in non-agricultural jobs must have occurred in the field of service occupations. So far the relative growth in population even in countries with a small though growing industrial sector has outstripped the relative increase in industrial earners. The shifting towards a greater weight of the industrial sector expresses itself in the rapidly rising value of industrial production relative to other branches and in higher per capita output.

THE PRODUCTION OF KEY-COMMODITIES: POWER AND MAJOR RAW MATERIALS

A criterion of considerable bearing in this context is offered by the increase of output in key commodities which determine the growth

[1] For details see tables Nos. 7 and 12 in Appendix II.

of a whole range of industries, such as electric power, coal, iron and steel, and relate them to the populations concerned.

Electricity

The production and supply of electricity assume an outstanding place in the progress of industrialisation. In an interesting article on 'Factors Affecting International Differences in Production', an attempt was made several years ago by E. C. Olsen to correlate the various estimates of the national income of several countries and the amount of energy, animate and inanimate, which each country consumed for productive purposes. When the countries were arranged in accordance with the energy consumption, their relative positions were substantially the same as when they were listed according to income.[1]

Total figures for national income and total production of electricity, however, are not yet conclusive since they neglect the population factor. We have to relate the totals to the number of inhabitants. Figures for the period 1937–54, calculated on a per capita basis, show an appreciable increase in per capita output—in many cases even a doubling of production—in spite of disturbing war conditions. Only a few countries which have been particularly affected by war devastation show a slackening pace

Electricity production can indeed be regarded as a good measure of the progress of mechanised goods production and its effects on consumption levels per capita.

In this sense the data of the table are relevant. They show:

(*a*) ·the enormous difference between per capita production of electricity in the advanced countries of the West and in underdeveloped areas throughout the world; per capita production of Canada, Switzerland and the United States, followed by all the industrialised regions, point to an output 50 to 500 times greater than that of the large underdeveloped countries in Asia and Africa.[2]

(*b*) notwithstanding these great gaps, the relative increase in per capita production of electricity over recent years exceeds that in developed countries. From this it can be concluded that there are good prospects for an approximation of the per capita supply in underdeveloped countries to the levels which prevailed about a generation ago in economically advanced countries. The latter levels were certainly far below the present per capita data in these countries; yet their attainment would nonetheless mean substantial progress in the underdeveloped areas. It should be added that the new

---

[1] *American Economic Review*, May 1948.
[2] See Appendix II, table 15.

developments in atomic energy may help underdeveloped countries to overcome the difficulties caused by paucity in traditional fuel resources such as coal and oil and in water supply.

A somewhat similar picture is revealed if we study trends in coal, iron, steel and cement production. The big industrial countries of the West leave the backward areas far behind in total production; the comparison of per capita figures shows even more clearly the appalling inequality in the relative availability of these products.

Contrary to the progress in generation of electric energy, there was after the war a setback in the production of coal in the whole region of Eastern Asia. China, which reached a war-time peak of nearly 56 million tons, was badly affected by flooding of mines, exhaustion and deterioration of mining equipment.[1] No figures are published in U.N. sources relating to recent years. As compared to the position in China, India could show a rising output of coal resulting mainly from the installation of mechanical cutting equipment. Expansion of production in China would have been quicker, but enforced reduction of output on account of the accumulation of stocks and the reduction in working hours from 9 to 8 slowed down the pace. The net annual production of coal per worker employed declined from 141 tons in 1938 to 92 tons in 1948. If we compare production figures per inhabitant for the United States, England and France with corresponding data for underdeveloped countries like India, Japan and Turkey which have a record of remarkable development efforts, the results are illuminating.[2] In all four production lines—coal, iron, steel and cement—we find the same situation: an exceedingly low per capita output for the underdeveloped countries, as against very large figures for the industrialised countries of the West.

Direction and Trends of Production in the Middle East up to the First World War

In Middle Eastern countries agriculture formed the basis of economic life; the majority of the population continued to live, as always, from its agricultural activities. The increase in the density of the population which began in the nineteenth century was maintained by the intensification of commercial activity which set in with the development of means of communication and an increase in the

---

[1] *Economic Survey of Asia and the Far East*, U.N., 1948, *U.N. Statistical Yearbook*, 1953, p. 105.
[2] See Appendix II, table 16.

contacts with abroad. Native handicraft had no particular part in it. In fact, its relative importance visibly declined as compared with that of the newly inaugurated machine production. According to contemporary sources the cleavage between these two forms of production became more acute year by year.[1] On the one hand native handicraft, with bazaars as its centre, tried to hold its own against the double onslaught of foreign goods and the new native industrial production, and to continue to function as in the past on the old traditional lines; at the same time the new factory system introduced by the foreigners was seeking outlets for expansion, and on the eve of the First World War had won a strong, even dominant, position in many branches.

Technical processes of handicraft production in most cases followed primitive methods practised in the trade for generations. Relations between employer and worker were on a patriarchal basis following old-established patterns. A large part of the work was wage work. Master-artisans undertook the execution of certain jobs on an entrepreneur's account, and frequently on the latter's premises; after the completion of the order they left for another place in order to do there the same work.

The new factory production, which developed alongside of and independently from this as a *transferred* form of production, grew slowly, here with success and there ending in failure. On the whole, Eastern industrialisation followed a somewhat spasmodic course in contrast to the development of machine production in European countries, which could establish itself on a broader basis within the framework of a society and regime which lent interest and support to the new venture. The limited industrial development in the Middle East initiated by native entrepreneurs suffered not only from the absence of active support by the authorities and from the hostile suspicion of the big landed interests towards the emergence of new classes in the towns; local industry was also confronted by political handicaps such as the strong position of foreign trade interests protected by foreign governments, and by internal obstacles such as a general indifference or even aversion to technical innovations.

The *direction* taken by industrial development in the Orient was determined by two factors: first, foreign capital aimed at rewarding novel fields of investments, such as that offered, above all, by public utilities (gas, electricity, port services, railway and other means of communication), with their good chances for a regular yield of interest on capital, and an often monopolist form of operation. Mining undertakings, usually on a concessionary basis and there-

[1] It should be noted that the most outspoken observers of these trends were Western writers.

fore mostly competition-free, were invariably a domain of foreign interests. With respect to their dimensions, most of these mining enterprises ranged far above the country's customary standards, their production being destined not for the local, but for the world market. A second preference of foreign capital was the large-scale production of essential consumer goods utilising local material for the local market.

The economic position of Middle Eastern industry at this period cannot be adequately appraised without giving full attention to the part played by imported goods from the West competing with local production. From the beginning of the nineteenth century almost up to the present time, there has been no end to complaints about the devastating effects of cheap machine-made products of foreign origin on local production. This was a period when European industry marched forward practically unhindered. Native handicrafts in Middle Eastern lands were everywhere exposed defenceless to its impact. The present writer has given a more detailed description of the effects of these influences in his *State and Economics in the Middle East*, where the reader can also find numerous references to contemporary sources. The essence of the experience during that period revolves around the position of the Oriental governments towards the indigenous producer: in the majority of cases their powers were too limited to give their citizens the necessary protection; in others, they were simply indifferent.

RECENT PHASES

Political and military events since the First World War have left deep marks also on the economic organisation of the Middle Eastern countries. In the economic field the immediate consequences of the new policies of industrialisation were an expansion of industrial production in general; increased imports of capital goods such as machinery, engines and fuel; an increase in the export of locally produced industrial goods; a decrease in the import of goods formerly bought from abroad and now produced within the country; and finally a diversification of production into many lines not existing hitherto.

The outlook for the long-term economic development of the whole area was deeply changed by the discovery that the Middle East represents one of the richest petroleum reservoirs of the world. It has been known since the beginning of the century that there are considerable petroleum resources in the area. Yet only in the forties did the scope of these reserves become evident. The concession companies lost no time in starting large-scale operations in Saudi

INDUSTRIALISATION

Arabia, Kuwait, Iraq and Qatar. By 1948, Middle East crude oil production was 3·6 times as large as that of 1938; in 1954, it was 9·3 times as large as in 1938, although the share of Iranian oil was in 1954 only a small fraction of its production in 1938. Daily average production per well at the end of 1951 was about 4,600 barrels in the Middle East (excluding Egypt), as compared with only 12·7 barrels per well in the United States and 225 barrels in Venezuela.

The three most important results for the region from this startling development can be seen in the following: the oil-bearing countries of the Middle East enjoy a practically unlimited supply of this key product at low prices for domestic purposes. Second: revenue from oil, sales and concession fees has become a major source for the finance of general economic development. Third: the technical installations necessary for the drilling and operation of oil wells as well as the refining plants themselves contribute in no small extent to the spread of industrial skill in the regions concerned.

With all the significance of oil production, it would be erroneous to regard the development and future prospects of the oil industry as the single focus of the Middle Eastern industrial future. Industrial production attained a fairly wide range of goods, primarily in the field of consumer goods, under the influence of war-time conditions.

EFFECTS OF THE SECOND WORLD WAR ON CONSUMER GOODS PRODUCTION

War-time difficulties in obtaining supplies from abroad led in most countries to a more extensive use of local industrial equipment, and to a substantial increase in locally produced consumer goods. Although some of the thus stimulated consumer-goods-industries showed severe declines after the war, the industrial output of the region as a whole at the end of the forties was considerably above that of 1938 and continued to rise.

Throughout the area the greatest expansion took place in the textile and food processing branches of industry. For food processing, surplus produce in Egypt, Lebanon, Palestine, Syria and Turkey offered good prospects. During this period numerous new techniques were introduced in food processing, such as pasteurisation of fruit juices, preparation of fruit concentrates, and dehydration, assuring the preservation of perishable goods for remote markets.

In the textile industries the number of looms and spindles increased considerably in most countries of the Middle East; productive capacity was gradually enlarged to cope with the requirements of domestic consumption, and even exceeded them. Notable progress was also made in the manufacture of certain key products such as sulphuric acid, superphosphates, soap, edible oils, etc.

In the analysis of Middle Eastern industrial data the familiar pattern of a definite order of consumer preferences emerges: textiles and food are everywhere the leading industrial branches from the viewpoint of numbers of employed and value of output. The limited range of raw materials in the Middle East and the low demand of Oriental societies for the more refined products of an advanced industrial civilisation did not encourage a varied production of industrial goods. On the other hand, requirements in textiles and clothing and the need for food—frugal as they may have been compared to developed economies—were of a magnitude sufficient to admit for the first time units of large-scale production. Industrial entrepreneurs could be relatively assured of a market in these fields. Dry textile goods had another advantage: for a substantial part of the population which maintains a high degree of mobility, dry goods have the quality of an investment commodity, as they are easily stored and transported, divisible, and marketable throughout the area.

Remarkable examples of such local industrial expansion are the development of cotton textiles in Egypt and Turkey and cement production in Egypt. The Economic Bulletin of the National Bank of Egypt published the following interesting data in 1951:

Development of Production in the Textile Industries*
(in mill. kgs.)

	1937	1938	1948	1949	1950
Local production of yarn	18·0	20·5	49·7	57·9	53·4
Imported yarn	0·7	0·8	0·3	—	0·1
	18·7	21·3	50·0	57·9	53·5
Less exported yarn	1·9	0·5	—	4·7	5·3
Net yarn supply	16·8	20·8	50·0	53·2	48·2
Less 2½% yarn wasted in the process of weaving	0·4	0·5	1·3	1·4	1·2
Production of cotton goods	16·4	20·3	48·7	51·8	47·0
Plus imported cotton goods	22·5	17·6	4·8	4·7	5·0
Total available supply	38·9	37·9	53·5	56·5	52·0
Population (in million)	15·9	16·1	19·3	19·5	19·7
Supply per capita (in kg.)	2·45	2·36	2·77	2·90	2·63

* National Bank of Egypt, Economic Bulletin, Vol. IV, No. 2, p. 102.

In its comment on these data, the article qualifies them as being rather rough and taking no account of quality. They are arrived at under the assumption that the totality of yarn available has been woven into cloth. Yet it can be concluded from the table that local production has more than filled the gap of reduced imports. Per capita consumption still remains relatively small when compared with Western countries; consumption of cotton cloth during the post-war years was about 14 kg. in the United States, 8 kg. in Belgium, 7 kg. in Switzerland, 6·5 kg. in the United Kingdom. In the East, however, consumption was lower than in Egypt; about 2 kg. for India/Pakistan and 1·2 kg. for Ceylon.

The cotton industry in Egypt has grown from humble beginnings early in this century, and after the rapid development of the last twenty years has become the leading industry in the country. The quantity of raw cotton consumed by local industry is the best indicator available to show its growth during the last 50 years.

Consumption of Cotton by Egyptian Spinning Mills*
(in 1,000 cantars)

	Five-year averages
1900–4	20·4
1905–9	25·8
1910–14	26·8
1915–19	54·4
1920–4	55·8
1925–9	55·8
1930–4	176·8
1935–9	513·4
1940–4	868·0
1945–9	1,171·0

* *ibid.*, p. 103.

If average world production of cotton is estimated at approximately 6 million tons per annum, the share of Egypt in the total is under 1%. Its further expansion depends primarily on the growth of the internal market; although there is little doubt that if the quality of production improves, a considerable share of production of finer counts could find markets elsewhere.

Turkey—A Case of State-imposed Industrialisation

In any appraisal of recent industrial developments in the Middle East special attention must be given to the case of Turkey. The outcome of the First World War and the Turkish War of Liberation had imbued the leaders of the new Turkey with the belief that a full measure of national and military independence was contingent on a high degree of self-sufficiency in goods indispensable for the country under conditions of an emergency. To realise this, the development of certain branches of industry became a *political* axiom, and economic considerations became not infrequently a secondary issue.

Statistics showing the development of industrial production in Turkey reflect a growth remarkable under conditions existing in that country, where the outlook for industrialisation from the view-point of readily available raw materials, skills and capital funds was far from promising. The number employed in industrial enterprises, the scope and range of production and the value of output show a steady growth since 1929, when the first steps for government-sponsored industrialisation were undertaken. In spite of considerable setbacks which have marked the course of industrial development in Turkey, the results of the new policy are important, as shown by the following data:

Index of Industrial Output in Turkey (1948 = 100)*

Year	General	Mines	Textiles	Sugar, Beer, Alcohol, Tobacco
1938	64	59	75	56
1945	92	83	108	108
1948	100	100	100	100
1950	115	122	116	112
1951	118	127	109	125
1952	133	146	128	129

* U.N., *Statistical Yearbook*, 1953, p. 86.

India

In a general way trends and problems similar to those experienced in the Middle East operated on a much larger scale in the great Far Eastern expanses: India and China. The effect of Western industrialisation, however, was felt somewhat differently here than in the Middle East. The economic philosophy of *laissez-faire*, which accompanied the spread of the Industrial Revolution, reached the Indian sub-continent at a time when it was under the domination of a Western power which had full powers and the greatest interest to create or maintain conditions conducive to a quick diffusion of the new machine-made goods. The concept of *laissez-faire* was extremely suitable for the elimination of brakes and obstacles to an expanding production in a technically superior country. Economic progress according to this concept was an inevitable process, drawing into its orbit every country which did not isolate itself, and tending, like water in communicating pipes, to even out differences in level of welfare. From this viewpoint British administrators acted in good belief when they belittled the possible repercussions and damages of the intrusion of foreign-made machine goods into India. They over-looked the fact that this country had an old-established system of local production which, though functioning on quite different foundations, had a remarkable record of quality output. For the Indians, British trade policy was a cruel and reckless onslaught on their native art, their economic institutions and habits. They were certainly not able to regard it as the realisation of a higher degree of economic efficiency and prosperity. Moreover, the British did not content themselves with opening Indian markets through the pro-motion of trade in English merchandise and the building of a widely spread railway network. They also intervened openly in favour of British industrial interests by removing the modest protective tariffs which could have given crucial support to local fabrics production.

Thus India's economic structure, based on a combination of agricultural production with a highly developed system of handicraft, was gravely upset. Towards the end of the nineteenth century the Indian economy was practically integrated within the network of the British Empire, and subjected to the interests of the home enter-prises. Despite the stipulated equality of all nations in respect of shipping, trading and investment, Great Britain continued to be in practically monopolist control of the field until recently.[1]

This development had, in fact, started in the first half of the nine-teenth century. Between 1814 and 1835 British cotton textile exports to India rose from less than one million to more than 51 million yards, while exports of Indian cotton goods to Britain declined from 1,250,000 to 306,000 pieces. In the middle of the century India was already importing one-fourth of Britain's cotton textile exports. These machine-made goods from England destroyed a large part of the Indian hand-weaving industry. Hand-spinning, too, was gravely affected. The mechanically produced yarn deprived the spinners of their livelihood. Similar effects were felt in other handicrafts.[2]

In spite of a wide range of valuable resources for industrial de-velopment, a diversified national industry able to cope with the country's urgent needs did not grow up. The economic relationship of India to the West was at the time based largely on the export of raw materials to the big industrial countries of the West, in particular to Great Britain, and on the import of manufactured goods from there. The development of an independent industrial economy of sensible size was thus delayed for a long time. To this day India suffers from the results of this policy of slowing down the pace of industrialisation.

[1] G. B. Jathar and S. G. Beri, *Indian Economics*, 7th ed., Vol. II, 1949, p. 199.
[2] Against the effects on home industries there were, of course, gains to the farming community which could now buy their goods much cheaper than before.

THE MOVE TOWARDS ADJUSTMENT

Even during recent decades, when foreign and Indian entrepreneurs co-operated closely and enlarged their promotive activities in India, the number of workers employed in all industrial occupations, including handicrafts, did not increase.

The delayed pace of industrialisation in India is not contradicted by the impressive figures relating to the absolute growth of Indian industrial production. As a latecomer in industrialisation India has developed a textile industry of amazing scope. The size of the cotton textile industry is imposing also in comparison with the national industries of other countries with a developed cotton industry. In 1948 it comprised 10·1 million spindles and approximately 200,000 looms, capable of spinning 1,615 million lb. of yarn and weaving 4,700 million yards of cloth. A major portion of the mills surplus yarn is devoted to hand-loom production on a cottage-industry basis. The cottage industry's present value of production is approximately 1,200 million yards, or nearly 25% of the modern mill production. Hand-loom industry is an integral part of the cloth production industry and supports approximately 10 million workers, including their dependents. The hand-loom industries are entirely independent of imported raw materials. Cottage spinning and weaving took a prominent place in the political movements preceding the separation of the ties connecting India to the British Empire.[1]

Per Capita Consumption of Cotton Piece-goods in India

Year	Net imports*		Net available† mill production		Hand-loom production		Net available for consumption	
	Actual	Per capita	Actual	Per capita	Esti-mated	Per capita	Total	Per capita
	Yards (crores)	Yards	Yards (crores)	Yards	Yards (crores)	Yards	Yards (crores)	Yards
1905–6	239	7·97	61	2·03	108	3·60	408	13·60
1923–4	142	4·30	154	4·67	101	3·06	397	12·03
1936–7	79	2·13	347	9·38	149	4·03	575	15·54
1939–40	56	1·47	379	9·97	182	4·79	617	16·23
1940–1	40	1·02	388	9·95	165	4·23	593	15·20
1941–2	10	0·26	372	9·54	207	5·30	589	15·10

* Imports of foreign goods minus re-exports of foreign goods.
† Mill production in India minus exports of Indian piece-goods.

[1] U.N. Economic Commission for Asia and the Far East: Report and recommendations of the Industrial Development Working Party, Study of Textiles, November 1948, p. 18.

INDUSTRIALISATION

The table on p. 110 shows the development of the cotton piece-goods sector during the period 1905–6 to 1941–2.[1] According to the data in the table this industry was at the beginning of the Second World War able to meet nearly the whole local demand owing to the rapid rise of local production.

The scope of other industries remained far below the scope of textiles, as shown by the following table:

Average Daily Number of Workers Employed in different Industries
in the Indian Provinces, 1939
(*Factories subject to the Factories Act*)

Industry group	No. of workers			
	In perennial factories	In seasonal factories	Total	Percentage of total
Textile	817,077	—	817,077	46·5
Food, drink and tobacco	97,407	150,048	247,455	14·1
Gins and presses	25,987	137,239	163,226	9·3
Engineering	148,424	—	148,424	8·5
Government factories	131,066	1,380	132,446	7·6
Chemicals, dyes, etc.	55,945	1,989	57,934	3·4
Processing of minerals and metals	55,123	—	55,123	3·2
Processing of wood, stone and glass	52,290	—	52,290	3·0
Paper and printing	44,377	—	44,377	2·6
Processing of skin and hides	12,906	—	12,906	0·7
Miscellaneous	19,712	167	19,879	1·1
Total	1,460,314	290,823	1,751,137	100·0

Source: Statistical Abstract of British India, 1930–1 to 1939–40, pp. 598–605.

Yet in all sectors the trend of production is clearly upwards. The general index of industrial production indicates a rise from 84 in 1937 to 128 in December 1952.[2] Index numbers for certain industrial groups show an even steeper rise, such as electric power and cement which reached in December 1953, 152 and 276 respectively.[3] Part of the expansion was certainly due to the war situation; the cutting of former supply lines and difficulties in obtaining import goods from former suppliers gave—as during the First World War—a certain push to local producers.

Yet if we analyse the expansion during the whole period of increased industrial activity in relation to population growth and

[1] G. B. Jathar and S. G. Beri, *Indian Economics*, 8th ed., Vol. II, 1949, p. 24.
[2] 1948 = 100. U.N., *Statistical Yearbook*, 1953, New York, p. 91.
[3] Monthly average 1948–9 = 100. *Tata Quarterly*, April 1954, p. 47.

levels of production and consumption in more advanced countries, the picture becomes rather different. Let us look first at the scope of employment. The following table shows that the relative size of employment decreased in the twenties, despite the temporary expansion of Indian industry during the First World War.

Proportion of Workers Engaged in Indian Industry*

	1911	1931	Percentage of variation 1931 against 1911
Population (million)	315	353	+ 12·1
Working population (million)	149	154	+ 4·0
Persons employed in industries (million)	17·5	15·3	− 12·6
Percentage of industrial workers in working population	11·7%	10·0%	− 9·1
Percentage of industrial workers in total population	5·5%	4·3%	− 21·8

* Source: Census of India, 1931.

It would be justified to doubt the accuracy of such comparisons, in view of the changes in definition of the labour force in industrial employment and the difficulties inherent in Indian statistical work. But the picture of a decreasing share of industrial employment in the total labour force emerges from other sources as well. The process of displacing workers in traditional occupations with mechanised production was certainly responsible for a considerable reduction in the number of those employed in secondary industries. But it does not appear that the displaced labour was absorbed in new industrial establishments, nor that the value of total production increased sufficiently to cope with the needs of a greatly increasing population.

As the figures of the table show, the number of workers in mill industries grew several times during the period 1901–51, against a decline in the labour force employed in 'unorganised' establishments. Yet in absolute figures the decline considerably exceeded the increase. The picture of a decreasing share of the industrial labour force may perhaps change if only the most recent period, in particular the changes brought about by the implementation of the Five-Year Plans, is taken into account. The available data are not yet sufficient to arrive at conclusions as to the effect on the labour force, though the growth of industrial production is spectacular. (See also p. 124 below.)

Working Force in Selected Indian Industries*

(thousands)

	Mill Industry			Unorganised Sector			Total		
	1901	1921	1951	1901	1921	1951	1901	1921	1951
Cotton ginning, cleaning and pressing	40	81	101	96	32	51	136	113	152
Cotton spinning, sizing and weaving	185	350	776	2,635	2,094	1,671	2,820	2,444	2,447
Cotton dyeing, bleaching, printing preparation and sponging	225	431	878	2,851	2,215	1,832	3,076	2,646	2,710
Wool carding, spinning, weaving and manufacture of woollen goods	—	5	22	165	104	57	165	109	77
Oil pressing	5	2	42	465	451	185	470	453	227
Leather, leather products and footwear	9	15	31	1,144	1,072	650	1,153	1,087	681

* From census data covering the period 1909–51, in a paper 'Relations between Population Growth and Capital Formation, etc.', submitted by K. N. Raj to the U.N. World Conference on Population, Rome, 1954.

113

Partition reduced the population of the new Indian Dominion. The modified figures, though considerably less than those for the un-partitioned sub-continent, show during the last inter-census decade an increase of no less than 44·5 million persons.[1]

Year	Population in millions*	Increase (+) or decrease (−) in millions*	Percentage increase (+) or decrease (−)
1901	238·4	—	—
1911	252·2	+ 13·8	+ 5·8
1922	251·4	− 0·8	− 0·32
1931	279·1	+ 27·7	+ 11·0
1941	316·8	+ 37·7	+ 13·5
1951	361·5	+ 44·5	+ 14·0

* Indian Union (including Jammu Kashmir).

To maintain the former percentage share of industrial earners (handicrafts included) in the working population—which amounted to 10% in 1931—the introduction into industry of two million earners during the period of 1941–51 would have been necessary. Yet according to the recent census results, of the twenty million new workers added to the labour force during that period, industry, commerce and transport combined absorbed only about one million.[2] Industry very probably did not take more than half of this number, and it seems very unlikely that the labour force newly absorbed in industry during any single year equalled the percentage of industrial workers reached in 1931.

Other tests can be used to demonstrate the inadequate pace of industrialisation. One is a comparison of the value of manufactured products per head of the population. Again, as the following figures

Approximate Manufacturing Per Head of Population in
Four Countries*

(in $ at 1926–9 prices)

	United States	Germany	Japan	India
1896–1900	160	120	5·70	1·50
1901–5	210	130	8·50	1·90
1906–10	230	150	12·00	2·30
1911–13	250	170	16·00	2·50
1921–5	300	130	31·00	3·10
1926–9	350	180	41·00	3·50
1931–5	240	140	48·00	3·90
1936–8	330	210	65·00	4·90

* *Industrialisation and Foreign Trade*, League of Nations, 1945, p. 58.

---

[1] Census of India, 1951, Part 1—A, p. 181.
[2] K. N. Raj, *op. cit.*, p. 3.

show the relative rise is indeed impressive: industrial output per head of the population more than trebled until the Second World War. But since it started at a very low level, it reached, after 40 years, no more than a trifling fraction of the values for economically advanced countries. To approximate their level of per capita production would have required an additional production of staggering size.

A similar rise of staggering dimensions is needed in respect of the scope of investment, taking into account the maintenance of present output levels for the growing population and the necessity of a rise in these levels. Again, to expand production for a decennial increase would require investment funds entirely out of proportion to the scope of local capital formation and existing investment. In 1938–9, according to *Industrial Capital in India*, capital employed in large-scale manufacturing industry in India was estimated at Rs. 6,748 million.[1] If we use the figure of 1·8 million industrial workers for a rough calculation of the capital–per worker ratio, we obtain a figure of Rs. 3,749 per worker. To provide for the decennial addition of 1·8 million industrial workers which we found would be necessary, the necessary capital would comprise an amount scarcely smaller than the total capital investment in modern industries hitherto.

This reasoning is admittedly not based on any refined calculation of average investment and employment needs, probable trends of development, etc. But it does give an idea of the towering problems which face the Indian economy in its effects to tackle the issue of raising levels of income through a decided policy of industrialisation.

AGENTS OF INDUSTRIALISATION

THE ROLE OF FOREIGN ENTREPRENEURS

The outstanding feature in the early stages of Eastern industrialisation is the dominating role of the foreigner. To the Oriental peoples industrialisation came not only as a new technique of production but as a new and strange way of life, out of line with established measures and modes of work and time-honoured habits of buying, selling and using new commodities. It needed a foreign element to institute such blatant departures from existing patterns of production and distribution.

During the first stages of industrial promotion in underdeveloped countries not only did the capital have to be advanced from without, but also the whole layout as well as the managing and technical

[1] M. V. Divatia and H. M. Trivedi, *Industrial Capital in India*, Bombay, 1947, p. 71. In present-day prices the amount would be much higher.

personnel to be employed in the establishment of the new plants. Throughout the countries of the Middle East, India and large parts of Eastern Asia, the beginnings of mechanical production were initiated by foreigners, who either came by invitation or otherwise became interested in the economic prospects existing in these areas. Foreigners assumed nearly everywhere the vital functions pertinent to industrial production: entrepreneurial, technical-operational and marketing. Yet we should keep in mind that scarcely any foreign enterprise was launched or capital investment made without contractual guarantees for the security of the investment or without backing by a foreign power. Without these safeguards most foreign economic activities would not have been realised.

THE MIDDLE EAST

The major, indeed the outstanding precondition for the sinking of foreign capital and employment of foreign manpower in the Middle Eastern regions during the nineteenth century was security of investment and law, and freedom of activities for foreign enterprise. The legal instrument to enforce this security and freedom was the capitulations. They guaranteed the existence of such a business climate that the investors need hardly feel the effect of an arbitrary, inefficient and corrupt administration and judiciary. The foreign enterprises were 'transferred' units, and existed more or less as a prolonged arm of their own national economy; they enjoyed a status of extra-territoriality, the jurisdiction of their own consular authorities and exemption from numerous fiscal burdens borne by the indigenous entrepreneur.[1] Where such conditions were not offered, no new economic development fed from without took place; where they were generously provided, they paved the way for the introduction of foreign techniques of production. As to the question of why the grant of political and legal security did not lead to economic, and particularly industrial, development on a larger scale, the answer is that this security was a necessary yet insufficient precondition for such development. Another vital precondition, the mass-market, was non-existent.

When the first concentrated attempt was made to introduce machine production on a considerable scale in Egypt, it was accompanied by the large-scale transfer of hundreds of foreign specialists from Europe.[2] That this attempt to launch an industrial revolution failed at the time cannot minimise the fact of the complete reliance

---

[1] A. Bonné, *State and Economics in the Middle East*, 2nd ed., p. 252.
[2] Cp. M. Clerget, Le Caire, *Étude de Géographie Urbaine et d'Histoire Econonomique*, Cairo, 1934, Vol. II, pp. 230 ff., and A. Bonné, *op. cit.*, Chapter XXII.

on foreigners during this phase. This was also recognised by contemporary observers of early industrial development in Egypt. 'The conservatism of local producers, their inclination to live for today, a rudimentary concept of accounting and a lack of genuine devotion' paved the way for the dominating role of foreigners. The role of foreigners in Egyptian industry, especially their share in industrial capital, remained prominent until a short while ago. For the last two or three generations the names of many leading industrial concerns in Egypt and of their main shareholders have testified to their origin. Even now, after pressure has been exerted for a considerable time to nationalise important business concerns in Egypt, guide books of industrial and commercial enterprises abound with names of foreign businessmen, who either have financial interest in Egyptian companies or are still active in the management of their affairs.

Foreign influence in Egyptian industry has been more conspicuous than that in other Middle Eastern countries. But parts of Ottoman Turkey, too, served as a field for the activities of foreign entrepreneurs and foreign capital.

In Middle Eastern countries local minority groups such as the Copts in Egypt, the Lebanese in other Arab countries and the Greeks and Jews in many parts of the Ottoman Empire fulfilled an important function as industrial promoters.

FORMS OF FOREIGN ENTERPRISE IN INDIA

Whilst direct participation of foreigners in the foundation and direction of business was widely practised in the Middle East, a remarkable system of delegated management developed in India under the name of 'Managing Agent'. The Managing Agents who came to India from the British Isles were originally representatives of trading companies working in various fields of import and export. Yet they soon became attracted by the many other business opportunities of the sub-continent. As Lokanathan put it, they found a country with vast underdeveloped resources; but unlike Canada and Australia, India had a large consumer population and a plentiful labour supply.[1] There were other differences as well. Whereas the New World had an incessant supply of enterprising European immigrants, India was lacking in industrial leaders and the newcomers had the whole field clear to themselves. They could well use the experience they had gained in international trade for industrial pioneering. They turned from one industry to another—not only because the experience gained in one was equally valuable in the other, so that all they needed was

[1] P. S. Lokanathan, *Industrial Organisation in India*, London, 1935.

to obtain the help of experts in the techniques of each industry—but also because each line of business opened the way for another and the market for the products of one line of business was found in another. Thus Managing Agents of jute mills started colliery concerns and found that the jute mills were good customers for their coal. Then again, when some of them floated inland steamer companies these latter were able to have their own jute mills and colliery companies and tea estates to send their goods by their own steamers. In this way they obtained a strong position in the markets of their own goods, which often comprised a wide range of products. For this reason managing agency firms in India have neither specialised in one or two industries nor developed a 'horizontal' form of organisation.

The relevant feature in our context is that the managing agency system offered great advantages for the maintenance and growth of strong, and frequently dominating, foreign enterprises on the subcontinent. Since the legal agreements which regulated the agencies' work provided for flexibility in membership, the owners or directors who wished to return to England could arrange for business talent from England to succeed them in India. Indian industry has thus afforded not only a remunerative outlet for British capital, but also exceptional opportunities for the young business brains of England to prove their worth. At the same time the Managing Agents performed a vital function in the early development of industry in India. According to Lokanathan they fitted the country admirably, and there was no alternative to them. Investors who had any money to invest in industries were willing to put their money in any enterprise promoted or backed by a reputable firm of Managing Agents. The lack of local leadership and capital gave the British Agent his chance; he was certainly the type of entrepreneur who could execute his job well.

It would be misleading, however, not to mention the important role certain local groups of entrepreneurs played in the development of Indian industry. In Western India merchant communities, such as the Parsees, the Bhatias and the Jains, proceeded along the lines of the managing agency system in the cotton mill and jute industries, and took prominent part in the development of the Indian textile industries. The conflicts and setbacks which later developed out of the expansion of the managing agency system cannot undo their pioneering function in the founding stages of Indian industry.

INDUSTRIALISATION

Industrial organisers and pioneers capable of fulfilling the tasks of entrepreneurs are dependent on another human element in the process of industrialisation in an underdeveloped agrarian economy. There is also a vital need for skilled workers who can fulfil the requirements of new techniques replacing old methods of manual production. These new processes are as a rule an entirely new experience for the workers, and demand considerable capacity for adjustment and acquisition of the necessary skills.

In the early stages of industrialisation labour is recruited from villages relatively close to the larger towns where the industry is located. In this way a certain contact is maintained with surroundings with which the worker is familiar. With increasing labour demands, the area of recruitment spreads over rural areas more distant from the centre of employment. In Egypt, where modern textile mills have existed for several decades, the majority of the workers were born outside the factory cities. From many new areas of industrial development difficulties are reported concerning the supply of operatives in sufficient numbers. Their regular attendance at work is difficult to assure. Minimum levels of productivity are hard to maintain. Experience in the new centre of Turkish heavy industry in Zonguldak shortly after the establishment of the plants is typical for this stage of industrialisation. After pay-day the workers disappeared from the plant for days and even weeks. This habit hampers, of course, the orderly functioning of the mills. Similar conditions exist, according to accounts given the present author during his visits, in many Indian factories to the present day.[1]

Large industrial centres have frequently been established in areas previously untouched by modern industrial development. Cases in point are the steel town of Jamshedpur (Tatanagar) in the heart of the Indian jungle, Kayseri in the centre of Anatolia, and Mehalla el Kubra in Egypt. The Indian steel town had to face the problem of creating a labour population out of nothing. The steel mills were virtually built in virgin forest, and considerable efforts had to be made to recruit the large number of workers who came from practically every province of India. In the majority of cases these workers were of rural origin and had to overcome the impact of time-old inhibitions such as caste restrictions, resistance to regular factory work, etc., before they could become adjusted to industrial employment.

---

[1] An excellent picture of labour conditions in India prevailing in the thirties is given in the Report of the Royal Commission on Labour in India, London, 1931, see in particular Chapter II for an account on these problems.

THE MOVE TOWARDS ADJUSTMENT

A basic difference between Oriental factory workers and the corresponding worker classes in Western countries lies in their relationship to their place of origin. The industrial worker in the West is now drawn largely from the urban population; the process of mass migration from rural to urban areas has largely subsided. Moreover, the workers who left their villages went away for good and started a new life in town. As against this, many Indian and Oriental factory workers stay in the cities as migrants, at least for a considerable time. They regard their connection to the industrial centres as temporary and hope to return to their former homes as their ultimate places of settlement. The observer is, however, warned against a generalisation of this impression. While it is true that the great majority of workers employed in the factories are villagers at heart, and even retain some contact with their villages, it cannot be said that originally they were all actively engaged in farming proper. Many of them were already employed in village crafts, either partially or fully, before they entered a factory. The institution of the joint family allows a certain rotation of employment within the same family unit. Members of the same family relieve each other in turn in the factories. The specific relationship of the Indian factory population to their place of employment shows all the criteria of a 'between-position':

a On the one hand this population is, generally speaking, not yet urbanised or fully divorced from the land as in the West; it continues to keep close contact with its home villages;

b On the other hand, with increasing length of their stay in town and industrial employment, factory workers gradually become integrated in the emerging industrial society and assume traits of its mentality.[1]

The nature of the contact between factories and villages is therefore not easily defined. In some cases the contact is close and constant; in others it is occasional and non-committal.

Many workers leave their wives in the country, and of the wives who come to the city all those who are able to afford it, return to their villages for their confinements. Many male workers, too, after having adjusted themselves to industrial employment, return to the village as often as they can. In fact, as indicated below, the time most feared by factory managers is the day after pay-day. The man who succeeds in his employment returns to his family even more frequently than the less successful. Leave periods of from one to three months are not at all rare; the duration of the holiday is usually limited only by the means available.

[1] Cp. on this and the following section the Report of the Royal Commission on Labour in India, pp. 13 ff.

INDUSTRIALISATION

The main motive for the decision to leave the village is the hope of finding a better livelihood in the new place. Scarcity of land can be regarded as one of the most impelling forces causing the Indian villagers to seek industrial employment. This pressure, however, is not confined to those engaged in agriculture; the village craftsman, too, owing to the improvement of communications and the growth of industry, finds himself constantly confronted by competition from the outside world. Textile mills, tanning and leather works, wood and metal factories are all drawing labour from the old village crafts, thus enjoying the advantages of an inherited skill in handling and processing material for once famous trades.

It is evident that the formation of a labour class in underdeveloped countries, a concomitant of industrialisation, has also meant a fundamental innovation for the indigenous society. The aversion of workers of rural origin to industrial employment, their low productivity performance and the problem of absentee labourers do not reduce the significance of this transformation. Similar phenomena have accompanied the process of industrial growth in the West.

More important from the viewpoint of international adjustment is the low share of the active population in secondary industries, which is still far below the percentage reached in semi-industrial economies. But against this it should be pointed out that it is only a relatively short period since industrialisation started in underdeveloped countries. Numerous outdated habits and arrangements from the early beginnings of the factory system—such as the jobber system (*sardar, serkal*) with its inevitable bribery, social disabilities such as the caste system, opposition to women working, and even traces of a bond system have not yet disappeared from the Asian continent. At the same time modern forms of class association and class struggle have come to stay, and are drawing their techniques and tactics from the best-informed and best-equipped centres of the Western labour movement. The considerable efforts now being invested in the improvement of labour skill and productivity with the co-operation of national and international agencies give reason to expect important adjustments also in the economic performance of the new labour classes.

THE GROWTH OF INDUSTRIAL PRODUCTION

A comparative analysis of pace and rates of growth of industrial production in economically advanced and less advanced countries could, if the data would be complete, offer an important contribution

121

to the understanding of problems of economic growth in under-developed regions. For the time being, however, comparisons can be made only by the use of crude figures and with the support of non-quantitative indicators; an analysis of trends of growth and certainly of industrial growth in underdeveloped countries and their explanation in the light of changes in production functions needs not only more reliable data; they should also relate to a more pro-tracted period. Whereas in recent decades conditions for the compila-tion of conclusive economic statistics have improved immensely for European and North American regions, the difficulties in obtaining data of such quality for underdeveloped countries are staggering. These difficulties will be reduced in the future, with the progress of statistical agencies throughout these regions. But though this will help us in the years to come, it will not do so with respect to the recent past, for which we have to rely on rudimentary data. If we believe in the value of tentative research efforts, we have no choice but to rely on such imperfect and short-term statistics and to treat the results accordingly as tentative and open to considerable modification.

A remarkable attempt in this field was made ten years ago by F. Hilgerdt, in the publication *Industrialisation and Foreign Trade*, issued in 1945 by the League of Nations. He calculated annual rates of increase in manufacturing for a number of countries for which data were available by using existing computations of national indices and supplementing them through intra- or extra-polations where necessary. His table includes three countries which rank among underdeveloped countries, namely, India and Burma, China and Japan.[1] It is reproduced in part in the Appendix II.

Since a comparison of rates of growth must in the nature of things be a comparison of percentage rates, absolute magnitudes are apt to be disregarded, and thus a wrong impression created as to the real scope of the processes which took place. The absolute figures for the scope of manufacturing per head show that there is a tremendous difference in the volume of production of the various countries. Whilst the rate of industrial growth of India from the end of the last century until the eve of the Second World War is quite impressive, and even higher than the rate of industrial growth in many European countries, the absolute volume of industrial production in India amounted to only a fraction of that of advanced industrial coun-tries. This difference is clearly shown when production is calculated per head of population. Compared with the United States, India

[1] The table also contains annual percentage rates of population increase and the ratio of annual increase in manufacturing to population, which is identical with the annual percentage increase per head of population.

produced only 1% of American industrial output, and less than 10% of the per capita production of Japan during the twenties and thirties.

The comment added by Mr. Hilgerdt to the data on the percentage annual increase in industrial production and in population gives various reasons for the difference in trends. The high rate of industrial growth in certain countries during specific periods has been hastened by the rapid growth of their population. Mr. Hilgerdt points in particular to the cases of the United States and Canada until 1929 both of which enjoyed abundance of natural resources available for exploitation as well as a rapid influx of newcomers into industrial occupations. From this the conclusion is drawn that it is in the sparsely populated areas that a rapid increase in population, especially through immigration, contributes to industrial expansion. On the other hand, in densely populated countries the increase in population does not necessarily hasten the pace of industrial growth if other conditions are not favourable. Furthermore, population growth is likely to slow down with growing industrialisation, because the latter effects a decline in fertility.

The figures available on the relative annual increase in manufacturing before the Second World War do not, however, support clear-cut conclusions. The correlation between population increase and increase in manufacturing in some of the sparsely settled countries is moderate. There are several countries—Russia, India, Burma and others—to which the conclusions do not apply. Russia shows an all-time record for average annual growth of industrial production; the reason lies, of course, in the fact that industrialisation was enforced through state authorities. Japan also shows a high rate of industrial growth, although it belongs to the densely populated countries and is not blessed by abundant natural resources. In the case of India, again, we find a densely populated area which shows a considerable rate of increase in manufacturing since the beginning of the century.

The experience available from more recent periods, too, is not uniform.

The cases of India, Japan, Turkey, Israel, all underdeveloped economies at varying degrees, point to the cardinal importance of the role played by governmental enterprise or initiative in this process.

This experience is of particular significance because of the lesson drawn from the Soviet Russian development. In most underdeveloped countries the difficulties standing in the way of a rapid rise in industrial growth are immense. The Russian example shows a remarkable rate of industrial growth and attracts thus the attention of economists in underdeveloped countries who are impressed by the results in industrialisation obtained by applying communist methods. The price paid by the use of such methods in terms either of human cost or wasted capital investment does not frighten political leaders in underdeveloped countries whose choice for improvement of marginal conditions of human existence is very limited. The relative easiness with which totalitarian regimes squeeze development funds out of a population living on very depressed income levels may even operate in favour of these regimes.

Average Annual Percentage Rates of Growth in Soviet Industrial Production*

Years	Revised Index	Official Index
1927/8–1932	14·5	23·6
1932–7	16·6	18·7
1927/8–1937	15·7	20·9
1937–40	4·7	11·6
1946–50	20·5	23·0
1927/8–1950	8·9	12·5

* From Donald R. Hodgman, 'Industrial Production' in *Soviet Economic Growth*, ed. by Abram Bergson, New York, 1953, p. 242.

There are however recent examples of industrial growth in non-totalitarian countries in which likewise high rates of industrial expansion can be noted. Recent experience in India is not less remarkable than that of Soviet Russia. The adherents of national planning will attribute the progress in India to the establishment of detailed targets within the framework of Five-Year Plans which is a certain adoption of Russian methods. In any case we are able to observe the progress made by comparing the rates of growth over time.

A source of usually sceptical appraisals, the London *Economist*, has at the beginning of 1955 expressed remarkably positive views on the success of the First Five-Year Plan.[1]

[1] 'There can be no doubt that the first three years of the Plan have seen startling improvements in India's economic position. The increase in national income has been three times greater than that of population and the per capita income of the Indian citizen has increased by about five per cent—a level which the plan did not foresee until 1956. This remarkable growth has been due to greatly increased output throughout the economy—an estimated 18 per cent increase over 1951 in agriculture, and in industry a 40 per cent rise above 1950. Particular benefit to the consumer has followed from the achievement of unusual advances in the two main items of consumers' expenditure—food grains and cotton goods. Food grains in 1953–4 increased by 11·4 million tons to 65·4 million, whereas the increase forecast for 1956 was only 7·6 million tons. Cotton reached 76 per cent of the 1956 target with an output of nearly 4 million bales. . . .'—From *The Economist*, January 22, 1955, p. 13.

INDUSTRIALISATION

In a most recent survey written by an Indian observer, the editor of the Indian Economist, E. P. W. da Costa, an even more optimistic appraisal is given.

Although part of the increase in Indian crops is due to the effects of good monsoons, the results of the First Plan are impressive both in respect of agricultural and industrial production. Yet if the success of agricultural planning may be attributed to good weather conditions, the expansion of organised industry has to be credited to the planners. 'The Interim Index of Indian Industrial Production recorded an all-time peak of 170 in December 1955—a gain of 53 points since the inauguration of the Plan. Average industrial production in organised industries has thus risen by more than 50% in five years; even if the new plan were not designed for industrialisation, the mere extension of this trend would have meant that about the same volume of industrialisation would have been generated by the "normal" growth of the Indian economy.'[1]

In the case of Turkey, a sparsely populated country with certain natural resources, a fairly high annual rate of increase in total production and per capita production would not have been possible without governmental efforts to industrialise its predominantly agrarian economy. For Egypt, in contrast to Turkey a very densely populated area, figures show a remarkably high rate of increase in industrial production during the period 1945–50.[2]

[1] See *Foreign Affairs*, July 1956, p. 667.

[2] Sources:

I. *Turkey:*

	1938	1947	1950
1. Industrial production index:	100	151	170

(U.N. Economic Survey of Europe in 1950).

	1937	1947	1950
2. Population:	16,825	19,250	20,930

(U.N., *Demographic Yearbook*, 1948, 1951).

II. *Egypt:*

	1937	1945
1. Manufacturing in £E.1,000,000:	13	54

(Dr. Mahmoud Anis, 'National Income of Egypt', p. 685).

	1950
(*b*) Manufacturing (£E.1,000,000):	110

[Estimate by Anis—AL-Ahram, June 14, 1952 (from *Middle Eastern Affairs*, Vol. III, Nos. 8–9)].

2. Index numbers of wholesale prices:

1937	1945	1950
100	318	330

(U.N. Monthly Bulletin of Statistics, Nov. 1951).

3. Manufacturing in £E.1,000,000 in 1937 prices:

1937	1945	1950
13	17	30

	1937	1945	1950
4. Population:	16,009	18,498	20,439

(U.N. Monthly Bulletin of Statistics, Nov. 1951).

The following calculations of the relative annual increases in manufacture and population are based on admittedly rough figures. They give an indication of the trends of growth in Turkey, Egypt and India. Their main deficiency is the shortness of the period covered by the calculations.

Percentage Average Annual Increase in Manufacturing and Population

TURKEY

	1929–1938	1938–1947	1947–1950
a Manufacturing	5·1	4·7	4·0
b Population	2·1	1·4	2·8
c Manufacturing per head of population	2·9	3·3	1·2

EGYPT

	1937–1945	1945–1950
a Manufacturing	3·4	12·0
b Population	1·8	2·0
c Manufacturing per head of population	1·6	9·8
d Industrial employment	3·2	2·2
e Production per worker	0·2	9·6

INDIA

	1937–1945	1948–1951
a Manufacturing	2·3	2·7
b Population	1·0	1·4
c Manufacturing per head of population	1·3	1·3

A somewhat similar situation prevails in Palestine and Israel, both of them having a fairly high density of population and a paucity of natural resources. The annual rate of growth was very high owing to the unique influx of a partly industrialised immigrant element and of large-sized capital import for industrial investment, sponsored by public institutions.

In the light of the available data it does not yet seem possible to formulate a generalisation as to the relationship between changes in population and rates of industrial growth. Apart from the obvious conclusion that a densely populated country offers better potential market prospects for industrial consumer goods no straight rule can be based on the available data.

Sources:
II. *Egypt (cont.)*

	1937	1945	1948
5. Industrial Labour force:	321,260	413,130	440,941

(Dr. Mahmoud Anis, 'National Income of Egypt', pp. 772, 773).

III. *India:*
   1. Index numbers of industrial production—U.N. Monthly Bull. of Statistics, October 1952.
   2. Population—Bulletin of Statistics, October 1952.

INDUSTRIALISATION

HOW WAS INDUSTRIAL DEVELOPMENT FINANCED IN THE PAST?

INTERNAL FINANCE

Western industrial development has essentially been encouraged by the forms and habits of saving and the organisation of credit and company finance as they have developed in Europe in modern times. The growth of industrial enterprises in the West is inseparable from the simultaneous emergence of the joint stock company with its sharing out of capital, and the deposit bank.

Throughout the countries of the East the progress of industrialisation has been greatly hampered by the lack of an adequate climate for the finance of new forms of goods production. The public which possessed or saved means had been accustomed for generations to investing them in land and buildings, rural and urban, in the hoarding of gold or jewellery, and in the lending of money for trade and mortgages. These preferences in the use of liquid money were common to people living in a region from the Mediterranean to East Asia.

During the first phases of industrialisation the scarcity of funds and the lack of an efficient system of banking restricted industrial activity to those fields of production which promised high profits. Yet the scarcity was not only a shortage of local funds; it was also a lack of willingness on the part of local investors to become interested in the new industrial production, in spite of attractive prospects for the utilisation of their means.

Other obstacles were implied in Eastern religious traditionalism, such as the aversion of Islam to banking and money operations based on interest. Difficulties of this kind existed in many Moslem countries practically until the present day, and increased the preference for investment in land and buildings.

In recent years changes in the attitudes towards industrial investment are reported from various areas. The change seems to be quite noticeable in India, though opinions as to the extent of these new habits are divided. According to one source a wide circle comprising all classes of people, from princes and millionaires to clerks and shopkeepers, are putting their savings into industrial securities.[1] More cautious observers maintain that industrial investment in India is still restricted to a relatively small class of urban investors. The same set of individuals hold the bulk of shares in all cotton, jute

[1] From Indian Central Banking Committee Report, quoted by P. S. Lokanathan, *Industrial Organisation in India*, London, 1935, p. 142.

127

and other concerns, and most of the bigger shareholders come from a few major cities, such as Bombay and Calcutta.[1]

Conditions in India at the time, indeed, contrasted sharply with conditions in Western countries, where ownership in joint stock companies through investment in shares had spread over many sections of society. Lokanathan gives interesting examples of the concentration of Indian holdings in a few hands about two decades ago. He reports on '42 jute mills which were managed by ten managing agency firms who own a considerable percentage of the shares in the concerns they manage, one of them controlling as many as 10 companies . . . We find similarly 75 coal companies managed by six managing agents. In individual cases the managing agents own more than 50% of the total shares and debentures.'[2]

Conditions in the capital market for industrial investments in India about 20 years ago were described by the Indian Industrial Commission as follows: 'Investors are few, nervous, and suspicious. The average rate of interest is much higher than in other industrial countries, and no local capital is available even for local industries, capital being mainly centralised in a few large cities and among a few wealthy classes.'[3]

The Report of the Indian Central Banking Committee has likewise given much attention to this question of capital supply for industry, and has arrived at similar findings. On the whole it may be said that the industrial investor is drawn from wealthy people in the bigger towns of India. Although some small investors, like city clerks, shopkeepers, etc., may be found among individual shareholders, the bulk of investments come from rich merchants and the more prosperous professional classes. As to the role played by big landowners, the Report of the Indian Central Banking Committee says the following:

'The wealth of the landed aristocracy consisting mainly of land contributed little to the capacity of the capital market of the country. Among the other well-to-do classes the salaried classes are on the whole content with a low but assured income from investments and prefer to invest in Post Office savings banks, postal cash certificates, or Government securities. A considerable section of the well-to-do classes also prefers gilt-edged securities. . . . The commercial community generally prefers to invest surplus funds in short-term deposits or Treasury bills when these are available. It also subscribes to the share of capital and debenture issues of joint-stock concerns. It appears, however, that numbers of merchants, and even certain

---

[1] Lokanathan, *op. cit.*, p. 145.
[2] Lokanathan, *op. cit.*, pp. 144 ff.
[3] Quoted by Lokanathan, *op. cit.*, p. 149.

classes of indigenous bankers, invest their funds largely in the purchase and mortgage of land and buildings.'[1]

This description is typical of the attitude of a pre-industrial society towards the use of its domestic savings, and could perfectly well fit conditions in many Middle Eastern countries. We shall revert to the problem of domestic sources below in the section on the finance of economic development.

CAPITAL INVESTMENT FROM FOREIGN SOURCES

The scarcity of domestic capital ready for industrial development paved the way for foreign capitalists and induced them to provide, on a steadily increasing scale, funds for various fields of investment.

On the eve of the Second World War India and China headed the list of debtor countries; they owed very considerable amounts to foreign creditors, as shown by the table, p. 130. But smaller countries like Japan, Turkey and Egypt as well drew considerable amounts from abroad, particularly when there were special conditions favouring the influx of such means. In the case of Japan, it should not be overlooked that this country had at the same time invested large amounts abroad.

It is of interest to compare the magnitude of the investments concerned. The absolute figures are impressive particularly if measured by investments made at the same time from domestic sources. Yet if the figures of the table are calculated on a per capita basis, they result in very low amounts. Considering the enormous size of the populations and areas concerned, an annual inflow of 500 million dollars[2] into the whole underdeveloped world in the twenties could not mean very much for an all-round development of recourses and activities. The gap between per capita investment in Western and underdeveloped Eastern countries was in fact not reduced by these investments, notwithstanding the concentration of foreign capital on a few specific fields of production. There were also significant differences in total and per capita foreign investments between the underdeveloped countries themselves; compare, for instance, Middle Eastern countries like Egypt and Turkey, on the one hand, with countries like China and India on the other. Whereas long-term foreign capital investment reached in the former countries in 1938 about $30–35 per head, approximately eight dollars per head were invested in India and China, even if we take the largest figures given in the estimates.

[1] Indian Central Banking Committee Report, pp. 432 ff., quoted by Lokanathan.

[2] *Measures for the Economic Development of Under-Developed Countries*, United Nations, 1952, p. 79.

Long-term Foreign Investments in Oriental Countries, 1938*

(all value figures in millions of $)

Turkey:

United Kingdom	185
France	299
United States	22·7
U.S.S.R.	6·5
Others	77·0
	$590 m.

Egypt:

France	280
United Kingdom	205
United States	22·8
Netherlands	5
	$512·8 m.

Egypt's investments abroad amount to $106 million—of which $94 million in U.K. in securities held by Egyptian Govt. and Banks.

Iran:

United Kingdom	115
United States	57·3
Netherlands	25
	$197·3 m.

All foreign investments are in oil. Iran's investments abroad are negligible.

Iraq, Palestine, Syria, Lebanon:

United Kingdom	60
United States	31·4
France	32
Netherlands	14
	$137 m.

These countries had $5·5 million in investments abroad, mostly securities held by residents of Palestine.

China:

Belgium	84 ⎫ about
France	124 ⎬ half in
Germany	130 ⎪ rail-
Netherlands	37·2 ⎭ ways
United Kingdom	841
U.S.S.R.	47·5
United States	230
Japan	1,060
Others	3·7
	$2,557 m.

China's investments abroad amount to $770 million, of which $200 in British Malaya, where Chinese companies produced 47% of Malayan tin, $150 m. in Netherlands East Indies, $100 m. each in Philippines and Siam.

* Cleona Lewis, *The United States and Foreign Investment Problems*, The Brookings Institution, Washington, 1948, Appendix A.

INDUSTRIALISATION

India, Burma, Ceylon:†

United Kingdom	3,050	
Burma	200	
Ceylon	125	
India 2,725‡	3,050	
United States	48·8	
(all in India)		
China (all in Burma)	14	

$3,113 m.
($2,774 India alone)

† Investments of these countries abroad $12 million; in U.S. by India $11 million.

‡ About half this amount in Government obligations, including $302 million in Government guaranteed rails and railway annuities.

Japan:

United Kingdom	250
United States	155·3
France	18·8
Others	110

$534 m.

Japan's investments abroad, $1,230 million ($1,060 million of this in China).

Where the growth of industry is dependent on foreign investments, certain extra-economic conditions are required in order to maintain or strengthen the flow of capital from abroad. These conditions usually lie in the political sphere, and affect also the mode, operation and control of foreign investment.

Apart from governmental loans, most foreign capital came in the form of direct investment, which is sunk largely in modern manufacturing enterprises. The majority of modern industrial establishments in Asian countries has, according to a report by the Indian Branch of the International Labour Office, not only been financed by such capital, but also owned, managed and operated by foreigners. In addition, considerable amounts of foreign capital have been invested in the development of internal transport, in banking and trade, and, more recently, in mining and oil production.[1]

The total investment from abroad in China was, according to the same source, estimated in 1937 to have reached the amount of U.S. $3,242 million; nearly 80% of this sum was direct business investment, i.e. an amount considerably higher than that given in the above table. Before the Second World War over half of China's coal industry, most of the iron mines, two-thirds of the inland shipping, and almost all the railways were financed by foreign capital. Of the textile industry in the middle thirties, comprising about five million spindles, 43% were in Japanese-owned mills, 4% in British-owned

[1] Report IV, *The Economic Background of Social Policy, including Problems of Industrialisation*, New Delhi, I.L.O., 1947, p. 93.

131

mills and 53% in Chinese-owned mills. Of 60,000 looms, Japanese-owned mills accounted for 50%, British for 7% and Chinese for 43%. According to an over-all estimate, 2·9 times as much capital was invested in foreign-owned modern manufacturing industries as in Chinese-owned industries.

In India the bulk of foreign investment available during the early stages of India's industrial development was British. Most of India's mining and transport enterprises and many of the jute, soap, cigarette, chemical and engineering industries were financed by the British. There were, however, also industrial interests owned by other Western countries; yet in the cotton textile industry, and later in the iron and steel industry, Indian capital and initiative have made great strides in recent decades.[1]

Conditions of individual investment in Egypt are perhaps more explored than those in any other Oriental country, owing to the large foreign interests which were focused on this country for several generations. In 1914 companies representing a total paid-up capital of £E.92 million—of which approximately 17·5% invested in mining, industry and commerce—were controlled by foreign interests. This figure has to be seen against the fact that the total paid-up capital of joint stock companies operating in Egypt in 1914 was only slightly more than £E.100 million.[2] Foreign interests were thus in control of 90% of the capital invested in joint stock companies in Egypt, to which must be added £E.16·2 million capital of the Suez Canal Co. and nearly £E.85·7 million Public Debt held entirely abroad. The year 1914 meant the culmination of foreign capital investment in Egypt, which comprised then considerably more than the capital of joint stock companies. But since the First World War the tendencies to reduce the predominance of foreign economic interests succeeded to narrow the position of foreign business. The economic effects of the war worked in the same directions. Many of the foreign investments were contracted in fixed amounts and could be repaid in such amounts. The increase of prices in the post-war period enabled debtors to get rid of their commitments at favourable terms. Between 1914 and 1933 occurred the reduction in capital shown in the table opposite.

A number of companies even completely disappeared since 1914. On the other hand, there was also a marked trend towards the increased participation of local capital. In 1934 an official inquiry regarding securities held in Egypt estimated that out of a total paid-up capital of £E.99·3 million, shares and debentures held within

---

[1] Op. cit., p. 94.
[2] A. E. Crouchley, The Investment of Foreign Capital in Egyptian Companies and Public Debt, Cairo, 1936, pp. 72, 77.

INDUSTRIALISATION

Companies	Reduction in Capital
Mortgage Companies	£E.10,512,000
Banks and Banking Companies	2,101,000
Agriculture and Urban Land	6,007,000
Transport and Canals*	1,570,000
Industrial and Commercial	3,943,000
Total	£E.24,133,000

* Excluding Suez Canal.

Egypt amounted to £E.49·7 million or somewhat more than 40% of the total. Not all the increase in local capital participation was due to an increase in holdings by Egyptian owners; there were also foreign residents of Egypt who enlarged their holdings. But the trend towards repatriation of investment is clear and continues to work up to the present date.

The impact of the Second World War and its aftermath on the scope and future of these foreign investments was of great consequence. In certain Far Eastern countries the extent of destruction through actual warfare was immense; but also the political upheavals and the changes in legislation, in external relations and in domestic social and political regimes have completely altered outlook and conditions for the evaluation of foreign investments. These changes do not affect the appraisal of the role of foreign capital in the industrialisation process in the past, but they had, as we shall see later, a considerable effect on the attitude of foreign interests towards future development projects in these areas.

SUMMARY OF CONCLUSIONS

The following conclusions sum up the contents of the preceding section.

1 In the early process of industrialisation in underdeveloped countries the entrepreneurs were foreigners; capital, management and skill were supplied from abroad. The price for these services was high: large profits were squeezed out and local sovereignty in economic matters was severely limited. At the same time the magnitudes in terms of volume of production and number of operatives were small.

2 The process of industrialisation in underdeveloped countries after the attainment of independence owes its drive in the first place to political motives. Political independence is regarded as incomplete

133

without economic self-subsistence. A second incentive is the evaluation of industrialisation as a means towards higher levels of living. Economic reasoning concerning industrialisation is in this stage frequently subordinated to or co-ordinated with political considerations.

3 Notwithstanding the remarkable rates of relative industrial growth and the spectacular expansion in individual industries, the size of the industrial sector in the underdeveloped economies is still modest. Since the process started nearly from zero, even a high rate of growth will not necessarily bring about more than a limited industrial expansion.

4 In the early stages of industrialisation the workers do not evince an acquisitive mind and are strongly tied up in village mentality. The lack of personal interest works against a rapid improvement in the level of productivity.

5 The present rate of local capital formation in most underdeveloped countries is so low that it does not suffice to raise the growth of national income to the extent that it would cover the rate of population growth as well as a rise in levels of living. Only in a few cases did trends of economic growth and population growth run in concordance; this happened in those cases where large natural resources helped to provide the large means necessary for an adequate level of investment. Where there are no natural resources of import, foreign capital is vital in order to secure a minimum rate of industrial growth.

6 The introduction of means of production, skill and knowledge and their co-ordinated organisation in the economic process—on a foreman and an entrepreneurial level—is a pre-condition for the drastic change in economic structure aimed at and maintained through industrialisation. Whilst this process was in earlier stages either completely or nearly fully implanted from without, several factors are now provided locally; yet many elements of the process, amongst them more refined means of production, such as highly developed precision tools, specialised production know-how and, as a rule, organisational skills remains to be supplied from without.

CHAPTER VIII

DEVELOPMENT PROSPECTS IN UNDERDEVELOPED AGRICULTURE

THE NATURE OF THE DEVELOPMENT PROCESS IN AGRICULTURE

AGAINST the break in production traditions which is implied in industrialisation and its transfer to underdeveloped countries as a process of implanted change, agricultural development offers a largely different scene. True, the potential of agricultural development too can be realised only through changes in the size and productivity of the stock of capital and the labour force. Yet the conditions governing the process of agricultural production differ obviously from those obtaining in the production of industrial goods.

Manufacturing, a mode of production widely subject to the command of man, has spread over the globe incomparably more rapidly than methods of rationalised agriculture. The main reasons for this are the early concentration of human inventiveness on the improvement of industrial production techniques; the immense range and elasticity of 'industrial' consumption; the relative ease in transferability and replacement of industrial capital goods. These goods can be brought to locations which enjoy optimum conditions for their successful operation; they can be increased nearly at will and thus increase the available output of consumer goods, as well as the stock of capital goods for further production.

Against this, agricultural production, which is bound to the land, progresses but slowly and gradually. Land, a major element of production in agriculture, appears as a capital good fixed in two senses: It is 'immovable' in terms of transferability; neither can it be increased at will, even if the demand for its produce should fully justify an addition to the land utilised now. Apart from the limits set by nature, there are man-made obstacles, too: it is difficult to imagine a radical change in agricultural production patterns without intervention by the State; the link between cultivator and landowner particularly in underdeveloped countries is itself part of an institutional pattern. If the landowning class does not co-operate in the development projects, single outsiders cannot change the situation.

These differences have all a great bearing on the potential of production in both spheres. The difference between the physical potential of industrial and agricultural production is particularly striking in countries with a rapid growth of population. Whilst an increase in output of industrial goods can always be envisaged, provided raw material and funds are available, fully utilised land resources mean, as a rule, a limit to further expansion of cultivation.

This is the issue which faces many regions with limited or apparently limited land resources. The regions which show a disproportion between the rates of population growth and agricultural growth are largely identical with the underdeveloped countries, and comprise some three-fourths of the present world population.

These regions embrace larger tracts in the Old World than in the New; but in Old and New Worlds alike, the main problems arising from the increase of population and the 'rigid' character of the factor of land in agricultural development are similar in many ways, and may at first sight indicate a grim perspective for future prospects of satisfying human food needs. Let us therefore consider the main elements involved in the scope of utilisable resources.

THE POTENTIAL OF AGRICULTURAL DEVELOPMENT

The elements generally recognised as most relevant to this issue are: (a) the extent of land, cultivated and potentially cultivable; and (b) the degree of its productivity. As to the first point, i.e. the extent of land cultivable, the difficulty in finding reliable data is evident, since no comprehensive or exact surveys have so far been undertaken on a universal scale. We have instead to rely on estimates, inferences from available experience, and some systematic studies of specific areas.

It is also difficult to ascertain the degree of productivity of land. Since it is technically feasible to improve practically all land, there cannot be an absolute measure of its fertility. Yet it is quite clear that in any economically consistent approach the aspect which matters is set by economic criteria to any outlay for the improvement of the quality of land. The problem revolves around the determination of that limit, which is called by the economist the marginal productivity of land. This marginal productivity is not a fixed datum.

Submarginal land has been improved on a large scale and made to serve the purpose desired for it on all five continents. The data of economic relevance in any project of land reclamation comprise first the outlay required for the reclamation work in relation to the available means. Yet the major consideration are data on the expected annual yields of the area after completion of reclamation; present and prospective price levels for the final products; the stability of the physical-biological results; and the net rate of interest required. Those who decide on the inauguration of a new reclamation project make their decision on the basis of comparisons of cost and physical and economic yields obtained through a more intensive use of already cultivated land, with analogous data for the new area to be cultivated. Owing to striking improvement in reclamation methods and new approaches to the investment of social capital, the decision will frequently be made in favour of expanding cultivation on hitherto unworked land.

Experience has shown that many of the traditional views on limits of economically feasible land reclamation can be ascribed to an outdated or inadequate consideration of three major aspects in land development: the time factor, changeability of the character of land, and advances in plant improvement and adjustment. The most frequent shortcoming is lack of sufficient consideration of the time factor. Some of the misunderstandings and difficulties in land potential appraisal might well be avoided by a clear distinction between short- and long-term evaluations. Both are necessary, though for different purposes. Contrary to the situation, for instance in industrial production, where output can be increased extremely quickly if the required means of production are available, the time element is a primary consideration in any long-term planning aiming at the transformation of arid land, either uncultivated or dry-farmed, into fully productive irrigated land.

As to the second point—the changeability of physical properties of land—decades ago Alfred Marshall dwelt at length on the essentially changeable nature of soil. Man can turn a barren into a very fertile soil by adding just those things that are needed.[1]

Today we have come to use the term 'cultivable' not as an absolute measurement, but as a definition of a property itself determined by the interaction of the soil's physical properties and the economic factors of production which are applicable to it and modify it. The full meaning of the definition, in countries with backward land regimes, would also have to include institutional adjustments. It is thus evident that there is no simple relationship between land resources and food production in the sense that an increase of food production presupposes an increase in the extent of cultivated land. The capacity of land to produce food becomes more and more dependent on the nature and amount of components added, to those

[1] Alfred Marshall, *Principles of Economics*, 8th ed., London, 1946, p. 146.

originally embodied in the soil; that capacity may be changed or adapted by the methods and approaches used in its 'productivisation'.

An obvious example is the strikingly higher production of irrigated land formerly under dry farming. The introduction of irrigation of course means a much higher capital outlay and/or a higher labour input per unit of land. There are also significant restricting factors, such as availability of water and surface conditions and the danger of salination, which limit possibilities of irrigation. But the fundamental point in our appraisal is the fact that all efforts to increase output per unit tend to decrease the importance of land in the aggregate of factors which produce national income, following increased application of capital and labour.

An increase of physical capital or labour input are not the only factors which can change the productivity of land. An inestimable amount of 'mental capital' has been invested over many years in efforts to improve farming results. Applied research in soil chemistry, new methods of fighting plant diseases, genetic improvement of food plants and the introduction of mechanical power have led to an amazing increase of productivity in modern agriculture, an increase expressing itself in the rise of output per unit of land and unit of labour. It is this remarkable increase in the production potential per unit of land and labour which explains the paradox of increased production of food in the face of a decreasing share of the agricultural segment in total national output in advanced economies. And it is not visionary thinking if one regards this development as still far from having come to an end.

The significance of these trends and potentialities has evaded the attention of writers who limit themselves to a short-term observation and those who draw their inferences from conditions in temperate zones. Unlike countries in the temperate zone, the agricultural potentialities of Oriental countries are largely marked by the fact that they include substantial territories which allow and require the use of artificial irrigation for cultivation and for the achievement of maximum yields. Irrigation makes regular farming possible in regions with insufficient rainfall, and permits cultivation in completely arid zones. Thus it has, first, a great stabilising influence on the outcome of farming activities in countries where drought is a constant menace to the farmer. But irrigation has another important effect: by requiring much greater physical effort and capital outlay, it leads to a ratio of labour and capital applied per unit of area which is basically different from that characteristic of dry farming, which requires no effort to supply its water needs. The high coefficient of manpower required in artificially irrigated areas thus results in a higher density of population; so that irrigated areas have a much higher potential with respect to labour input, yield, and earning power than un-irrigated land. Where irrigated crops have been introduced, the absorption of labourers is greatly facilitated; the capacity of newly irrigated tracts to employ new farm hands during the first phase of expansion usually exceeds the number of those living in the region.

The implications of introduction of regular irrigated farming, either in formerly uncultivated arid areas or as a conversion from dry farming or occasional irrigation, are of great significance in appraising the agricultural potential of the regions under discussion. They have been studied for the principal irrigation countries, and it is worth while to mention some of the findings in this field. We begin with India, where the dimensions of the problem are staggering. Sir William Stampe assesses the increased yield attributable to systematic irrigation in India, where the monsoon is usually erratic and sometimes fails completely, at an average of 60 to 100%.[1] This is a conservative estimate; even so it means a tremendous increase in production for the huge sub-continent.

The Director of the Gokhale Institute of Politics and Economics, Mr. Gadgil, reports on the results of a survey of the direct and indirect benefits of the Godavari and Pravara Canals in the province of Bombay.[2] The investigation was based on a selection of sample areas in which a secure and plentiful water supply has been brought to fields previously dependent on an uncertain rainfall. The character of the cultivation and the degree of its intensity have thereby been profoundly changed. The main changes have been the introduction of new and more valuable crops, and in higher productivity of crops previously cultivated.

According to the results of the survey, the construction of the canal system of irrigation has made possible an increase in the value of agricultural production from an average of Rs.680 in a typical dry-farming unit to about Rs.1,500 under second-class irrigation, and to Rs.4,000 in intensive irrigation dominated by sugar cane.[3] The table on p. 140 shows the difference between yields of canal irrigation, and dry-farmed fields.[4] The increase in production on the irrigated farms is, of course, dependent on higher investment in both working and permanent capital. A number of tables in Gadgil's treatise demonstrate the relationship for the various types of farms.

[1] Sir William Stampe, 'Irrigation from the Ground Water for Stimulating Food Production in Desert Areas', *Empire Journal of Experimental Agriculture*, January 1948, pp. 46 ff.
[2] D. R. Gadgil, 'Economic Effects of Irrigation', Poona, 1948.
[3] *Ibid.*, p. 54.   [4] *Ibid.*, pp. 100, 105.

THE MOVE TOWARDS ADJUSTMENT

Yields of Crops per Acre

	Canal-irrigated	Dry-farmed only
Sugar cane	37 pallas	
Pastory plantation	31 pallas	
Jowar grain	8 maunds	3½ maunds
Wheat	7½ maunds	3 maunds
Groundnut	20 maunds	8 maunds
Gram	5 maunds	3 maunds
Bajri grain	6 maunds	2½ maunds
Cotton	3 maunds	1 maunds

One maund = 82·3 lb.
One pallas = 1⅞ maunds.

The author sums up the economic effects of irrigation by a hypothetical calculation of the difference between the gross produce of the irrigated land and that of a corresponding area of 'dry' land, arriving at the following figures: The canal-irrigated area of 53,400 acres yields a total produce value of Rs.13,219,775, or Rs.8,277,494 more than the value of crops would have been from an area of 80,000 acres composed of 13,000 acres of land irrigated by wells and 67,000 acres of dry land. The area of 80,000 acres corresponds, according to the author, to the potential of the canal-irrigated area of 53,400 acres.

A higher yield from irrigated crops in a general phenomenon in areas with developed irrigation. It is particularly striking in those countries where dry as well as irrigated farming is practised, owing to differences in local conditions such as topography of soil, supply of water, etc. The data on p. 141 refer to conditions in Israel.[1]

In respect of labour needs there exist great differences between the various cultures. Wheat crops, either in dry-farming areas or in irrigated belts, do not require intensive preparation and therefore imply a relatively low density of farm workers; specific irrigation crops like bananas, oranges, sugar cane and rice demand considerable attention on the part of the cultivator. Preparation of levelled grounds or terraces and seed beds, the need for repeated watering and numerous other operations make irrigated farming a particularly labour-intensive form of agriculture. This aspect of irrigation has been well noted in areas short of manpower. Soubhi Mazloum, in discussing problems of irrigation in Syria, emphasises the importance of a labour force sufficient to cope with the additional labour requirements of irrigated farming as compared to dry farming.[2] Since one hectare of irrigated crops needs five times as much

[1] According to information supplied by Professor Sh. Hurwitz of the Agricultural Experimental Station, Rehovoth. The variations in yields indicated in the table under the same column head result from differences in sowing-time.
[2] *L'Agriculture Richesse Nationale*, Beyrouth, 1942, pp. 66–7.

Irrigated crops in Israeli agriculture	Yields in tons per hectare		Number of working days required per hectare	
	Irrigated crops	Dry-farmed crops	Irrigated crops	Dry-farmed crops
Tomatoes	30–40	7–12	250–350	100
Potatoes	20–30	0·8–1·5	100–150	
Carrots	30–40		150–250	
Eggplant	30–50		150–250	
Cucumbers	20–30	5–10	150–200	100
Cauliflower	10–20			
Onions	30–50	10–15	210–250	150
Groundnuts (seeds)	3–4		90–120	
Fodder Crops:				
Beets (fodder)	120–200	30–50	80–150	40–50
Clover	60–90	30–40		
Vetches (winter)	20–30			
Corn	3–4	1·5		
Barley	3	1		

work as one hectare of dry-farmed land, areas with a low density of population should be transferred only stage by stage to irrigated agriculture, in accordance with the growth of the population. Reports from the large irrigation zones of China and India point to the same difference in relative requirements of labour; in these countries, where there is a considerable density of population, dry farming leaves the cultivator a period of several months of absolute leisure during the year. According to data available for India, the maximum employment in agriculture worked out at 258 to 280 days per annum in canal-irrigated and wheat tracts in the northwest and central regions. In the unirrigated non-wheat tracts employment was available for only about 114 to 118 days, or roughly four months of the year.[1]

Professor Buck arrives at similar conclusions with respect to China. In that country human labour on grain crops is greatest for rice, amounting to 117 man-work units per hectare for ordinary rice and 122 for glutinous rice; the amount of labour on other grains and on crops grown for their seed products does not differ greatly from that on wheat, which requires much less than rice: an average of 60 man-work units per hectare, or the equivalent of 24 ten-hour days per acre. There are obviously considerable variations in the number of man-work units required per hectare, because of different farm

[1] *Agricultural Wages and Incomes of Primary Producers*, International Labour Office, Geneva, 1949, p. 16.

practices and differences in soils, topography, climatic conditions, availability of animal labour, etc. Incidentally, in many advanced economies employment of 200 to 250 field days per year is regarded as 'full time' employment in farming, because there are many other labour requirements aside from work-on-the-field to be coped with during the year.

So far only the physical aspect, i.e. the effect of additional input on physical output, has been dealt with. Economically speaking, additional input would be feasible as long as the price of the produce continues to cover outlay for work, interest and amortisation. This holds good under conditions of stable as well as changing price levels. It goes without saying that a lasting increase in farm prices enlarges the scope for additional outlay on cultivation and the extent of the cultivable area, because it directly affects the marginal return from land.

These conclusions apply in particular in countries where industrialisation has already had considerable effect on the economics and techniques of agricultural production. The experience of the last hundred years of soil cultivation in such countries has been that the capacity of land to produce crops is becoming more and more dependent on the nature and size of added components other than those originally embodied in the soil. This capacity may be varied a great deal by the methods and approaches used in this method of increasing production. In fact, were it not for this development we should have had to face a very different situation in respect of the world's food supply situation. The phenomenal population growth during the last hundred and fifty years, bringing about a continuous and accelerating demand for food, would have caused an enormous increase in the price of cultivated land, expressing itself either in the form of high land values or higher land rents. This, however, has not happened at all. Land values have as a rule not risen beyond modest scales: in many Western countries the land factor has shown itself to be of decreasing importance in the aggregate of inputs into food production, whilst the share of other factors of production has become larger.

It may be argued that this phenomenon is primarily a characteristic of well-developed economics. Here the majority of the population is engaged in non-agricultural activities which also bring about a constant improvement in methods of agricultural production. Farming becomes mechanised; it owes more and more to man-made agents of production. This argument, however, just confirms the point being made here. Improved methods in agriculture and a simultaneous reduction of the relative share of land as against that of other production factors are results of economic rationalisation,

DEVELOPMENT PROSPECTS IN AGRICULTURE

culminating in countries where industrial progress is intensive. Even where a policy of industrialisation has been enforced for a limited period only, effects similar to these have been observed. In the Middle East, for instance, new employment opportunities during the war brought down the share of agricultural net income in the national income of Egypt and Palestine. Following reduced pressure on land, the level of rent, which had been excessive for generations, became lower, with a corresponding improvement in the tenants' standard of living. After the First World War rent tended to return to the old level.

The practical meaning of these developments becomes clear if we study the figures for yield of essential crops in main areas of food production. The United States certainly has the most impressive record in the expansion of food production, in terms of both quantity and plant improvement. The introduction of new wheat varieties produced by U.S. Experiment Stations and grown by farmers is responsible for an increased production of 170 million bushels per year above what would have been possible with the varieties available 25 years ago. In the Central Spring wheat area of the U.S., around North Dakota, actual yield per acre for the 25-year period, 1919–1944, shows an increase of about 50%.[1]

Where hybrid corn has been introduced in the United States, yields have increased by at least 30%.[2]

With regard to another major crop, potatoes, although the improvements have centred primarily on the development of disease-resistant varieties, the results also express themselves in conspicuous increases in yield per unit of land. The table on p. 144 gives a general picture of crop yield averages in the U.S., and shows the nearly general upward trend prevailing in that country over the last 50 to 80 years.[3]

Notwithstanding fluctuations in yield for individual years, the upward trend is impressive. A recent report of the U.S. Department of Agriculture estimates the present production of American farms to be higher by 45% than in the pre-war years, 1935–9.[4]

Upward trends can be reported from other areas as well. In Japan, rice yield improvement has been a foremost issue, rice being the most

[1] M. T. Jenkins, 'Genetic Improvement of Food Plants for Increased Yield', Proceedings, Symposium on Scientific Possibilities for Increasing the World's Food Supply, 1951, p. 85.
[2] M. T. Jenkins, op. cit., p. 86.
[3] Figures from Statistical Abstract of the United States, annual issues, 1949–51.
[4] Herald Tribune, New York, 'Economic Review', August 2, 1954.

THE MOVE TOWARDS ADJUSTMENT

Yields of Major Crops in the United States—1866–1950
(*yields per acre in bushels*)

	Corn	Wheat	Oats	Rye	Barley
1866–75	25·6	12·3	26·5	10·8	21·7
1911–15	26·0	15·0	30·8	13·4	23·5
1926–30	—	—	—	—	—
1941–45	32·8	17·5	32·3	12·3	24·1
1946	36·7	17·2	34·7	11·7	25·2
1948	42·7	17·9	37·1	12·6	26·3
1950	37·6	16·6	34·9	12·6	26·9

	Tobacco*	Cotton*	Potatoes	Sorghum	Soybeans
1866–75	754	162·6	86·9	—	—
1911–15	816	200·7	100·6	—	—
1926–30	—	—	—	12·5	12·8
1941–45	1040	262·2	140·9	17·7	18·5
1946	1182	235·3	186·3	15·8	20·5
1948	1234	311·5	212·4	18·0	21·4
1950	1277	265·4	237·9	22·9	21·6

* In lbs.

important single crop and the basic food of the people. Yield records as reported by Salmon indicate that acreage has increased by about 25%, yield per acre by 70%, and total production by 113% during two generations.[1] In the Middle East, Egypt and Israel have achieved remarkable results in attempts to increase wheat and other cereal yields through the use of selected seeds. In Java, the introduction of hybrid varieties has resulted in a very considerable rise in sugar cane crop yields.[2]

Mention must also be made of another important achievement: the reduction in working time related to the volume of output. Again, figures for the U.S. are illuminating: between 1800 and 1940, the number of man-hours needed to produce 100 bushels of wheat dropped from 373 to 47. Since the pre-war years output per man-hour has risen through increased use of machines by no less than 78%.[3] In 1820, one farm worker supported 0·5 people; in 1946, the figure was 14·5.[4]

These impressive improvements have all taken place in recent decades. They are due not only to the work of soil and plant specialists; the agricultural economist and the expert for technical services in farming have also had a share in the introduction of new methods of crop rotation, soil tilling, planting, watering, harvesting and

[1] M. T. Jenkins, *op. cit.*, pp. 87–8.   [2] M. T. Jenkins, *op. cit.*, p. 91.
[3] *Herald Tribune, loc. cit.*
[4] M. R. Cooper, *et al., Progress of Farm Mechanization*, U.S. Department of Agriculture, 1947.

storing of crops. Though it cannot be proved that such agricultural progress can be transferred to all underdeveloped areas, it seems safe to assume, on the basis of experience gained hitherto, that a considerable increase in world food production is possible through improvements along the same lines, in regions where yields have so far remained below levels obtained in the West. The global trend towards higher production has not changed, despite such disturbing events as the last World War which affect the pace of its expansion and per capita supply. The table on page 49 presents a comparison between pre-war and post-war data on food crops. Yet an increase in productivity alone would not suffice to raise present consumption standards in underdeveloped regions, and at the same time to satisfy the needs of the additional hundreds of millions of new human beings to be fed. An increase both in productivity per unit of land and in cultivated area must be aimed at.

POPULATION GROWTH AND FOOD PRODUCTION

The unprecedented growth in the world's population, when viewed in relation to the world's food supply situation today, has been a source of alarm; and apprehensions of future calamity and starvation are strongly felt. Assuming a global rate of increase of only 1% per annum, the 1951 world population of approximately 2,400 million would reach 2,600 million in 1960 and 2,900 million in 1970. We may thus calculate, even allowing for the differing methods of making population projections, that within 15 years from today 500 million additional mouths will have to be fed. A projection of future growth on this scale, moreover, is a conservative appraisal. During the next two decades the rate of growth may accelerate, since the increased application of scientific methods to the prevention of epidemics and cure of diseases will reduce mortality rates, while reproduction rates will remain more or less unchanged.

There have been frequent attempts to relate possible expansion of food production to the requirements of the growing world population during the coming two or three decades. Such calculation of the production potential should be based on data on the actual and potential yields of cultivated land and on surveys of unused cultivable land.

Some writers on the subject tend to disregard land not already under the plough, and to consider only the size of cultivated land and average crops obtained in the past as data of relevance. They conclude that, considering the many obstacles to full use of land not yet cultivated or prepared for utilisation, not much additional food production can be expected from such areas. Yet the available data do not lend themselves to such gloomy conclusions. Indeed, among the

145

fields of knowledge which have been much affected by the advancement of science in recent years are those pertinent to agricultural production. Any projection of future developments must take into consideration the experience in this sphere which has been accumulated from many areas of research.

To give an example: millions of acres of sugar cane and vegetables are now grown in humid regions on soil naturally so sterile that these crops could not have been grown there before. Now these areas belong to the important supply regions of the world. The lesson to be drawn from this is vitally important. In the light of such experience it was demanded at the U.N. conference on Conservation and Utilisation of Resources, in 1949, not to concentrate on the restoration of lost fields to production: 'We can convert into productive fields land which has hitherto never contributed to our food supplies. It is reasonable to assume that about half of the world's land surface is unsuitable for cultivation. This includes the mountains, the snow-covered areas of the Arctic and Antarctic and some of the sandy desert regions. But of the half which is potentially cultivable, only about one-fifth is now being farmed.'[1]

ESTIMATES OF PRODUCTION POTENTIAL OF UNDERDEVELOPED AREAS

Probably most of the good land in temperate regions is occupied—though by no means all of it. In the United States, Kellogg estimated, present cropland of about 370 million acres could be expanded to a total of about 450 million acres, or possibly even 500 million, under conditions of full employment. To this should be added another 300 million acres of new land to be utilised in the region of Podzol soil north of the temperate zone.[2]

The determination of the production potential of underdeveloped soil areas offers more difficulties owing to many unknown factors in the areas concerned. According to Kellogg, it may be assumed that at least 20% of the unused tropical soils of the Americas, Africa and the great islands, such as New Guinea, Madagascar and Borneo, are cultivable; this would add one billion additional acres to the 300–400 million acres in the temperate zones.[3] This area of 1,300–1,400 million additonal acres would indeed be a tremendous reserve for increasing food production. To translate this potential into reality will mean a complex and difficult job which is bound to employ humanity for many years. It will require careful planning and in

[1] Sir Herbert Broadley, U.N.S.C.C.U.R. Proceedings, Lake Success, New York, 'Critical Shortages of Food', 1951.
[2] Charles E. Kellogg, Journal of Farm Economics, 1949, p. 257.
[3] Charles E. Kellogg, Food, Soil and People, published in co-operation with U.N.E.S.C.O., New York, 1951, p. 23.

particular simultaneous development of transportation and secondary industries.

However, expansion of cultivated area, as is mentioned above, is not the only method of increasing the volume of production. A rise in yield by 20–50% per unit of land has been obtained *de facto* in many countries, and it is reasonable to assume further yield increases given the existence of favourable terms of trade, a co-operative labour force and a progressive farmer element. Should these increases be forthcoming, only part of the 1,300 million acres of new land would be needed.

Estimates of increased yield through the use of improved practices as given by Salter are shown in the following table for some of the world's most heavily populated areas:

Estimated Attainable Increase in Yield through Improved Practice
(after Salter)[1]

Crop		Yield per Acre 1935–9	1960
	U.S.S.R.		
Wheat	bushels	10·0	12·0
Rye	bushels	12·7	13·5
Corn	bushels	16·3	20·0
Oats	bushels	22·2	28·0
Barley	bushels	14·9	18·0
Sugar beets	tons	6·1	8·0
Potatoes	bushels	121·5	180·0
	INDIA		
Wheat	bushels	10·7	20·0
Rice	bushels	26·2	40·0
Corn	bushels	12·9	20·0
Barley	bushels	16·5	20·0
Peanuts	pounds	400·0	600·0
	CHINA		
Wheat	bushels	14·9	18·0
Rice	bushels	52·2	70·0
Corn	bushels	24·2	35·0
Barley	bushels	21·8	24·0
Peanuts	pounds	769·0	1,000·0
Soybeans	bushels	16·8	20·0
Dry beans	pounds	730·0	1,000·0
Potatoes	bushels	100·0	150·0

Many of the yield increases in Europe and the United States were due to the scarcity of workers, which led to a more efficient use of

[1] M. R. Salter, *Science*, 1947, p. 533.

available labour; it is therefore not certain whether in under-developed countries with their cheap labour supply the same in-centives for raising output will operate as they did in Western countries. Many farming improvements require additional outlay of capital, which is very scarce in underdeveloped economies. But since present-day yields are frequently extremely low, even small incentives are apt to effect yield improvements; such improvements can indeed be observed in a number of Oriental countries, though they cannot be taken for granted everywhere.[1]

POTENTIAL AND REALITY

Against the approach just presented the argument is frequently advanced that data on the food growth potential of underdeveloped regions are long-term projections and in a sense comfortable generalisations which evade the real difficulties of today and tomorrow. It is one thing to compute figures of arable land classed as utilisable on account of its soil condition, topography and irrigability and to elaborate calculations of possible yields from such land; it is another to meet the increasing concrete demand of a growing population for additional food. Though it remains true that the starting point for any practical plan must be a set of data and figures determining the magnitude of cultivable land, manpower and water, the issue which counts in a long-term appraisal is the ratio between population increase and food production increase. Calculations of cultivable land do not take into account obstacles such as backward political and social conditions particularly in the spheres of land tenure; the

[1] Salter has also calculated the data given in the following chart on potential increases of food production which might be derived from more intensive use of existing cropland plus the development of unused land:

Prewar Food Production as Compared with Potential Increases from More Intensive Use of Existing Cropland plus Development of Unused Land

(in millions of metric tons)

	Pre-war production	World food needs in 1960	Production attainable from present cropland	Production attainable from present cropland plus 1,300 million new acres
Cereals	300·4	363·5	360·0	753·0
Roots and tubers	153·2	194·5	230·0	535·5
Sugar	30·0	33·6	34·5	178·1
Fats and oils	15·2	20·4	18·0	70·9
Pulses and nuts	36·2	65·2	43·4	56·2
Fruits and vegetables	156·3	411·0	211·0	470·0
Meat	65·6	95·8	78·7	96·8
Milk	150·2	300·0	180·2	323·2

According to the table, the potential food production attainable from higher yields on present cropland plus 1,300 million new acres exceeds by staggering figures world food needs which would arise in the year 1960, with the exception of milk and meat, where the requirements would just be met.

absence of regional agreements between neighbouring countries on the use of common water resources; deficient transport conditions; and lack of capital for large-scale projects, credit facilities for individual farms and marketing facilities for cash crops.

The present writer, though fully recognising these qualifying conditions, does not share the fears that the world is heading for a universal crisis in food supply. Nor does he believe that it is sensible to depict now conditions which might prevail in three or more generations.

Present expert opinion as expressed at various conferences of F.A.O. regards an increase of 1 to 2% per annum in world production of basic food and other essential agricultural products *in excess* of the rate of population growth as a minimum necessary to achieve some improvement in nutrition standards. This annual increase of 2 to 3% in world food production appears feasible in the light of recent production trends. Moreover, the assumption that world population will continue for a considerable time to grow by more than $1\frac{1}{2}$% per annum is far from certain. It is justified to assume in the not-too-distant future a slight decrease in this reproduction rate, taking into account the trend towards birth control which has become manifest in urban sections of certain Eastern countries. A comparison of numbers of children under 5 years of age per 1,000 women in age groups from 15 to 49 years shows a considerably lower figure for women in urban districts in underdeveloped countries.[1]

This reduction in the reproduction rate, which shows the population's capacity of adjustment, will be one of the factors instrumental in improvement of the long-term ratio of increase of population to increase of food. The other factor is the advance in methods and techniques of agricultural production.

Many changes in the resources factor which have occurred in the past were not expected at all, such as the discovery of underground water and cheap techniques for raising it, the effect of new fertilisers, plant improvements, etc.[2] There is also an exaggerated fear of bringing marginal resources into use. Today's marginal resources are tomorrow's normal resources, just as many of our present resources were marginal yesterday.

[1] *Demographic Yearbook*, 1952, U.N., Table F, p. 17.
[2] The potential effects of continuous use of commercial fertilisers are well covered in the Paley Report, a five-volume study of the resources of the U.S., published under the title, *Resources for Freedom*, A Report to the President by the President's Material Policy Commission, Washington, 1952. If American agriculture should continue to increase its use of fertilisers at the same rate as in recent years, agricultural production would rise by 75%, by 1975. An additional input of 900,000 tons of nitrogen and corresponding quantities of phosphate and potash would increase cereal production by 27 million tons, which equals the total turnover of cereals in the world's cereal markets.

THE MOVE TOWARDS ADJUSTMENT

For this very reason the insistence on rigid equations expressing ratio of growth of population to food supply which marks the arguments of many pessimistic observers is misplaced. Time and again experience has proved the unpredictability of rates of human procreation and rates of progress in global and regional food production, developments which play a vital role in adjustment of food supply to the demand. An instructive instance is what is now termed the Indian 'Rice Revolution'.

In India rice production is of crucial importance to the physical existence of the people, and the deficit in rice production constituted for years a grave issue in India's efforts to secure vital supplies needed to maintain its population. Indian agronomists were worried because Indian rice crops were so hopelessly behind the levels of crop yields per unit of land attained in other Asian countries, particularly in Japan. Yet it was taken for granted that the Indian farmer, for a number of reasons, would not achieve the results obtained by his Japanese counterpart.[1]

Following the initiative of a few enterprising Indians who did not accept the fatalistic conclusions of the observers, experiments were made recently in the transferring of Japanese methods of rice cultivation, first on a limited scale and later on a much more extensive one. According to a report published by Suresh Vaidya, the results were extraordinary. In most cases, Indian crops reached a multiple of former yields on the same plot, and equalled Japanese yields. In 1953 the Indian Ministry of Agriculture supplied and supported the campaign for transfer of Japanese methods to thousands of Indian villages. The effect of these measures was that 2 million acres of Indian paddy land were cultivated by the new methods and an additional million tons of rice were produced in 1953. Plans are now being worked out to extend the new methods gradually over the whole of India's 75 million acres of paddy land.[2]

LAND AND POPULATION GROWTH IN THE MIDDLE EAST

The countries of the Middle East are a good demonstration of particular aspects of the general problem. On the one hand we see Egypt, where rapid population growth during the last decades has so outstripped expansion of the cultivated area as to promote a serious case of rural overpopulation. The Egyptian Government has devised impressive long-term development schemes for expanding Egypt's

[1] K. Ramiah and M. V. Vachhani, 'Features of Rice Work in Japan and how they differ from those in India', *Indian Farming*, February 1950, pp. 54 ff.
[2] Cp. the article by Suresh Vaidya, 'India's Rice Revolution', *Christian Science Monitor*, July 19, 1954.

DEVELOPMENT PROSPECTS IN AGRICULTURE

irrigated area, but they will not affect the situation in the immediate future. On the other hand we find such countries as Iraq, Syria, Iran and Turkey in which the present population is not yet making full use of available land reserves. They possess vast territories, and a wide range of agricultural potentialities, primarily in the field of irrigated crops but also including dry farming, animal husbandry, plantations, afforestation, etc. They have large potential resources of land and water, the exact extent of which has not yet been fully determined.

Political considerations have in former years injected a controversial aspect into discussions of Middle Eastern agricultural potentialities. 'The region is overpopulated', was the generalisation frequently submitted. I do not hesitate to confess that upon my first contacts with this region, I arrived at a very positive appraisal of its potentialities, an appraisal supported by impressions of many journeys throughout the area and on-the-spot studies.

In a computation of available figures based on conservative estimates which I attempted several years ago, interesting data were obtained. The cultivable area of the eight countries covered in the survey (Turkey, Egypt, Iran, Iraq, Syria, Israel, Lebanon and Jordan) totals 118 million hectares. Of this area, less than a third was cultivated, leaving 85 million hectares as land reserve for future cultivation. This total does not take into consideration the specific potentialities of irrigation, for which I then submitted an estimate of 15·7 million hectares; of these 7·5 million were utilised and another 8 million were still open to irrigated cultivation. This is a very large potential.

I had further assumed, on the basis of rates of natural increase given in the U.N. publication, *World Population Trends, 1920–47*, that the population for this region will reach 80 million in 1967.[1] We have to relate this figure to our data on potentially cultivable land. Since irrigated land is at least twice as productive as dry-farmed land, we attach to it a weight of one as against 0·5 per unit of dry-farmed land and have then a total land potential of 67 million hectares. This divided by a population of 80 million gives us 0·84 hectares, or approximately 2·1 acres, per capita.

According to recent calculations, the amount of land per capita

---

[1] The rate of natural increase for the above computation is 1·1 per annum. In a recent memo of the population division of the United Nations the current rate of natural increase in South-west Asia has been estimated at 1·35. In the same source, however, a higher increase is envisaged for the following decades. Projections of populations over decades are highly speculative. The assumption of a very substantial increase in Oriental populations does not take sufficiently into account the effects of urbanisation on the birth rate, which shows a decrease in Oriental towns. There are other restricting influences, too, which all lead to the conclusion that such a substantial increase of population is not at all certain.

required to produce adequate diets in the United States is from 1·8 to 3·1 acres. Professor L. D. Stamp, in a paper submitted to the U.N. World Conference on Population, Rome, September 1954, regards the produce of one acre of average improved farm land as sufficient to support one person at the standard of living current in North-Western Europe. Considering our very cautious rating of irrigated land as only twice as fertile as dry-farmed land, we may still say that a per capita amount of two acres for the region as a whole must not cause concern over the relationship between land and population for a considerable time to come. The only exception is Egypt. In this country there indeed exists, for the present decade at least, an acute problem of a population increase which outstrips natural resources.

The above data on land resources do not tally with figures in a recent U.N. survey of economic conditions in the Middle East, which includes, in addition to the countries referred to above, Afghanistan, Sudan and Aden.[1] Although the differences are not too far-reaching, and in the case of a number of countries are even irrelevant, a few comments on these differences themselves should be added. Unused potentially productive land totals 54·2 million hectares, as against 85 million according to my findings. The main discrepancy is due to different data for Turkey, owing to a narrower interpretation of the term 'cultivable' in the F.A.O. Report as against the broader definition used by Turkish authorities. The latter include 44 million hectares of meadows, pastures, and grazing land under productive lands, whereas the F.A.O. Report lists only 21·8 million hectares altogether as cultivable. The research mission sent by the International Bank in 1950 regarded nearly 20 million hectares of pastures as potentially good grazing areas, whilst attaching little value to the other half for grazing purposes.[2] There is no cogent reason not to include pastures under 'productive land', since they certainly substitute for the growth of fodder crops for animals' maintenance.[3] In the case of Iran, too, there is a different evaluation. The large cultivable area of this vast country, with its great water resources, needs, as do practically all other regions, much more investigation before a definite estimate can be given with sufficient authority.

[1] Food and Agricultural Organisation of the U.N., 'Current Development of, and Prospects for, Agriculture in the Near East' (Rome, 1951).
[2] I.B.R.D., 'The Economy of Turkey' (Washington, 1951), p. 14.
[3] Wilhelm Salomon-Calvi maintains in an interesting paper 'Die Wasser-verhältnisse Agyptens verglichen mit denen Anatoliens' published in the periodical *Maden Tetkik ve Arama*, 1939, Sene 4, Sayi 2, that the irrigable area of Turkey would suffice to feed a population five times as large as its present size. He believes, on the basis of measurements of the volume of river flow of 15 Anatolian rivers in 1936, that the water sources of Anatolia are at least 15 times larger than the Nile. He adds that there are, of course, considerable fluctuations in the water flow year by year.

DEVELOPMENT PROSPECTS IN AGRICULTURE

PRODUCTION PLANS AND POTENTIALS

What is the meaning of these figures? Is it reasonable to present regional calculations of production potentials when practical requirements of food appear in the form of concrete market demand for individual areas and must be met as such? And, in addition, are there not many deficiencies and gaps in methods of calculating these potentials; and even if the estimates are acceptable, are there not many obstacles of a socio-political and physical nature which may prevent or slow down the immediate utilisation of the land in question? Yet, though these qualifications are readily admitted, they are not the relevant point here. First, we are not concerned in this context with the elaboration of concrete and practical schemes for the immediate utilisation of individual areas. Our main point is the following: for years prospects of food supply in Middle East countries were, in the light of their population increase, depicted in gloomy terms. Yet the actual trends so far have shown a very different picture. Figures of food production for the area as a whole and per capita point to an encouraging trend. Gross food supplies in the Middle East as expressed in index figures rose from 100 in the pre-war period to 137 in 1952–3. At the same time, population grew from 100 to 124. This means that food supplies per capita available for domestic consumption rose from 100 to 108.[1] In other words, in spite of a very substantial increase in population, food production has not only kept pace with but has actually exceeded it.

All this happened, I may add, even before the area began to benefit from the execution of recent agricultural development projects. There has never before been such an awareness on a national and international plane of the significance of large-scale development schemes in the field of land and water utilisation. Entirely new concepts have been worked out which will serve as guiding lines for the drafting of development plans on a scale without precedent in the Middle East. The second half of this century will see a fundamental alteration of the water geography and land utilisation of the region, and very probably of the socio-economic structure of its society as well.

In Egypt the revolutionary concept of 'century storage' has been devised. This concept envisages the use of Central Africa's huge lakes for long-term storage of water. A small increase in the water level of these immense bodies of water, primarily Lake Victoria and Lake Albert, would mean an enormous volume of additional water stored up. A rise of one metre would add 5·3 billion cu.m. to Lake Albert and 67·5 billion cu.m. to Lake Victoria. This and other projects

[1] F.A.O., *Problems of Food and Agricultural Expansion in the Near East*, Rome, 1955, pp. 26 ff.

153

which would completely harness the Nile could, over a period of 25 years, increase the cultivated area of Egypt from 6 million to about 10 million acres. Considering the present ratio of land to population in Egypt, however, even this expansion of cultivation will not solve the Egyptian problem, if the same rate of population increase should prevail during this future period.

In Israel the order of magnitude is of course much smaller. Still, existing plans for development of the country's land and water resources envisage within a six-year period an increase in the irrigated area from its 600,000 dunams in 1953 to 1·8 million dunams, or, in acres, from 150,000 to 450,000. These plans have as their economic starting point the reduction of the country's dependence on foreign supplies to a fraction of its present degree.[1]

In Iraq impressive schemes have been worked out in recent years. Some of these are now in the process of preparation and some are being completed. The Iraq Development Board is in charge of the following major projects, which do not, however, exhaust the potential of land reclamation in Iraq:

1 The Wadi Tharthar Scheme, which aims at elimination of the recurrent disastrous flooding of the Tigris and Euphrates, through construction of a canal with protective dykes and a dam on the Tigris. The work should be completed in 1956.

2 The Habbaniya Flood Control Project, which aims at diversion of the water of the Euphrates into Habbaniya Lake, and includes the building of channels and a barrage. This work will be completed in 1956.

3 Construction of the Diyala Dam. This project is to provide water for the irrigation of the Diyala basin. It is in an early stage of preparation.

4 The Irrigation Project of the Lesser Zab, near the Iranian border. This project aims at the construction of a dam with a storage capacity of 5·8 billion cu.m., which is regarded as sufficient to irrigate an area of 2·8 million acres.[2]

A remarkable case of an accelerated development of land resources has occurred in Turkey. Here a fortunate combination of political and economic circumstances has operated to bring about a unique expansion, primarily in the sphere of agriculture but also in other sectors of the economy. The results are surprising, even if measured in terms of achievements in more advanced countries. Production of wheat rose in index figures from 100 in 1950 to 194 in 1953, barley

[1] Cp. *Data and Plans* submitted to the Jerusalem Conference (October 1953), pp. 111 and 143 and *Israel Agriculture*, Jerusalem 1955. The irrigated area will reach 1,000,000 dunams in 1956.

[2] Iraq Development Board, Annual Report for the Financial Year 1952–3 (Bagdad, 1953).

DEVELOPMENT PROSPECTS IN AGRICULTURE

from 100 to 164, and maize from 100 to 175. The increase was due partly to an extension of the area and partly to an improvement in size of crop per unit of land. Both achievements, however, were made possible by the rapid mechanisation of Turkey's agriculture and improvement in its road system. The following table shows the increase in utilisation of arable land in Turkey for selected years in millions of hectares:

	1934	1951	1952	1953
Cereals	5·9	8·8	9·9	11·1
Fallows	3·7	5·0	5·6	
Other	1·1	2·0	2·1	
Total arable land (excl. pastures)	10·7	15·8	17·6	

Source: Annuaire statistique de la Turquie, and Agricultural Structure and Production, Central Statistical Office, Ankara, 1954.

Most of the projects mentioned above aim at expansion of the area under cultivation and irrigation, at drainage schemes, and the like. Yet there is, as mentioned before, another potential of improvement which has so far been tackled in only a few cases: namely, the expansion of food production through plant improvement, fight against disease, efficient use of fertilisers, new methods of crop rotation, etc. Until now these new techniques have been tried only to a limited extent. But experience in Egypt, Turkey and Israel certainly indicates that there are indeed great possibilities in the further development of the new methods. Progress achieved in certain Western countries under conditions not too different at the time can serve as demonstration of the possible margin of advance.

LAND AND POPULATION IN INDIA

With respect to extent of land area and size of population, the magnitudes of the Indian sub-continent are staggering in comparison with those of Middle Eastern countries. At the same time the scope and level of statistical work in India are impressive in comparison and contribute to the clarification of problems deriving from the unique growth of India's population over the last 50 years. As we have seen above (p. 114), the population of the Indian Union grew from 238 million in 1901 to 361 million in 1951, i.e. by no less than 123 million or 51·6% in 50 years. Since the Indian population is primarily engaged in agricultural occupations, our first question concerns the effect of population growth on per capita land resources.

155

THE MOVE TOWARDS ADJUSTMENT

In a study of the development of the ratio of land to population in India during the first half of this century, the first impression is distinctly discouraging. The increase in population exceeds by far the relative expansion of cultivation, with the result that the cropped area, calculated on a per capita basis, shows a steady decline. The decrease in the per capita area coincides, it is true, with a substantial increase in the total crop area, a situation well known from other agricultural countries with a rapid growth of population. The important fact in India, however, is that in comparison to the substantial rise in the number of people maintained in agriculture and industry, all other factors of production lag behind during the above period.

The Census Report for 1951 contains the results of a study based on 13 selected districts with a population of about 120 million. The following table shows the trends with regard to growth of total and per capita area:

Development of Total and Per Capita Area in 13 Indian Districts*

	1891	1921	1951	1891	1921	1951
	(in million acres)			(per capita area in acres)		
Net area sown	89	92·7	99·7	1·09	1·11	0·84
Double cropped area	9·9	10·9	12·5	0·12	0·13	0·10
Irrigated area	12·8	15·2	16·9	0·16	0·18	0·14

* Census of India, 1951, Part I —A, pp. 140 ff.

The data indicate a substantial decline in per capita area during the last three decades, owing to an increase in population which was unaccompanied by a corresponding extension of cultivation. Taking into account also the immense amount of livestock, which is to a large extent not productively utilised at all—cattle and buffaloes alone number 199 million—the conclusion of a most severe pressure on existing land resources is inevitable, and it is only a small step from here to a prediction of hopeless doom and starvation. Indeed, the common feature of nearly all appraisals of India's economic and social future, including those originating in government quarters, is one of extreme concern. The official Indian Census Report warns that there will be a catastrophy after 1969 unless India's population can be stabilised at 450 million through restriction of what is called 'improvident maternity', i.e. maternity in women who have already had three children. The degree of reduction in the birth and death rate, which is regarded as the principal remedy, would be indeed far-reaching: a limitation of the birth rate nearly to the level of the death rate, which would, at a rate of natural increase of 0·1%, produce a kind of stationary population of about 450 million.

Such a radical change in demographic trends does not seem feasible.

156

DEVELOPMENT PROSPECTS IN AGRICULTURE

It cannot be conceivably assumed that recommendation and introduction of restrictive measures of this kind would have effects as drastic as those proposed in the Report, though it is justified to expect a certain decrease of the present birth rate as a result of recent beginnings of family planning throughout India.

The gloomy approach of the authors of the Census Report as well as of other schools of thought with a similar orientation do not take sufficiently into consideration recent experience in other countries. The conclusion of hopelessness might be acceptable if the existing set-up of resources and their utilisation, available skills, customs and habits which have such a close bearing on the economic process were to be regarded as static. The truth is, however, that we cannot view these conditions as static. But this does not mean that the immense obstacles in the way of changing the 'static' set-up of India's economy are ignored. From the following comparison it appears that the greatest obstacle to a basic improvement in the sphere of agriculture lies in the small size of arable land per capita.

Land Area Per Capita
(in various countries in acres)

Country	Total	Arable land (including fallow and orchards)	Permanent meadows and pastures	Forests and woodlands	Other land area
India *	2·25	0·97	—	0·26	1·02
China	5·03	0·48	1·03	0·45	3·07
Indonesia	6·40	0·37	—	4·06	1·97
Japan	1·09	0·18	0·62	0·74	0·15
France	3·22	1·23	0·72	0·65	0·62
Italy	1·56	0·82	0·27	0·32	0·15
U.K.	1·19	0·37	0·60	0·07	0·15
U.S.S.R.	30·46	2·87	1·61	11·71	14·27
U.S.	12·64	3·02	4·39	4·14	1·09

* Census of India, 1951, Part I—B, pp. 61 ff.

This average per capita area is indeed much lower in India than, for instance, in important industrial countries such as the United States, or the U.S.S.R. But it is larger than that in China, Indonesia, Japan, and even in Italy and the United Kingdom. Yet the difference between these figures alone is not crucial. The question as to what measuring rod should be applied in order to determine the viable lot leads us back to the point dealt with before: namely, that it is not the physical extent of land resources which is decisive but a combination of production factors and conditions, including the level of prevailing production techniques and the country's economic organisation.

157

THE MOVE TOWARDS ADJUSTMENT

Under the conditions prevailing in India, i.e. at a 'rudimentary' level of production as compared with developed economies, the available per capita area can in the best of cases hardly offer more than a marginal existence to Indian peasant farmers. With improvement of technique and economic organisation the prospects for increased output rise. In this respect the Census Report has underestimated the considerable potential which is existent in India no less than in many other underdeveloped economies. Dr. Sen rightly comments on these shortcomings of the Census Report,[1] and would probably have been even more critical if he could have referred then to information contained in the Reports of the Indian Planning Commission on progress made during the period of India's first Five-Year Plan. Instead of 61·6 million tons of cereals, a target for the first three years, which was regarded as over-optimistic at the time, 65·5 million tons were harvested in 1953–4.

This result may have been largely due to the effect of favourable weather conditions. Yet a further discussion of the potential of India's land resources would in any case be needed before we are able to arrive at conclusions regarding this central problem of the subcontinent.

HOW MUCH LAND IN INDIA IS CULTIVABLE?

In some respects the problems of land utilisation in India resemble those of the Middle East. Excessive density in large parts of the main agricultural areas, sparse population in others and above all the signal importance of irrigation for further development give their imprint also to the Indian scene. Yet there is, as mentioned before, one conspicuous difference: the order of magnitude in terms of area, size of population and diversity of cultural and historical landscapes.

The various reports and investigations which deal with the problem of Indian land resources are unanimous as to the existence of a considerable area as yet unutilised. But views vary greatly as to the extent of these unused land resources. Whilst some authors estimate the unused potential at no less than 50% of present net sown areas, sceptical observers express the fear that owing to population increase the available margin of land, i.e. those land resources which the average peasant can profitably bring under cultivation with the means at his disposal, will shortly be used up. The issue apparently turns, as in many other countries with a great increase of population

[1] See S. R. Sen, 'The Problem of Population and Agricultural Productivity in India', paper submitted to the World Population Conference, 1954 (mimeogr.), pp. 8 ff.

and largely stationary farming systems, on the concept of the productivity of land, meaning land already cultivated and land not yet under the plough, and on the ability of the population to develop these resources.

Large divergencies exist in respect of the extent of cultivable land termed in official reports 'cultivable waste', the meaning of which is not clear. In an earlier publication of the Indian Government Economic Adviser it is explained as 'culturable waste and current fallows'.[1] This would allow for the interpretation that before the war there were about 170 million acres of cultivable land not under the plough. Some authors have gone even beyond this. Dr. Maclagan Gorrie of the Indian Forest Service estimated the area that could be immediately reclaimed as 170 million acres, out of which 140 million acres were in British India. M. R. Masani wrote of 360 million acres as 'at present sown with crops, about 80 millions kept as fallow, and 170 millions as cultivable waste'.[2] According to him there are thus 250 million more acres which might theoretically be brought under cultivation. In another publication the following data are given for British India before partition: out of 512 million acres, 210 million acres are actually cultivated, 158 million are occupied by forests, houses, roads, water, etc. Current fallows cover 47 million acres, and the balance of 97 million acres remains an uncultivated area. But the same author warns against an indiscriminate approach to the question of reclamation of this land, which might require efforts beyond the financial resources and strength of the country.[3]

A classification of India's surveyed land area *after partition* includes the following data.[4]

	Average for five years 1945–50 1,000 acres	%
Sown area	268,430	43·0
Fallow land	59,370	9·5
Area under forest	93,390	15·0
Land not available for cultivation	99,570	16·0
Other uncultivated land	102,660	16·5
Unclassified	60	—
	623,480	100

Though the figures of this table are not comparable to those of

[1] *Recent Social and Economic Trends in India*, New Delhi, 1946, p. 33.
[2] *Tata Studies in Current Affairs:* 'Your Food', Bombay, 1944, p. 56.
[3] Sir T. Vijayaraghavacharya, 'The Land and Its Problems', *Oxford Pamphlets on Indian Affairs*, p. 4.
[4] *Statistical Outline of India*, 1953. Published by Department of Economics and Politics, Tata Industries Ltd., Bombay.

pre-partition India, they also show a very substantial area of un-utilised land available for cultivation.

Two conclusions emerge from these figures:

(a) Even according to conservative estimates there is a consider-able margin of land available for further cultivation.

(b) The present state of knowledge, based on past experience as well as on data contained in recent surveys, does not yet allow us to determine the exact total of cultivable lands. Most observers in dealing with this question stress the obstacles standing in the way of utilisation of uncultivated areas. Part of the land has an excess of water; part of it is too saline; other tracts are in remote areas and practically inaccessible. This means that in many cases it would be possible to make the soil into fully exploitable farm land only by a very considerable capital investment.

Yet a discussion of the extent of cultivable land resources in a country which is partly semi-arid and partly fully-arid would be inadequate if due consideration were not given to the enormous potentialities of irrigation. According to an official British source less than 6% of the available water wealth of India's rivers is utilised, whilst the balance of over 94% runs waste into the sea.[1] In addi-tion there is a vast underground reservoir of water, of which only about 30,000 cubic feet per second are being utilised at present for irrigation; and a very large reserve is available for still further extension.

Yet the balance of over 94% of surface waters is not readily avail-able for use. Most of the supply is concentrated in the monsoon months, and except for snow-fed rivers emerging from the Himalayas, the rivers run almost dry during the dry months. In most parts of the country there is either too much water, resulting in disastrous floods, or too little water when it is most needed. The only solution to this problem is to equalise the supply throughout the year as far as possible, conserving water during periods of excess for release during periods of shortage. The estimates of the Indian Planning Commission arrive at the conclusion that out of a volume of 1,356 million acre-feet of water—the total annual available—it should be possible to raise about one-third or 450 million acre-feet as compared with 76 million acre-feet used now.

PROGRESS OF IRRIGATION IN INDIA'S MODERN HISTORY

In undivided India over 70 million acres of land were irrigated each year; this was the largest area irrigated in any country in the world, being more than three times that in the United States and more than

[1] Cp. *India*, Overseas Economic Surveys, London, March 1949, p. 97.

the combined total of any other ten countries of the world.[1] This is an outstanding achievement. The lesson it imparts is so significant that it is justified to dwell somewhat on its background and history.

The differences in physical and climatic conditions of the sub-continent have produced very distinct systems of farming in the various regions. There is an extended area of dry farming over all the arid uplands, covering large parts of the Western and North-western provinces of India, where only one cereal crop every two or three years is possible without irrigation. As against this, irrigation farming assures regular cultivation in arid and semi-arid districts at least once a year; in many places even two crops are obtained. The main areas concerned are the upper Ganges plain, the Punjab plain and Sind. Wet farming is characteristic of regions which receive very heavy rainfall (more than 80 inches), such as the central sub-Himalayas, lower Bengal and the Malabar coast; in the central Ganges plain and the Central Provinces, which receive between 40 to 80 inches of rainfall, humid farming is practised. To what extent irrigation was apt to change farming prospects is perhaps nowhere better demonstrated than in the Punjab, i.e. the land of the five rivers.

Until nearly the end of the nineteenth century, the greater part of the Punjab consisted of arid waste and desert land sparsely populated by nomad tribes of camel and sheep graziers. The Indian Government appropriated these unclaimed lands and inaugurated a project of colonisation, in order to bring these areas, where disturbances occasionally flared up, into the orbit of its laws, and at the same time to alleviate the pressure on land resulting from over-crowded tracts elsewhere.[2] It was a policy applied in other Oriental countries as well, with varying results. In India, however, it met with great success; thus irrigation schemes followed one after the other, and already before the First World War caused the transformation of a steppe and desert country into a highly cultivated, prospering area. The inter-war period immediately saw a resumption of large-scale efforts to utilise the surplus water of the great Indus, Beas and Sarda rivers. The largest project was that of the Sukkur Barrage in Sind, which includes a network of seven canals with a total length of 6,564 miles, and a gross area of no less than 7·5 million acres to be supplied

[1] *Ibid.*, p. 98.
[2] The Punjab has an area of 135,880 square miles and was partitioned in 1947 between India and Pakistan. Its climate is of a continental type and shows extremes of heat and cold; in the western and northern parts arid features predominate. The dry western plain of the Punjab, which comprises 59,000 sq. miles, exhibits the wor'd's most remarkable system of canal irrigation. The change from dry to irrigated farming has created a new agricultural region from practically nothing, and points to promising developments wherever similar natural conditions exist. From A. M. Lorenzo, 'Atlas of India', *Oxford Pamphlets on Indian Affairs*, Sect. 11.

by these canals. It is the biggest single scheme of this kind in the world.

There are other large-scale irrigation schemes in India, part of them fully executed, part still in the process of execution. So far the area benefiting from irrigation by government projects amounts to 30 million acres.

But irrigation on the sub-continent is not dependent on river and canal water supply alone. The large quantities of subsoil water, too, are an invaluable source for irrigation purposes. The most common instrument for lifting this underground water is the well, which assumes all forms from a simple hole in the ground to an imposing masonry well raising water from a depth of many hundreds of feet. Power is provided by manpower, animals, bullocks and oil engines. Nearly 30% of the irrigated area of India is under well-irrigation. The wells are frequently a complementary source of irrigation, in many places serving together with canals. There are also ingenious devices which make it possible to switch over from one source of water to another in order to utilise to the utmost the available quantities; a high level of the water table allows the release of surplus canal water for agricultural expansion elsewhere, and vice versa.

A third method of utilising water for irrigation purposes is the tank, a kind of water reservoir, usually in the form of a pool of varying size which collects rain water, frequently from a fairly extended area. During the rainless season it provides drinking water for men and animals and irrigation water for farm lands in the neighbourhood. Though the tank system cannot be compared in size or efficiency to other systems of collection and distribution of water, it still has great significance owing to its widespread use, especially in Madras. The area irrigated by tanks is estimated at no less than eight million acres; though in many cases these lands are irrigated on a very precarious level.

India's irrigation projects have been promoted with vigour since the turn of the century. After the First World War the area under irrigation was substantially expanded: the table opposite shows the development in the inter-war period.

During the Second World War a new phase in irrigation planning set in, following the new impetus in the field of projecting long-term economic development.

An interesting example is offered in the approach to the Damodar Valley project, as described as early as 1945 by Dr. Sudhir Sen, who assisted the Agricultural Adviser to the Government of Bengal, 1944–5.[1] The economic benefits to be expected from perennial irriga-

[1] L. K. Elmhirst and Sudhir Sen, *Collected Notes on Agricultural Problems in Bengal*, published by the Government of Bengal, Alipore, Bengal, 1945, pp. 55–6.

DEVELOPMENT PROSPECTS IN AGRICULTURE

Development of Irrigation in the Inter-war Period*

Year	Area under irrig.	Area in % of net area sown	Irrig. from Govt. canals	In % of net area sown
	BRITISH INDIA AREA			
1920–1	47,783	24	19,558	10
1932–3	48,453	23	21,524	10
1941–2	56,714	27	26,150	12
	INDIAN STATES			
1920–1	8,048	15	2,401	4
1932–3	10,056	14	3,206	5
1941–2	11,169	15	4,337	6
	TOTALS			
1920–1	55,831		21,959	
1932–3	58,509		24,130	
1941–2	67,883		30,487	

* *Recent Social and Economic Trends in India*, p. 38. Figures for the Indian States refer to 1940–1.

tion in the Damodar Valley were seen by Dr. Sen as follows: 'If 800,000 acres, as proposed, are serviced with year-round irrigation so as to ensure two crops a year over the whole area, the rice output per acre in the unirrigated area (say 620,000 acres) will be brought to the level of output in the irrigated area (say 180,000 acres). Owing to frequent crop failures as a result of droughts and floods, the long-term average yield of clean rice in the unirrigated area would at present work out at something like 12 maunds per acre. In the irrigated area the yield is at least 50%, probably 60 to 65%, higher. In view of the fact that a substantial area under rice is already irrigated, though inadequately, from tanks, the additional rice output to be expected as a result of extensive canal irrigation may be placed at 6 maunds per acre or 3,720,000 maunds in all. The value of this additional output, at the pre-war price of, say, Rs.5-0-0 per maund, would be Rs.186 lakhs. At the price of Rs.10 per maund (the present price being substantially higher), the value would be Rs.372 lakhs.

'In addition, the twice-cropped area will increase from 58,210 acres to 800,000 acres. The output of the second crop from 58,210 acres may also be expected to increase as a result of improved irrigation, though this need not be included in our calculation. . . .

'The acre yield of all crops is at present extremely low. This is due, above all, to lack of irrigation facilities and failure to apply manure. Once perennial irrigation has been assured, the farmer will have every incentive to use manures on a substantial scale. Besides, once the

163

intensity of cropping has been raised, it would be possible to introduce a scientific rotation of crops so as to conserve or enhance the fertility of the soil and thus to improve the yield per acre. If at the same time the present small-scale farming under an open field system is replaced by large-scale scientific farming along modern lines, the acre output of crops might eventually rise by anything from 200 to 300%.

'Even if these long-term considerations are left out of account and the framework of Bengal's agriculture remains substantially unaltered, the provision of year-round irrigation alone would render possible the creation of additional wealth, the value of which would at the rate of pre-war prices, amount to Rs.7·5 crores a year. To this should be added the money value of fish that may be grown in the reservoirs and canals, of additional water transport, of electricity that may be produced in the area and of the gains which will result if malaria and floods are brought under effective control. Judged in terms of wealth-producing capacity, hardly any scheme could hold out better promise than the proposed scheme for the comprehensive development of the Damodar Valley.'

Eight years later when these lines are being written the Damodar Valley project is in full stage of execution. Details of the expected results may be different from those assumed in the original blueprints, but the belief and the reasoning of those who first envisaged the scheme was certainly justified: it gives bread and hope for a better living to countless destitute people.

Conclusions

To sum up, our considerations lead us to the following conclusions:

1 World population will grow for several decades to come and thus increase the demand for food by very considerable quantities. The efforts towards improvement of diets throughout the world will further strengthen this trend.

2 In economically advanced countries, progress in agricultural techniques resulting in higher yields per unit of land has at least balanced the impact of population growth on food demand. The economic weight of the land factor component in food production has been substantially reduced by increased capital outlay.

3 In many areas of the world there exist large reserves of unused or not intensively used land, which open vistas for a greatly increased food production. Calculations of production potentials based on the attainable yield increases, as well as on the possible expansion of cultivated land, justify the view that a balance between food demand and production is possible for the populations of underdeveloped areas.

4 The land issue is thus not the primary question for the future fate of world population. The crux of the problem turns on the density of the population in relation to the cultural and material stage which such populations have reached.

There is sufficient evidence to show that a higher level of political and social organisation accompanies or is followed by a higher degree of productivity and a decreasing birth rate. Such a development is, however, not an automatic process, but needs strenuous and conscious efforts and permanent vigilance towards the relation between available and creatable resources and their consumption.

It is part of the underdeveloped state of the economic and social organisation of the countries under review that most of them are burdened by an obsolete system of land tenure. We shall deal with this issue in the following section.

CHAPTER IX

LAND TENURE CONDITIONS AND ECONOMIC DEVELOPMENT

IT follows from our general concept of the nature of economic progress that the institutional aspects of agrarian development will have to be taken fully into account; in the first place the distribution of rural property and the nature of ownership relations.[1] Even now the majority of the Oriental populations earns its living by working on the soil. Yet land is, as a rule, extremely unequally distributed. Since the main income of the population derives from it, the income distribution in Oriental countries reflects a similar degree of inequality.

Inequality in land distribution is not the only aspect of deficient land tenure conditions. Landed property in underdeveloped countries is also an expression of social and political influence; those who possess land possess power. The political regimes of most underdeveloped countries show the overriding position of wealthy landowners in the hierarchy of power.

A further major aspect is the effect of the possession of property on the accumulation and flow of capital in the economy. Landowners who have managed for generations to amass wealth from land revenues have become the money lenders and bankers of the community, in the first place of farmers who possess no funds of their own to keep up their production. Interest rates for rural credits reach usurious levels in many of these countries—from 30 to 100%—adding another nearly unbearable burden to excessive land charges. The issue of land distribution is thus not only the problem of allotting a sufficient piece of land ('viable lot') to each farmer and of his title to this piece of land. Land tenure conditions refer to the whole

---

[1] The importance of this issue finds expression in the increasing number of studies devoted to it by national and international bodies. Among these studies the U.N. publication *Progress in Land Reform*, New York, 1954, should be mentioned. It contains an analysis of replies by Governments to a United Nations questionnaire.

166

institutional framework of agricultural production. The institutional features included in this framework comprise:

a Conditions of ownership, i.e. land tenure relations in the legal sense of the word;

b The inheritance system according to which land is passed on from the owner to his heirs;

c The system of crop distribution which regulates the division of the product between the landowner and the operator;

d The national distribution of farm property by criteria of farm sizes;

e The habits and systems by which agricultural production, marketing and extension are organised and financed;

f The system of taxation imposed on the rural population.

It would be impossible to describe here in detail the manifold systems and features of agrarian structure which prevail in underdeveloped areas. For a considerable time it has been recognised that obsolete land tenure conditions and related issues present a formidable obstacle to projects of rural development. It is from this general viewpoint that the following sections dwell on some of the characteristic features of a backward agrarian structure, and indicate some of the recent approaches to overcoming these obstacles. It goes without saying that, owing to the extreme variation of conditions from region to region, no general recipe can be applicable indiscriminately to all the areas concerned.

FREEDOM OR CONTROL OF LAND DISTRIBUTION

The demand for a basic change in land tenure conditions ranks high in all modern programmes for betterment of economic and social conditions in underdeveloped countries. Where such demands have remained without response for a protracted period, forceful changes in land ownership have quite frequently been imposed on the landowning class. There are two main viewpoints in discussions of a remedy for the problem: one is that measures to change the situation have to aim at the restitution of private ownership to all those who cultivate land not owned by them. Modern development in the free world, it is argued, is marked by the restitution of the individual liberty of man and his right to own and control property. Without the appropriation of land to the tenant and worker on the soil in complete individual ownership, the problem of inequality and poverty cannot be solved.

This is essentially the viewpoint of certain American schools of thought, which rely on experience in the development of land tenure and related problems in the North American continent.[1] This view does not, however, take into sufficient consideration the experience in countries of the Old World, pointing decidedly to the dangers inherent in such a preference for complete and uncontrolled right of ownership. It was precisely by insistence on the absolute character of rights in the land that the most abhorrent misuses in Eastern lands became sanctioned, and that the old customs of land and crop distribution prevailed for centuries and left the heritage of rural destitution to the reformers of the twentieth century. Only very recent developments have brought about a more penetrating approach to problems of land tenure in many Oriental countries. The present concept is, then, to change the existing distribution of land by limiting the size of the farm unit owned by a single proprietor, and redistributing the resulting excess lands to tenants and farmers who have no land of their own. But this redistribution is not always intended as a transfer of land from one owner to another. In some legislations the new beneficiaries should not become full proprietors, but should instead have the assured *usufructus* of the land. Whatever the various solutions propose, they take for granted the right of the community to contest and abolish legal titles to ownership if their maintenance would violate modern notions of economic and social justice.

Recent years have seen a considerable increase in the interest devoted to problems of the agrarian structure in backward regions. The conference on world land tenure problems held at the University of Wisconsin, Madison, Wisconsin, in October 1951, with the participation of governmental departments and many foreign institutions and experts, was an effective expression of international concern for these topical issues. The proceedings of the conference were an important contribution to the clarification and solution of problems of land tenure on an international plane.

International agencies, and in particular United Nations institutions, had already evinced their interest in the various issues of the agrarian structure in underdeveloped countries. Following discussions in the sub-committees of the fifth session of the U.N. General Assembly in 1950, the Department of Economic Affairs of the U.N. submitted a report entitled 'Land Reform: Defects in Agrarian

---

[1] Cp. the following passage in *Land Reform, a World Challenge*, p. 10: 'The United States historically has followed the policy that it is desirable for the farmer to own the land he cultivates or have opportunity to become a land-owner. This ideal was already imbedded in American life and thought at the time the nation achieved its independence. Thomas Jefferson, who drafted the Declaration of Independence in 1776, considered small landholders "the most precious part of a state". Succeeding leaders actively championed the cause of farm ownership by the individual cultivators.'

LAND TENURE CONDITIONS

Structure as Obstacles to Economic Development' to the 13th session of the Economic and Social Council. This report was prepared in co-operation with the F.A.O. of the U.N., and gives a representative survey of the main features of the agrarian structure in these countries.[1] In addition to official publications of international and national bodies, there is an increasing number of individual monographs dealing with recent developments in land tenure conditions.

CONDITIONS PRECEDING LAND REFORMS

To convey an idea of the land tenure situation which faces the legislator and land reformer in the countries under discussion, conditions preceding land reforms in the regions of the Middle East and India will be very summarily outlined.

Middle East
In most Middle Eastern countries present-day land tenure conditions are oppressive although, potentially, they are given to improvement, since the unutilised land reserves are considerable. Yet the individual tenant who is involved in the network of traditional land tenure relations and obsolete production techniques is not affected by the potential surplus of land. A good example is Iran where abundant land reserves are available. For an analysis of conditions in Iran, we may use the results of a sample survey in the Teheran and Demavent areas, comprising 1,300 villages.[2] This survey revealed that in 1949 60% of the rural families possessed no land at all. Another 25% owned less than 1 hectare and about 10% owned between 1 and 3 hectares. The 95% of the rural families surveyed who held 3 hectares or less owned only 17% of the total land. On the other hand, one-fifth of the families in the group of holdings exceeding 20 hectares, possessed holdings of 100 hectares and more, including 34% of the land surveyed. There were two major landowners in the country: the government, which actively controlled from 9 to 13 million acres of land, and the royal family, which controlled from 6 to 10 million acres. The nature of the claims on government land is not always very clearly defined, and the government has not challenged what it considers the illegal basis of doubtful

[1] Reference is made here to the following sources in particular: Proceedings of the Conference on World Land Tenure Problems, the University of Wisconsin, Madison, Wisconsin, October–November 1951 (four mimeographed volumes); Land Reform, Defects in Agrarian Structure as Obstacles to Economic Development, U.N. Department of Economic Affairs, New York, 1951; Land Reform, a World Challenge, U.S. Department of State publication 4445, February 1952. Since completion of this book, the Madison proceedings have appeared in book form.
[2] G. Hadary, 'The Agrarian Reform Problem in Iran', *Middle East Journal*, Vol. V, No. 2, Spring 1951.

claims. Many of the government lands are leased to wealthy individuals who sub-lease the land to tenants or establish a management of their own on the lands.

As usual in Oriental countries, the predominating group among the deputies are the landlords, about two-thirds of the members of the Majlis. Though the tenants are not compelled to remain in the villages where they were born, they are bound to stay on in their localities by the lack of alternative employment, initiative and urges of improvement, which do not easily grow in people with such poor health and widespread illiteracy.

The traditional tenure arrangement is to allocate crop returns to each of the five main 'factors' in production, i.e. land, water, work animals, seed and labour. Since the landlord often contributes land, water, animals and seed, he is entitled to as much as four-fifths of the crop; but there are other arrangements as well. Hadary gives a rough estimate of 7,750 rials as the average annual income per tenant family, as compared with approximately 75,000 rials per average landlord family. For the country as a whole the share of the landlords is estimated, after deduction of outlays, at about one-third of the crop. Incidentally, the planting and growing of trees is discouraged by landlords, because trees traditionally belong to the peasant.

Syria

In Syria the main characteristics of the land tenure regime is the dominant position of the large landowners. There are neither accurate nor complete statistics available. The scanty data point to the prevalence of absentee ownership in many districts of the country, particularly in the northern parts and to the usual exploitation of the tenants and share croppers in the agreements for the distribution of the crops. El Ricaby mentions the following conditions:[1]

   i If the landlord provides the land and habitation only, he gets about 30% of the produce.

   ii If the landlord ploughs the land with a tractor and pays 50% of the expenses for clearing water canals, etc., he gets 50%. Cost of manure is born equally between landlord and and tenant. All other farm operations, seeding, etc., are done by the farmer.

   iii If the landlord farms his lands, he employs labourers and pays a foreman who also works for a salary ranging from $250 to $300 per annum with about 400 kgrs. of grain for his

[1] Cp. Akram el Ricaby, 'Land Tenure in Syria', paper presented before the Conference on World Land Tenure Problems, Wisconsin, 1951.

bread. When there are fruit trees, the tenant, in addition to the foregoing, receives 25% of the value of fruits but has to look after the trees in accordance with the directions given to him.

According to another source, rents average about 60% of the produce.[1] Since rent is paid on about two-thirds of the land of Syria, only about 60% of the total produce remains in the hands of the rural population working on the land. The proportion of large landed property to the total area of cultivated land is very considerable; thus the regime of the country is, of necessity, the regime of the large landowners of the country.

Lebanon

Land tenure relations in the Lebanon are not too different from the conditions just described, although very much at variance in point of farm sizes. The Lebanese farmer very frequently has less than two acres of land, and since he has to rent it from an absentee landlord he has to pay him up to two-thirds of the crop for rent. There is no security of tenure, and where the farmer has to borrow money from a professional money lender he has to pay from 30 to 40% interest, again narrowing down his share in the yield from the soil. The excessive fragmentation of the land is a great obstacle to efficient cultivation also in the Lebanon; one case is cited by Mr. N. Alamuddin, according to which in one village the number of parcels is 32,000, the number of parcels per property 56, and the area of each parcel about 0·17 acre.[2] The width of each parcel does not exceed a few metres, whereas the length is a few kilometres. 44% of the 250,000 hectares of cultivated land belongs to 1,700 owners, 16% to 8,500, and 40% to 74,500 owners in holdings of less than five hectares, according to an official source given in an Egyptian periodical.[3]

Data from other sources confirm the picture as given here. According to the paper by Charles Issawi and Carlos Dabezies, almost half the total area of the Lebanon, including some of the richest agricultural land in the country, is owned by a few large landlords.[4] The share of the net produce accruing to the landlord can be put at a minimum of 50%.

[1] Ch. Issawi and C. Dabezies, 'Population Movements and Population Pressure in Jordan, Lebanon and Syria', *Milbank Memorial Fund Quarterly*, October 1951.
[2] Cp. his paper presented at the Madison conference, 'Proposals for the Solution of Land Tenure Problems in Lebanon'.
[3] Cf. *La Revenue de l'Egypte Economique et Financière*, May 28, 1949, p. 12.
[4] *Milbank Memorial Fund Quarterly*, Vol. XXIX, No. 4, October 1951, p. 397.

Egypt
The data for the development of land tenure conditions in Egypt could serve as a fitting demonstration of the effects of high population pressure on the limited land resources of an underdeveloped country. The following table shows the distribution of land holdings in Egypt:

Egypt: Distribution of Holdings according to Size, 1949

Size group	Number of holdings (thousands)	Per cent of all holdings	Area in holdings (thousands of feddan)	Per cent of farm area
Under 1 feddan*	1,956	71·59	789	13·26
1 and under 5 feddan	618	22·62	1,305	21·94
5 and under 10 feddan	80	2·93	527	8·86
10 and under 20 feddan	43	1·57	589	9·90
20 and under 50 feddan	22	0·81	662	11·13
50 and under 100 feddan	7	0·26 ⎫	456	7·66 ⎫
100 and under 400 feddan	5	0·18 ⎬ 0·47	826	13·88 ⎬ 34·90
400 and under 1,000 feddan	0·6	0·02 ⎪	353	5·93 ⎪
1,000 feddan and over	0·2	0·01 ⎭	442	7·43 ⎭
Total	2,732	100·00	5,949	100·00

Source: *Statistical Pocket Yearbook*, 1951 (Cairo, 1952).
* One feddan equals 1·038 acres.

As the data indicate, more than 71% of the holdings are in the lowest group up to one feddan and add up altogether to only 13·20% of the total area. As against this, less than one-half per cent (0·47) of the holdings occupy 34·9% of the total area. The consequences are not surprising: excessive fragmentation, sub-standard size of holdings, inflated rent level, low wages and, as result, destitution and poverty in the villages. H. A. Dawood has shown in an interesting article in *Land Economics* that, as a result of the enormous pressure on available land resources in Egypt, an agricultural worker would in 1945 have had to invest wage earnings of 10 years to buy one feddan of land.[1] His average daily wage was then 10 piastres, while the price of one feddan was £E.300, or 3,000 times that wage. In the United States, where the average value of farm land in the same year amounted to $40.63 and the average wage per day was $4·12, the average farm labourer could buy one acre of land with the wages of less than 10 days.

This appalling inequality of chances is not limited to the farm worker who wants to acquire land. The tenant farmer, too, would

[1] H. A. Dawood, 'Land Ownership and Tenancy Systems in Egypt', *Land Economics*, Vol. XXVI, August 1950.

find it extremely difficult to pay the inflated land prices. This inflated rent level is the reason, according to Dawood, why many capable landowners who reside in rural villages prefer to rent their land to small farmers rather than work it themselves. The landlord can insist on such high prices because there is always a great demand for leased land on the part of the landless tenants who have no other chance of making a living; thus he obtains a higher income from leased land than from such land when worked by himself.

To give an idea of the magnitude of the problem it should be mentioned that the share of rent on land amounted in some years to half, and sometimes more than half, of the total revenue from agriculture and to nearly 20% of the national income.[1]

India

It appears that the most difficult situation in the field of land tenure conditions exists in India. Professor M. L. Dantwala of the Bombay University, one of the foremost students of land tenure conditions in India, brought the disturbing trends in the distribution of land property in India well into relief.[2] For many years there was a marked tendency for land to pass into the hands of non-cultivating owners. In the State of Bombay the proportion of non-cultivating owners to the total increased between 1916–17 and 1947–8 from 9·3% to 22·6%, the percentage of area held by them from 12 to 30. At the same time the number of landless labourers has been continuously on the increase. In 1882 the number of landless day-labourers in agriculture was estimated at 7·5 million. An estimate for 1933 puts the figure at 35 million, and one for 1944 at 68 million. Unfortunately, simultaneously with this increase in the number of landless workers a rise in the number of rent-seeking intermediaries took place. So-called sub-infeudation and rent-racking has further narrowed down the share of the landless worker who has to live from the fruit of his toil.

Another important implication is the inability of agriculture to absorb the excess population withdrawing from secondary and tertiary into primary industries following the spread of machine-made goods. A considerable proportion of the rural artisans— according to the 1931 census, no less than 64%—were compelled to give up their traditional occupations and seek their livelihood in agriculture.

The situation prevailing at the beginning of the fifties was also far from reassuring with respect to the size of holdings owned by the farmers. 82% of holdings in Madras, 81% in the United Provinces,

[1] Cp. M. A. Anis, 'A Study of the National Income of Egypt', *L'Egypte Contemporaine*, November/December 1950, Tables 1 and 2.
[2] Cp. his paper, at the Madison conference, on 'Land Tenure Problems in Countries with Heavy Pressure of Population on Land' (1951).

79% in Orissa, 71% in Bengal, 64% in the Punjab and 66% in Assam were below five acres. In the State of Bombay, 42% of the total number of cultivators had holdings below five acres, 30% of the holdings were below three acres, and most of them severely fragmented. Living conditions and in particular family and per capita income placed the villagers on the verge of starvation. In many areas the percentage of rural families with deficit budgets amounted to two-thirds and more of the total number of families in the village. This does not invalidate the fact that a small percentage of farms could improve their position either by reducing debts or expanding assets, or both. Professor Dantwala arrived in his paper at the following conclusions:

'When the most frequent size of holding is less than five acres and there is no prospect of any substantial increase in the same in the near future, it is obvious that tenancy has no place in the agrarian set-up in India. Probably not more than five per cent of farms are of a size which will admit of double interest of the owner and the tenant. The units are too small even for the owner-operator to eke out a decent living. Tenancy under the circumstances must result in the exploitation of the tenant and mining of the agricultural land. Theoretically, if the rent is no more than interest on the value of land and equipment on it, the tenancy arrangements may not be considered exploitative. But in countries where land hunger is so acute, rents are always extortionate.

'Yet, in contrast to what is desirable, probably more than two-thirds of the land under cultivation in India is tenant-cultivated and rents certainly represent returns higher than interest on investment by the landlord. Tenancy legislation under the circumstances can at best be ameliorative—except to the extent it provides for the buying up of land by the tenant and prevents further extension of area under tenancy. . . . "Land to the tiller" is not just an idealistic political slogan—it represents a basic economic necessity.'

RECENT APPROACHES TO LAND REFORM

The political and social crises which marked the situation in many underdeveloped countries after the Second World War affected also the position of the various inherited land tenure systems nearly everywhere. Land reform movements thus sprung up throughout the underdeveloped world, with varying degrees of strength and success. This outline does not aim at an analysis and enumeration of the various attempts undertaken hitherto. Yet some of the new approaches will be discussed here, either because of the original methods applied or the magnitude of the changes involved.

LAND TENURE CONDITIONS

India

From the viewpoint of the magnitudes involved and the novelty of the approaches the abolition of the Zamindari institutions in the Indian State of the United Provinces deserves particular attention.[1] With the United Provinces Zamindari Abolition and Land Reforms Act 1951 a basically new method to the solution of land tenure problems has been applied in part of India. The new Act evolved a simple and uniform system of land tenure which combines the features of peasant proprietorship with the development of self-governing village communities.[2] These village communities will become the owners of all common lands and will have the powers of land administration and management. The rights and interests of the intermediaries on land shall be acquired on payment of compensation amounting to eight times their net income to all the Zamindars and of rehabilitation grants at a graded rate ranging from twenty to two to all the small Zamindars paying annual land revenue up to Rs.5,000. The difficulty of financing these payments shall be solved, *inter alia*, by asking the tenants to make voluntary contributions of ten times their rent. Future re-emergence of the landlord-tenant system should be prevented by the restriction of sub-letting to disabled persons, minors, widows, etc. An important provision is directed against the accumulation of large holdings and the exploitation of farm labour. No person will be permitted to acquire by sale or gift a holding of more than 30 acres.

The remarkable feature in the new legislation is the restoration of the rights and freedom of the cultivator combined with the re-establishment of the supremacy of the village community which it once exercised over all the elements of village life.

The attempts to improve the agrarian structure in India by legal measures such as land reform, have been recently supplemented by the institution of pilot development projects for the raising of food production and the encouragement of the village population to generate capital and resources of their own. It is a comprehensive programme starting with numerous demonstration schemes; although directed entirely by Indians, it is aided by the United States with a substantial grant. The programme provides for instruction in

[1] The term *Zamindar* refers to a specific class of landowners in certain Indian provinces, who owe their position to their service as tax-farmers. The original institution of the *Zamindar* dates back to the end of the eighteenth century when hereditary proprietary rights were conferred on revenue collectors. These revenue collectors became owners of land on condition that they paid fixed amounts of rent directly to the government. They soon developed into a powerful class of landlords.

[2] Cp. the paper on 'Agrarian Reform in the State of U.P. India' by Aditya Nath Jha presented before the Conference on World Land Tenure Problems, Madison, 1951.

175

co-operative organisation, in the use of machinery, improved irrigation techniques and fertilising, and will be enlarged later on.[1]

A review of conditions of land reform in India has to mention the
unprecedented movement 'Bhoodan Yagna' (Land gift movement)
which aims at obtaining gifts of lands by a voluntary or spontaneous
act on the part of the landowners.[2] A disciple of Ghandi, Acharya
Vinoba Bhawe started in April 1951 a walking tour of villages
throughout India asking landowners to give away one-sixth of their
land as a gift for redistribution among the landless. The gifts which
followed this unique appeal range from one-tenth of an acre to
100,000 acres. At the end of 1954 an amount of $1\frac{1}{4}$ million acres was
acquired in this way under the 'Bhoodan Yagna'. The head of the
movement, Vinoba, who exerts such an extraordinary influence on
landowners, operates by way of addressing the villagers in open-
air meetings. The land put at his disposal on this occasion is distributed among the landless by the general consensus of the people
assembled on the spot. All observers of this movement are agreed
that it is an experiment without parallel in social and economic
history. Without any coercion by state law and authority a unique
contribution to economic reconstruction is being made by the
genuinely non-violent technique of social change. The acquisitive in-
stinct which is supposed to prevail universally is disregarded and,
in the light of the astonishing results of the appeal, even visibly
weakened. At the same time it must be observed that although the
aim of this offspring of Ghandian concepts is to acquire 50 million
acres of land, the results hitherto do not justify the belief that India's
land problem can be solved in this way. The signal importance of the
movement lies more in its educational impact than in its immediate
effect on the distribution of land. Because of its contribution to the
creation of a proper atmosphere for land reforms it has been given a
definite place in the Five-Year Plan.

Opinions differ widely as to the success of the land reforms introduced hitherto in India. Considerable criticism is directed against
the efficiency of the measures which were designed to implement the
land reform. Their deficient execution brought about a state of affairs
which is remote from the spirit in which the reform was originally
conceived. The lack of clarity in the provisions of the law as to the

[1] The former American Ambassador in India, Chester Bowles, gives a remarkably positive appraisal of the prospects of this programme in his 'Ambassador's Report', New York, 1954, pp. 201 f. According to Bowles, it is 'the
greatest development effort of its kind ever launched in a democratic nation'.

[2] Cp. 'Progress in Land Reform', p. 92; M. L. Dantwala, 'Programmes and
Plans for Rural Development in India', in *Programmes and Plans for Rural
Development in Tropical and Sub-tropical Countries* published by I.N.C.I.D.I.,
Bruxelles, 1953, p. 217, and G. Weller, 'Vinoba Bhawe, India's walking Messiah',
Yale Review, Vol. XIII, No. 2, 1953.

exact nature of the rights of tenure, ownership and intermediaries is regarded as one of the major reasons for the failure of the reform legislation. These deficiencies made it easy for those whose position was bound to be affected by land reform to evade its immediate consequence. The majority of executives and bearers of responsible office in local and central government and of the members of congress are landowners themselves. Many of them were not and are not prepared to execute faithfully a policy which robs them of their main substance of wealth and their position of social prestige and influence.

The present state of the land reforms in India offers therefore many severe features of open and concealed evasion of the law and shows in particular the use of skilful devices to forestall the application of the law by reckless eviction of the tenants.

These reactions are no surprise to those who are familiar with the course of similar attempts of reform in Oriental lands. Indeed, many attempts to introduce new systems of land tenure in Egypt, Syria and Iraq during the nineteenth century ended in failure because of the absence of certain prerequisites for a successful execution of the new laws.[1]

On the other hand, the experience available hitherto should not lead to the conclusion that the present phase of reform in India must inevitably produce the same results. A more patient and detached appraisal, although taking into account all the negative features and difficulties prevailing today, would probably point to the achievements attained hitherto and stress that temporary deficiencies are the price which has to be paid when means of peaceful evolution are chosen for the promotion of progress and change in a society with a time-honoured social stratification.

Iraq.

The Dujayla settlement project is an interesting experiment in the field of land reform in Iraq though it does not, so far, exceed a very limited scope; and it is not even a land reform act in the proper sense but a limited attempt to establish on a certain area a land settlement project.[2] Beyond its local importance it has, however, a considerable significance as a pilot project for Iraq's agrarian and land tenure conditions.

The basic feature of the Dujayla project is to be seen in the provision of landless tenants with an average plot of 62·5 acres of land

---

[1] Cp. A. Bonné, *State and Economics in the Middle East*, London, 1955, 2nd ed., Chapter XVII.

[2] Cp. Norman Burns, 'The Dujayla Land Settlement in Iraq', *The Middle East Journal*, Vol. V, No. 3, Summer 1951.

free of rent and other charges for 10 years. After 10 years the tenant is granted full legal title; the land will be registered in his name without cost, subject to the condition that he cannot sell or otherwise dispose of it in favour of any other party for another 10 years after registration. If the old cultivator dies within this period his legal heirs inherit his rights.

The farmer-tenants must have had previous farming experience, must be married, between 18–50 years old, and have at least one child. The individual contract specifies the names of all male members of the family and commits them to cultivate the land and not to enter leasing or mortgaging agreements that might endanger their rights on the land or its produce. The farmer has to build a house with his own resources, a stable for his animals and storage bins for his crops. He has to dig small canals through his land from the feeder canals and to buy seeds, trees and animals. If a tenant loses his rights by violation of the regulations it means loss of all his rights to his contract, buildings, trees and crops without claim to compensation.

The extent to which the project found ready response can be seen from the fact that 50,000 land-hungry fellahin applied for the 1,200 Dujayla farm plots. Since the inauguration of the project further land distribution schemes have been worked out and although only a few years have passed since then, the venture appears to have a certain influence on the socio-political conditions in the agrarian sector of Iraq.

Iraq is a country where 70 to 80% of the cultivated land is owned by the State; this means that powerful intermediate holders such as absentee landlords and tribal chiefs control the utilisation of this land and receive at least half of the crop as their share from an impoverished peasant class. The scope of the problem of land tenure conditions remains therefore immense and one of the outstanding issues of Iraq's internal policy.

Egypt

After the coup d'état the new regime, in July 1952, turned to land reform as one of its first measures to improve social conditions. A land reform law was enacted in October 1953 with a view to enable cultivators of small plots of land who suffer from the shortage of land and other defects of the agrarian structure in this country, to adjust their holdings and rights and to attain a decent level of living. The main points of the reform are the following: establishment of a limit of size for individual land property which was fixed to 200 feddan (200 acres); 'surplus' land, i.e. that part of the property of a landowner which exceeds 200 feddans should be expropriated and distributed among those entitled to receive additional land. The reform should be carried out within five years. The procedure should start from the largest estates.

The landowners are entitled to a compensation for expropriated land to the amount of 10 times the annual rental value. The value of buildings, trees and machinery will be considered in the determination of the compensation. The farmers who will be provided with the expropriated land will obtain between 2 and 5 feddan of land in units varying in size according to soil quality. They must be Egyptians by nationality, cultivators by profession and own less than 5 feddan. Farm workers who do not know anything about managing a farm are not entitled to claim land out of the surplus. Certain groups of people are entitled to preferential treatment in the distribution of the expropriated land: those who worked on it before, family fathers who support many dependents, etc.

The price to be paid for the land by the cultivators should equal the price obtained by the sellers plus 3% annual interest charge. The latter receive the purchasing price in government bonds to be redeemed in 30 annual instalments.

A most important provision of the reform is that all farmers who own 5 feddan or less, whether they obtain expropriated land or not, must by law become members of an agricultural co-operative association which will handle marketing of the crop, buying seeds, machinery, etc. Another important clause is the introduction of wage regulation for farm workers and the sanctioning of unions which will take an active part in wages bargaining.

These are remarkable provisions for a country which has for generations become proverbial for the destitution and exploitation of its rural population.

Measured in terms of land reforms carried out in countries with a progressive social regime, the picture becomes somewhat different. The number of tenants without land is so large that only a small percentage of them can be provided with titles from the land taken away from the large land-holders. The expropriation of land from estates which exceed 200 feddan is thus not at all a measure of extreme radicalism. A landed property of 200 acres is still a substantial property and its owner can regard himself as a member of the gentry and as a large landowner, particularly in a country where all the land is under irrigation and produces high crops per unit.

Perhaps the most crucial issue is that of the qualifications of the administration which has to carry out the programme of land reform. It certainly does not yet possess the stern qualities needed to tackle comprehensive and ambitious projects of social and economic reconstruction. And once this first project has been executed, there will still be a great mass of landless tenants in Egypt paying exorbitant rents to the landowners who retain their property.

Complicated problems of implementation face the legislator, the administrator and the farmer in every phase of the reform under such conditions.

Israel

Conditions in the new State of Israel were favourable to the emergence of a progressive agrarian structure. The hampering legacy of old and frequently outworn institutions did not exist in this case; moreover, the strong social impulses in the Zionist Movement worked since its inception towards the creation of free and healthy land tenure relations. Israel is the only country in the region where a remarkable form of not-compulsory land nationalisation has developed. Land is regarded as the property of the nation and is leased out to the individual tenant-farmers with a view to promoting a bond of attachment between him and his piece of land. An institution founded by the Zionist Movement, the Jewish National Fund, became the central body for the acquisition and administration of land.

The allocation of the land to settlers is based on several principles: the first is the national (or public) ownership of the land itself. This principle implies a prohibition of re-sale of land and a right of control through the Fund if the *usufructus* passes from one tenant to another. The lease is contingent upon the annual payment of rent, which means at the same time that the National Fund retains its position as landowner, and the tenant acknowledges his status as tenant with all the rights and duties involved. The tenant is subject to certain obligations and restrictions; thus the land is protected against over-utilisation; if there is a rise in land values, a new evaluation may take place and lead to a higher fixation of the rent. If by changes in the technique of cultivation the size of the farm proves to be too large—which happened frequently in the past with the spread of irrigation—the tenant has to consent to a reduction of the area allotted to him.

In the lease contracts the use of the land is always specified: for agricultural cultivation, for the establishment of a factory, for a house or school building, etc. These terms cannot be changed without the permission of the Fund. Likewise, the tenant cannot transfer his rights to another tenant if the Fund is not agreeable. The contract is made for a period of reasonable length (49 years) in order to create a sense of confidence in the heart of the tenant and to encourage him to invest. If a tenant reaches the final year stipulated in the contract, he can ask for another 49 years' prolongation, which means that the property may be easily held in one family for generations.

The annual rent depends on the value of the estate. In the case of agricultural land it is usually 2%; for urban land the rate is 4%. As mentioned above, there are, however, from time to time, new assessments and the tenants may have to accept a higher burden if the general conditions justify the rise.

Nationalised land has become the basic form of land ownership in Jewish agriculture. The main results of this development can be seen in the following:

 a Farmers and settlements on national land are in secure possession of their land and are interested in the improvements of their farms as much as settlers on private land.

 b The land is allotted to each farmer in equal portions, the size varying in accordance with the requirements of cultivation in different zones (about six acres for irrigated farms and 25 to 40 acres for dry farming).

 c The use of land is under control.

 d No accumulation of such land by wealthy owners has taken place.

The aspect of nationalised land finds it counterpart in the social organisation of the new settlements. The social structure of these settlements is again an original device to solve the complicated problems which presented themselves with the realisation of the Zionist goals, namely to settle on the land essentially urban people who came into surroundings very different from the countries of their origin in their physical, economic and social configurations. The paucity of capital, the lack of skill and experience, the decision to return to the soil and to stay on the land and a certain utopian urge for an improved social order were all responsible for the development of the new collective and co-operative types of settlement.

The most important of these new types are the *Kvutzah* and the *Moshav Shitufi*. In the Kvutzah, the representative collective settlement, not only land but all means of production and the whole range of domestic appliances, including kitchen supplies, is owned collectively; production and consumption are organised on behalf of the community on a collective basis. Domestic and social services are likewise provided communally. The privacy enjoyed by the members of the settlement is the individual living quarter.

The Moshav Shitufi is a settlement based on collective ownership in means of production and collective (pooled) work as in the kibbutz. Each family, however, as in the co-operative and private villages, has its own house and is responsible for its own domestic services, such as feeding, laundry and care of the children. Payment is based on the principle: 'To each according to his needs and from each according to his capacities'—each family, for example, *receiving money* in accordance with the size of the family.

Conclusions

Most of the land reform projects outlined above have been in force for a short time only and do not yet allow us to judge their results in full. But several conclusions can be already drawn now:

1 There cannot be any uniform or single recipe for the solution of land distribution problems. For this reason projects to reform land tenure conditions must be tackled not only country-wise, but for every region of each country individually.

2 To be successful, land reform must have an incisive and compulsory character. Land reform will always affect vested interests which, practically everywhere, yield only to the dictation of power. If the legal use of power for the purpose of such changes does not forthcome, land reform in underdeveloped countries will continue to be the objective of attempts to introduce it by violence.

3 Land reforms aim at the execution of basic changes in land tenure relations, not only with respect to the rural sphere immediately concerned, but for the fabric of the underdeveloped society as a whole. This means that the institution of a land reform is not only a single legal act; it implies a complete reshuffling of economic and social relations, and therefore requires for its successful execution the existence of an adequate socio-political regime.

4 The following immediate targets of land reform are common to all underdeveloped countries where there is pressure of population on insufficient land resources:

   a limitation of individual property and redistribution of surplus land—from expropriated or newly reclaimed areas;

   b abolition of fees, rents and other charges resulting from the existence of a hierarchy of powerful intermediaries between the soil and the tiller, and abolition of the intermediaries;

   c establishment of village co-operatives for various purposes of self-help such as marketing and joint purchasing, credit, etc.;

   d rise of the living conditions for farm workers.

5 Redistribution will not solve the problem of land scarcity in

countries like India or Egypt where the basic ratio of land to people on the basis of the present farming methods is unsatisfactory. Yet though a redistribution in such countries does not offer a full solution, it will substantially reduce the burden of rent hitherto borne by tenants. With the extension of the area under cultivation and an improvement in productivity through new techniques and capital investment the ratio of land to population may become more favourable even in congested rural areas.

6 There is in fact one serious argument against the introduction of restrictions in the size of property and the subsequent redistribution of surplus land to smallholders in overpopulated rural regions. Redistribution of land in underdeveloped countries along the lines of a modern land reform could under certain conditions cause a decline in productivity. It would have this effect in the case of substitution of large-farm management by the usually less experienced individual farmers. Such a danger of decrease in efficiency on the smallholdings is real, yet the answer to it lies in the re-organisation of these small units within a co-operative association. With a competent manager as its director, it will be able to perform a number of services that have hitherto been performed by the manager of the large-scale holding. There are also many cases of large absentee proprietorship in which the smallholder—tenant or share-cropper—already cultivates a small unit as a separate entity, and all that the land reform would have to achieve is to legalise his claim to full, unrestricted property or, in case of dwarf-units, to complete his possession to a viable size. One could add that in numerous underdeveloped countries there are large estates which are not at all models of efficient farm management; the distribution of their land among individual farmers would not affect the volume of crops.

A change in ownership may move the landlord to an improvement of efficiency and output as well. If redistribution would affect the efficiency of farming without prospects for an immediate remedy, the choice in our days cannot be in doubt; it must still be made in favour of the restoration of security of possession and viable size—even at the price of a delay in the attainment of economic rationality.

CHAPTER X

THE FINANCE OF ECONOMIC DEVELOPMENT

GENERAL CONSIDERATIONS

DURING the period of colonial expansion and until the eve of the First World War, the major purpose of export of capital from economically advanced unto underdeveloped area was the promotion of primary production. Primary products formed the main interest and target of development activities deployed by the manufacturing centres. Since the thirties, and in particular since the Second World War, measures to raise the level of living of the local population have become a central objective of development programmes in underdeveloped countries. Changes in the motivation and targets of economic development in such areas offer an instructive lesson on the changeability of ideas and principles when the specific conditions which influenced their formation no longer apply.

For the economist of the classical tradition capital investment was fully justified if it paid interest and amortisation. Economic development was regarded as a question of cost and yield, the latter had under given conditions also to cover a high risk premium. If the estimated cost was too high, development was not regarded worthwhile. Many national development goals which appear essential today were then not seen or fulfilled at all. The great stream of European capital which spread overseas in the eighteenth and nineteenth centuries was indifferent to the living conditions of the capital-receiving country. This indifference changed into an attitude of slowly growing interest in the years preceding the Second World War, and has even developed into a position of considerable concern since the end of the last war. This change in interest has placed the capital factor in the centre of modern development problems. As we have found in several of the preceding chapters the scope

184

of capital available for new investment determines to a large extent the scope of economic progress. The mobilising of real capital has thus become one of the vital prerequisites of economic development. The answer to the question of how to mobilise and use funds is an essential part of development approaches and plans. Recent literature devotes considerable attention to discussion of the various avenues and methods of obtaining and utilising the necessary financial resources, domestic as well as foreign.[1]

It will be impossible to review here even the gist of the literature dealing with these problems, yet we must discuss some of the more important problems of development finance under the following main headings:

A. The scope of financial requirements:

B. Sources and methods of capital mobilisation.
   I. The potential of domestic resources.
  II. The potential of lending from foreign sources.
    (*a*) Chief sources of foreign lending in the past.
    (*b*) Grants-in-aid and international capital.

C. Lessons of the period.

THE SCOPE OF FINANCIAL REQUIREMENTS

THE EMERGENCE OF NEW MAGNITUDES

In the United Nations Report, 'Methods of Financing Economic Development in Underdeveloped Countries', issued in 1949, statements and views of various international agencies regarding domestic and foreign financing are summarised for the first time in the postwar period. The following observation apparently represented the predominant attitude of these agencies on one of the vital issues treated in the Report, namely domestic versus foreign resources.

'There is general agreement in the reports that domestic savings in most underdeveloped countries are very low and are unequally distributed, that domestic finance will, nevertheless, be required to cover the bulk of total investment needs and that there is a dearth

---

[1] After the completion of this manuscript Professor W. A. Lewis's new book, *The Theory of Economic Growth*, came to my attention. Professor Lewis's book is a mine of wisdom on many of the problems dealt with or touched upon in this treatise.

I wish to mention in particular the often brilliant comments of Professor Lewis on cardinal issues of financial policy, without necessarily accepting all his conclusions.

of mature projects actually ready for financing'.[1] As we shall see later, this view is maintained until today by leading international agencies.

Whilst the first part of the statement of the level of domestic savings will meet with little opposition, the observation referring to domestic finance has not achieved general recognition. It is only reasonable to demand that domestic finance should contribute substantially to the satisfaction of capital requirements; yet to assume that the financial resources of the underdeveloped countries themselves should cover the bulk of total investment needs means to ignore the remarkable lesson of international economic relations since the end of the war. Owing to an entirely changed world situation unique economic relations developed between the countries with surplus funds and those in need of capital import and had also considerable influence on the size and nature of this capital flow.

The view expressed at the end of the above quotation, that there is a dearth of mature projects actually ready for investment does not differ much from the approach customary in previous phases of economic development, where investors concentrated on a few specific projects the realisation of which had only a limited effect on the economy of the country as a whole. Yet the present writer believes that the situation today, i.e. the needs of economic development in backward economies, require a basically different approach. I have for years advocated an 'aggressive' approach to the issue of economic development, conceiving it as a comprehensive process of economic and social change and placing its necessities high in the scale of priorities in international economic policy implying also the use of unorthodox means of financing.

Important and effective as many of the former investments were in respect to individual areas of production, they amounted to irrelevant figures if calculated in per capita terms for the total population, and left the well-being of the majority of inhabitants unaffected. A few examples will support this contention.

For China an estimate of capital invested in modern industries before the Second World War amounted to only 3·8 billion Chinese dollars, or U.S. $1·2 billion—i.e. about $2·70 per capita.[2] For India a figure of about $1·7 can be calculated, on the basis of the estimates of Divatia and Trivedi of the amount of industrial capital invested in Indian factories in 1938–9.[3] Middle Eastern figures are somewhat

[1] 'Methods of Financing Economic Development in Underdeveloped Countries', U.N., 1949, p. 5.
[2] H. D. Fond, *Postwar Industrialisation of China*, p. 55.
[3] M. V. Divatia and H. M. Trivedi, *Industrial Capital in India, 1938–9*, 1947, pp. 9, 26.

higher; but all of them point to a fraction of the industrial equipment which marks the economy of Western countries.[1]

Against such a paucity and erratic flow of capital investment must be viewed the situation in developed countries, where much higher levels of capital investment per earner (and per head of the total population) are indicative of the fulfilment of this crucial precondition of higher productivity. The gap in per capita investment can certainly not be bridged in the near future. In terms of size, pace and character the process of capital formation which changed Western economic history was a unique phenomenon and cannot be repeated elsewhere. But we have not to aim at a close similarity of this process; to achieve a partial reduction of the gap in capital equipment would mean a great improvement of conditions in underdeveloped economies. Let us thus first discuss the scope of capital requirements to be regarded as essential for such an improvement.

SCOPE AND PROJECTION OF REQUIREMENTS

To obtain an idea of the order of magnitude of financial requirements if conditions of poverty in underdeveloped areas are to be remedied, a hypothetical calculation of these requirements will be useful. This is based on a number of assumptions, including certain data which can be regarded as feasible in the light of recent surveys. Let us take as the area of demonstration underdeveloped Asia outside the Soviet-dominated areas, which has an estimated population of about 700 million. About 30% of the population, or 210 million, are gainfully employed in agriculture, industry and services. The estimated distribution is as follows: in agriculture, fishing, etc., 80% or 168 million; in industry, 10% or 21 million; and in services the same proportion, 10% or 21 million.[2]

[1] Cp., *Review of Economic Conditions in the Middle East, 1951–52*, U.N., 1953, Ch. 2.

[2] The figures used in the text deviate from a similar calculation included in a paper delivered by the author in April 1951, at the Annual Conference of the American Academy for Political and Social Science and published in the July 1951 issue of *Annals of the Academy*, 'Lessons from Asia'. In that paper an average investment of $500 per agricultural earner, as against $250 here, was assumed. Though the main intention of these figures is to demonstrate the order of magnitude, they are based on certain empirical data.

One of them is the remarkable difference between average investment requirements in agricultural and non-agricultural branches. While, as a rule, the investment per worker implied in the setting up of a modern industrial plant is also high in underdeveloped countries, substantial improvement of farming results can be achieved with a modest outlay. The explanation lies in the generally lower capital requirements of small-size and middle-size farms, which are by far the majority in underdeveloped countries. Thus an additional investment of the order of $250 appears adequate in order to enable an agriculturist to raise his present low income of $150–180 by an additional $100 to $150. The capital:

THE MOVE TOWARDS ADJUSTMENT

What should be the average addition in productive equipment to effect an essential rise in net output? For the purpose of this very general calculation we may ignore far-reaching differences in the economic resources of the various areas and their actual levels of development in terms of per capita equipment and production. Two methods offer themselves for our purpose. One would be to apply a capital–output ratio of 4 : 1 and to deduce that an annual increase of 1 per cent in income requires an annual net investment of 4 per cent. On the basis of this assumption and taking into account the natural increase we need an annual net investment of approximately 15 per cent if we want to achieve a rise in per capita income of 2·5% in net income per earner in agriculture and 4% in industry and services. The additional assumptions are specified in the notes to the tables on p. 190.

What are the results of the first method? The investment requirements for a period of 15 years calculated in this way amount to $170 billion. To assess the meaning of this sum, it must be related to the national income produced by the population concerned. Given an annual net income of $43 billion at the beginning and the other assumptions specified in the notes to the tables, it would be highly unreasonable to assume that more than 10% or approximately $4–5 billion p.a. can be saved from this flow of income during the initial stages of the development period. The gradual rise in national income would provide an additional source in later years; but even in the fifteenth year it would hardly exceed 10% of $85·5 billion, or approximately $8·5 billion. Against the potential contribution of $4–8·5 billion p.a. from local sources, an optimistic assumption, we have to hold our all-round capital requirements of $170–175 billion, the bulk of which will have to be met during the first phases of the development period because it will take time until the investments bear fruit. It is clear that an investment programme of such a scale cannot be executed during a 15-year period if the bulk of needs must be financed from domestic sources.

The tables on p. 190 show the scheme and data according to the various projections of population, earners and national income.

output ratio is low, as a rule between 2 and 3, owing to the large influence of the manpower factor in small-size farms.

The figure of $2,500 per industrial worker engaged corresponds to the level of industrial investment in countries with a moderate degree of modernisation in equipment. The same amount has frequently been used in calculations of U.N. committees. A capital outlay of $1,000 has been assumed as investment per earner in services such as public buildings, education, hospitals, etc. (Cp. also the data given by Colin Clark in *Conditions of Economic Progress*, 1951, p. 487.) It goes without saying that in concrete cases of national planning, key figures for average investment have to be inserted in accordance with the specific conditions prevailing in each country.

THE FINANCE OF ECONOMIC DEVELOPMENT

As a result of the investment, total net income rises in our projection from $43 billion to $67 billion after 10 years, to $85 billion after 15 years and to $108 billion after 20 years. The annual average rise over both decades is $3·2 billion. The average net income per earner in industrial and service occupations shows a spectacular growth: in industry it rises from $400 to $592 after 10 years, to $720 after 15 years and to $876 after 20 years. The corresponding figures for service occupations are $209, $309, $376 and $458. In agriculture the increase is smaller: from $180 to $295 in 20 years.

The second method of calculating capital requirements is based on the use of average rates of net investment per earner in main occupations. This approach introduces at once an element of arbitrariness, in addition to the difficulty presented by the considerable differences in the equipment value per individual farmer or industrial earner even in the same country. Still, we have to ignore these differences for our purpose of a very general calculation.

Starting with capital needs of farmers we will find that the value of present-day equipment per farmer (implements, animals, farm buildings) ranges between a few dollars and many hundreds of dollars. It is certain that an average addition of real capital amounting to $250 per unit of agricultural earner will substantially change the production potential—either by putting the dairy, plantations or cereal branch or a combination of them on a different footing.

A wide range exists also between the equipment values per worker in industry. An additional investment of several hundred dollars into the outfit of an artisan can perform great changes in output whilst in the case of modern industries the addition of several thousands of dollars per worker may turn out as inadequate. An average additional investment of $2,500 per earner would make possible the mechanisation of production or a spectacular improvement in practically all lines of manufacturing, excepting those in which large-size, highly capital-intensive units dominate. Long-term capital requirements for the present population would, on the basis of these figures, be $52 billion for agricultural development and $52·5 billion for industrial development including power and transport. Adding $21 billion for investment in services (health, education and so forth) on the basis of an outlay of $1,000 per earner, we would arrive at a total of $115·5 billion for primary, secondary and tertiary occupations.

However this is not the full account. There is also the factor of increase in population. Within a 15-year period it would grow more than 16%; this would add 34 million to the number of earners. This increase should be employed in non-agricultural occupations, half of it in industry and half in services. Thus an additional amount

THE MOVE TOWARDS ADJUSTMENT

Projection of Population Growth and National Income Development

Period	Population (millions)	Earners (millions)	Net national income		
			Total ($ billion)	Per capita ($)	Per earner ($)
I Initial year	700	210	43	61·5	205
II After 10 years	773	232	67·4	91·2	290
III After 15 years	813	244	85·5	105·0	350
IV After 20 years	854	256	108·3	126·7	423

Break-up of National Income by Occupations

Period	Net National Income (in $ billion)				National Income per Earner (in $)			
	Agri-culture	Indus-try	Ser-vices	Total	Agri-culture	Indus-try	Ser-vices	Aver-age
I Initial year	30·2	8·4	4·4	43·0	180	400	209	205
II After 10 years	38·6	18·9	9·9	67·4	230	592	309	290
III After 15 years	43·8	27·4	14·3	85·5	261	720	376	350
IV After 20 years	49·6	38·5	20·2	108·3	295	876	458	423

Assumptions: (1) Population increase—1% per annum for the whole period.
    (2) For the whole period the proportion of gainfully employed is assumed to remain stable—30% of total population.
    (3) Of the gainfully employed—80% are in agriculture, 10% in industry and 10% in services, in the initial year.
    (4) The annual increase of the earning population shifts half to industry and half to services.
    (5) No change in price levels will occur.
    (6) The annual rate of increase in net income per earner is 2·5% in agriculture, 4% in industry and services.

of $42·5 billion would be needed for the transfer of 17 million additional earners to industry and $17 billion for the transfer of the other 17 million additional earners to services. Thus the total investment requirements would rise to $175 billion.

What is the value of these figures in view of the reservations which can be made against practically all the assumptions from which the calculations start? Our answer is that they should show the magnitudes involved if certain not excessively ambitious targets are to be achieved. The approach used in the above calculation leads to proportions which exceed by far former data of this kind. The common feature of most development schemes is indeed a different order of magnitude of the objectives regarded as essential and reflecting itself in the projections of requirements which have been worked out in recent years for individual regions. Yet this fact of a departure from established magnitudes should not be the crucial criterion. The criterion should be whether there exist reasonable prospects for the implementation of the schemes. If such prospects can be proved to exist, economic policies will adjust themselves to the new concepts and sizes in the field of economic development.

The U.N. publication, 'Methods of Financing Economic Development in Underdeveloped Countries', already quoted above, contains a statement of the F.A.O. including calculations and estimates of investment requirements needed to secure a minimum rate of economic development for the whole world, excluding North America.[1]

The investment plans which were available at the time comprised 42 countries and 32 dependent territories; in the F.A.O. statement the investment needs were adjusted to a uniform four-year length and 1948 price levels. For countries which have not issued plans, data have been compiled on the assumption that they would invest at about the same rates as similar countries which have prepared plans. The following tabulation sums up the estimated investment needs for the whole world, excluding the capital-exporting parts of North America.

Estimated Aggregate Investment Needs over the Next Four Years by Regions—Based on Official Plans where Available in 1,000 Millions of U.S. Dollars*

Region	Estimated total	Total investment agriculture	Estimated foreign investment
Developed regions:			
Western and Central Europe	105·2	8·5	17·3
Oceania	0·8	0·3	—
Sub-total	106·0	8·8	17·3
Underdeveloped regions:			
Southern Europe	9·7ᵃ	1·6	3·7
Eastern Europe	11·3	1·3	0·8
U.S.S.R.	17·7	3·5	—
Africa	6·8†	1·0†	2·9† ‡
Latin America	8·5	2·8	2·3
Near East	1·7	0·5	0·8
Far East	10·9	1·1	5·8
Sub-total	66·6	11·8	16·3
World total, excluding North America	172·6	20·6	33·6
N. American cotton belt	8·5	§	—

* At 1948 price levels.   † Including public and private investment.
‡ Excluding investment from metropolitan countries for development in their colonies and dependencies.
§ Not available.

[1] 'Methods of Financing Economic Development', etc., pp. 51–2.

In the comment to the table it is pointed out that the planned investment provided for underdeveloped countries is much lower per capita than the average figures for more highly developed countries. Difficult as the proposition is for poor countries to save for new investment a larger proportion of their national income than do most highly developed countries, the poorer countries have inserted such high investment rates into their development schemes. The range of savings planned for European countries was found to be 11% of national income in Denmark, 15% in Italy, 23% in Hungary and 27% in the Soviet Union.[1] The needs for the underdeveloped regions were estimated at about £17 billion a year—as compared to aggregate national incomes amounting possibly to £150 billion or 11% of current income. After deduction of planned foreign investment the rate of domestic investment is 8½% of national income in the same regions. The report does not discuss the question of how underdeveloped countries with their restricted possibilities for saving can adjust their domestic saving potential to the levels required by development needs referred to in the scheme.

From a hypothetical calculation presented in the same report it appears that the amount of $1,000 has been assumed as the average investment necessary to provide capital facilities for each worker added to industrial employment. In agriculture the investment figures given refer to investment per unit of land. Whereas the investment shown per hectare of cropland per year is $101 in the Netherlands, the corresponding amount to be spent in Mexico is $34 per hectare, and falls to as little as $2–3 per hectare per year in many underdeveloped arid countries.[2] Here it must be asked whether an additional investment of a few dollars per hectare can serve any purpose at all.

In the U.N. Report, 'Measures for the Economic Development of Underdeveloped Countries',[3] a much higher per capita amount has been used in determining the scope of industrial capital requirements. In this calculation the shifting of a substantial percentage of earners to industrial employment and the ensuing investment needs take pride of place. The authors of the Report assumed an amount of $2,500 as capital requirement for each earner to be absorbed in non-agrarian employment. This figure represents an average which takes into account the different requirements of light and heavy industries. Other assumptions are that a rate of 4% of the national

---

[1] 'Methods of Financing Economic Development', etc., p. 52.
[2] *Ibid.*, p. 53.
[3] 'Measures for the Economic Development of Underdeveloped Countries', Report by a Group of Experts appointed by the Secretary General of the United Nations, U.N., New York, May 1951.

income be spent on investment in agricultural production and agricultural services.

Such a rate of total rural investment would mean low per-capita amounts of investment; the Report does not expressly mention per capita figures, but they can be calculated from the table in the Report and its explanations. The average amount of investment lies between $50 and $190 per agricultural earner over a 10-year period.

The large margin between these two figures is to be explained by the differences which exist between the individual regions in respect of levels of national income.

The authors of the Report saw the main purpose of the calculation in a demonstration of the capital needs if national income should be raised in two ways: by transferring population from agricultural into non-farm occupations, and by increasing agricultural yields.

The tabulation of the data shows capital requirements totalling $19 billion per year to be covered by net domestic savings, rising from $5·4 billion to approximately $9 billion annually, and by a annual capital import of over $10 billion. As to the question of how much such an investment in industry and agriculture would yield in terms of annual production increase, the authors of the Report expect an annual net increase in national income of 2%, following a shift of 1% of the total working population into industry in countries which have surplus labour in agriculture. In other countries net increase of national income will be lower, being equal only to the difference between the productivity of labour in industry and the productivity of labour in agriculture from which it has been withdrawn. Over the whole underdeveloped world, the authors conclude, the shifting might increase national income by only 1·5% per annum.

The authors of this U.N. Report did not expect that the figures used by them in their calculations would be readily accepted by the more conservative schools of finance which dominate the field. They have also inserted a number of criticisms on the subject of government lending, directed at the policies of the new international institutions which have been set up to promote development in underdeveloped countries. In particular, the International Bank for Reconstruction and Development was criticised because of the small scope of its lending activities so far (then less than $300 million annually). The Bank had not met the challenge of the circumstances: it is accused of attaching excessive importance to foreign currency aspects, and of putting 'the cart of foreign exchange difficulties before the horse of economic development'. The Bank is also blamed for being somewhat slow in giving technical assistance and in the preparation of plans, and in general for its emphasis on the limited capacity of underdeveloped countries to absorb capital. To accelerate the flow of capital into underdeveloped countries, the authors of the U.N. Report strongly recommend the creation of a mechanism for transferring from developed to underdeveloped countries, in the form of grants and aids, an amount which should eventually reach a level of about $3 billion a year. It would be equivalent to rather less than 1% of the national incomes of Western Europe, Asia, the U.S. and Canada.

This criticism immediately evoked a rather pointed rejoinder on the part of the Economic, Employment and Development Commission of the Economic and Social Council. The tenor of its comment was that the estimates of the financial needs and especially of the scope of foreign financial assistance as given in the Report were not substantiated, and that in general too much stress was laid on the need for international financial assistance. Although the majority of the Commission agreed that the international flow of capital to underdeveloped countries will have to be augmented, they took exception to the specific figure of $1 billion, which was set up in the U.N. Report as the target to be reached within five years in the International Bank annual lending programme to underdeveloped countries. In general, however, although certain specific criticisms were refuted by the Commission and other observers, there was a measure of willingness to accept the broader meaning of the Report.

The reaction of the International Bank for Reconstruction and Development is pervaded by the same spirit, paying tribute to the work of the authors of the Report and accepting some of its findings and recommendations. Exception is taken, however, to the criticism of the Bank's policy; the authors are censured for their unjust belittling of the lending programme of the Bank. The Bank has in fact lent money to the limits set by several factors over which it has no control; thus the rate of Bank loans for development does not depend primarily on decisions of the Bank at all. 'It will depend, in the short run at least, upon the ability and willingness of the industrialised nations to make equipment and materials available. It will depend also upon the ability and willingness of the underdeveloped countries, with such foreign technical assistance as may be made available to them, to push their development programmes ahead along the lines the experts have discussed, and particularly to prepare programmes and projects ready for financing. It will depend to some extent, too, on whether the more developed countries, other than the United States, make available for lending purposes a greater part of their 18% capital subscriptions to the Bank—for many of the less developed countries are in a position to service a greater amount of non-dollar indebtedness than of dollar indebtedness. Finally it depends upon what action may be taken by the more advanced countries on the various proposals now under consideration for additional developmental assistance in the form of grants—for obviously grant funds, if available, could be so used as to increase the ability of many countries, particularly some of the Asiatic countries, to service additional foreign debt.'[1] The reply emphasises also that there seems to be no likelihood that the amount of the Bank's development loans will approach the figure of $1 billion annually suggested by the experts.

The above answer formed the immediate reaction to the proposals included in the U.N. Report at the time of its publication. They were not the only rejoinder which the report met. Incisive criticism was directed against specific points as well as against the tenor of the report by Professor S. H. Frankel in his essay 'United Nations Primer for Development' and by P. T. Bauer in his review article in *The Economic Journal*.[2] The discussion is of considerable interest to this day. Without belittling the importance of these critical comments, I feel strongly they do not take sufficiently into account the wider issues involved in numerous cases of proposed development. The views expressed in the U.N. Report and those of its critics represent in a way two different schools of thought. The authors of the U.N. Report as well as numerous other adherents of an aggressive approach to economic development claim a high priority for the satisfaction of development needs because of the political urgency of the latter, or because of the possible—though not certain—pioneering effect of the investment. They are at this stage less concerned with the necessity of fulfilling strict economic criteria and are prepared to advocate grants which cannot be justified on economic grounds alone. As against them, there stand the economists who insist throughout on the strict application of established economic principles and demand the most careful appropriation of subsidies, if at all. To the present author economic development in most underdeveloped regions implies nearly always a political issue and the economic and political aspects have to be appraised on different grounds. It is one of the functions—and admittedly a highly responsible one—of the development economist to determine in each particular case whether and to what extent, in addition to the means which can be made available through 'normal' channels of capital mobilisation, grants should be given to increase or speed up prospects for the success of a development programme.

[1] U.N. Economic and Social Council, Methods of Financing Economic Development, Replies of specialised agencies', etc., E/2029, June 20, 1951, p. 10.
[2] Professor Frankel's essay is included in his 'The Economic Impact on Underdeveloped Societies', Oxford, 1953. Mr. Bauer's review article was published in the March 1953 issue of *The Economic Journal*, pp. 210 ff.

The Effect of the War on Government Receipts*

	Year	Total Receipts (in millions of local currency)	Per Capita Receipts	Total Receipts (in millions of local currency)	Per Capita Receipts
				1937 prices	
			Rupees		Rupees
India	1938/9	1,571·7	4·2	1,746·3	4·7
	1942/3	2,757·9	7·0	1,826·3	4·6
	1943/4	3,515·6	8·9	1,706·3	4·3
	1948/9	4,100·5	11·9	1,117·2	3·2
				1939 prices	
			£L.		£L.
Lebanon	1939	7·20	7·4	7·20	7·4
	1942	15·50	14·6	2·48	2·3
	1943	26·65	24·4	3·19	2·9
	1947	85·53	72·5	10·73	9·1
	1948	78·66	65·0	10·12	8·4
				1938 prices	
			£T.		£T.
Turkey	1938/9	266·9	15·6	266·9	15·6
	1942/3	895·0	49·2	262·4	14·4
	1943/4	866·4	47·1	146·3	8·0
	1947	1,258·5	65·3	289·3	15·0
	1948	1,291·8	66·2	276·0	14·1
				1938 prices	
			£D.		£D.
Iraq	1938/9	7·55	2·2	7·55	2·2
	1942/3	15·77	4·2	3·6	1·0
	1943/4	18·35	4·6	3·2	0·8
	1947/8	22·28	4·6	4·2	0·9
	1948/9	23·37	4·8	4·4	0·9
				1938 prices	
			£E.		£E.
Egypt	1938/9	37·62	2·3	38·00	2·3
	1942/3	67·14	3·8	33·57	1·9
	1943/4	77·77	4·4	30·62	1·7
	1946/7	109·96	5·9	35·70	1·9
	1948/9	142·48	7·3	45·09	2·3

* Per capita figures computed from U.N., *Statistical Yearbook*, 1951, and U.N., *Public Finance Information Papers*, for individual countries.

SOURCES AND METHODS OF CAPITAL MOBILISATION

The preceding discussion was primarily devoted to the quantitative aspects of the financial requirements implied in the new concepts of economic development. We have now to discuss this problem from the viewpoint of the potential of the financial resources.

THE FINANCE OF ECONOMIC DEVELOPMENT

THE POTENTIAL OF DOMESTIC RESOURCES

(a) Voluntary Savings

First it will be necessary to define the term 'potential' of domestic savings as it is used here, in order to prevent misunderstandings from the beginning. If we were to limit the meaning of potential savings to those means which can be saved because the population in under-developed countries is willing and able to save, we should have to be content with a small volume of savings. Neither their present willingness nor their ability to save would yield amounts of the magnitude mentioned in the preceding section in respect of the domestic contribution. We are, however, on good grounds when we assume the possibility of changes in existing spending habits and also in income levels, particularly after the execution of development projects. Whether this saving potential is utilised or not, it is greater than the low rates of domestic saving usually mentioned in discussions of this kind. Notwithstanding the depressed average net income of the population in most underdeveloped countries, considerable amounts are still diverted away from consumption without affecting the state of health and the income-producing capacities of income earners. There are also chances for the mobilisation of idle resources and surplus income, e.g. gold, jewellery, stocks and unused deposits. In all underdeveloped countries there are substantial amounts of sterile capital hoarded away from utilisation in the production of goods and services.

The Clapp Report mentions in respect of the gold hoards in Syria, for instance, that though no official estimate of their scope is available, their 'total is believed in some well-informed quarters to be no less than $150 million (1949). To hoard gold is an ancient habit in this region, accustomed as it is to seeing wealth in other forms lose its value. Indeed, many Syrians prefer to have recourse to bank over-drafts, for which they pay heavy rates of interest, rather than invest capital that lies idle in gold.'[1] Gold hoarding and investment in jewellery and land in South and South East Asia are deep-rooted habits of all sections of the population. The wealth which lies idle in this form in numerous palaces and temples all over the Asian continent defies the imagination. It is difficult to assess, on the basis of accumulated wealth in the form of gold and jewellery hoards, the potential financial contribution of a population to needs of current national production. This does not mean, however, that such wealth cannot be of considerable importance in the financing of economic development.

Hoarding of precious metals and precious stones has reached

[1] Final Report of the United Nations Economic Survey Mission for the Middle East, 1949, Part 1, p. 41.

particularly large proportions in India. In the Annual Report of the Bank for International Settlement for 1934-5, the gold hoarded in India from 1493 to 1930 was estimated at at least Rs.1,450 crores, or close to £St.1,095 million.[1] This estimate does not include, of course, the immense value of hoarded and worked silver and precious stones. Visitors to India who have attended social affairs have been impressed by the display of beautiful ornaments made of fine and expensive gems. The lavishly shown jewellery points to a remarkable accumulation of wealth in certain strata of Indian society. In addition there are millions of small hoards of jewellery scattered over the large expanses of the sub-continent, which together add up to very substantial amounts; though it would be unwise to regard these scattered little possessions as assets which could be used for purposes of financing development. According to Indian custom—which, incidentally, prevails also in other Oriental regions—women possessing jewellery made from gold and silver are entitled to hold it as their personal property. It is for this reason that the hoarding of gold coins, which can serve the double purpose of safeguarding wealth and adorning the womenfolk, has become particularly popular in many underdeveloped countries. A visit to the Cairo gold market, for instance, during the daily rush hours (i.e. from the arrival of the train from Upper Egypt to its departure) is quite instructive to the economist. The fellahin of the villages arrive with their bank notes and return after a few hours with their choice of coined gold or gold jewellery. The motive of the hoarders is not just to substitute one form of wealth with another, but to increase the degree of safety of their savings without reducing the liquidity of this investment. Gold fulfils this purpose but also fits other purposes well. The custom has become established owing to the satisfactory experience of many generations acting in the same way. For the same reason, appeals to the peasants to use banking facilities for their cash surpluses have so far had only a limited effect.

The prospects for utilising the hoarded treasures of the wealthy classes, of merchants, landlords and princes are, theoretically speaking, much better; they have already developed a sense of acquisitive interest in investment operations, often combined with a remarkable skill in their handling. However, practical difficulties in using these hoards are considerable; they are frequently not the property of individuals but of families. In addition different practices in the evalua-

---

[1] The question of hoarding has been dealt with frequently in recent discussions of the subject. Most writers seem to regard the hoards as a valuable completion—but not a major source—of potential financial resources in underdeveloped countries. Cp. also the interesting observations on this issue in *Indian Economics* by G. B. Jathar and S. G. Beri, Oxford University Press (Indian Branch), 1945, Vol. II, pp. 420 ff.

tion of precious metals on the home and foreign markets are apt to prevent the sale of privately hoarded gold and silver.

Still, if even part of the hoardings could be mobilised, the problem of development finance would be alleviated in countries where hoarding continues to absorb considerable surplus reserves. But this source would in any case cover no more than a limited part of the requirements. A long-term development programme has to rely on large recurrent contributions from current income. Since savings are produced from income, it goes without saying that they are much lower in underdeveloped, 'low income' countries than in more advanced countries with higher income levels. The differences are remarkable. Domestic savings vary from a few per cent of the national income in many underdeveloped countries, to 15 to 20% and even more in highly developed countries of the West, and in those controlled economies where a stern policy is practised to extract a maximum degree of compulsory savings from current income. Colin Clark has collected and elaborated on an interesting series of data concerning the relationship between levels of real income and savings, and found that a close positive correlation exists between them. 'At an income level of a little over I.U. 0·1 per man-hour accumulation commences and the curve rises steeply. Then the curve rises in such a way as to keep net savings about 10% of income as income continues to rise.'[1]

	Real Income per Man-hour in I.U.	Net Per Capita Savings in I.U. p.a.
U.S.		
1918–20	0·674	173
1940	0·971	264
1941	0·999	386
ITALY		
1914	0·134	32
1939	0·213	52
SWEDEN		
1913	0·226	90
1925–30	0·305	103
JAPAN		
1913–19	0·049	89
1924–30	0·122	140
1938	0·192	155

The data presented by Clark refer primarily to economically advanced countries. But as already pointed out above, there must be a degree of saving in underdeveloped countries. For were it not so, the rural population, particularly in agrarian countries which suffer

[1] Colin Clark, *op. cit.*, p. 506.

from a chronic state of population pressure on land resources, could not have continued to exist as they have. Owing to their constant increase in numbers the population could be maintained even at the prevailing marginal level only by an expansion of production, which in turn has been made possible only by a measure of capital formation. This assumption of an inherent capacity to save even under most oppressive conditions is supported by historical evidence. Most Oriental countries have experienced recurring capital losses, i.e. substantial dis-investment during wars and protracted periods of famine with ensuing cattle mortality; they have also been affected by natural disasters which destroyed substantial parts of their productive resources. Though it appears inconceivable to expect any factual saving among destitute populations of regions visited by such calamities, a limited degree of saving must nevertheless have occurred over large areas if the effect of the above-mentioned disasters were to be offset. Exact statistical material of the extent of this saving is not available, which makes it impossible to elaborate on this significant issue. The explanation of the apparent contradiction must be sought in the behaviour of the peasant everywhere, who in spite of a nearly chronic state of poverty does not easily change his consumption level when an improvement in prices or in crop yields occurs. Nor do occasional outbursts of spending change this situation. In any case it seems wrong to ignore the phenomenon of a certain accumulation of capital, even in the rural sections of Oriental populations, which transforms a varying share of the farmers' small real income not currently consumed into hoarded wealth or productive assets. Sources relating to these problems for India tend also to confirm that improvements in the conditions of the people are going on at various levels in rural sectors of underdeveloped countries.[1]

Professor Datta refers to investments reported by the Punjab Board of Economic Inquiry, which show an average saving of about 14% of income among tenant cultivators.[2] To be sure, the tenants considered in this inquiry belong to a category of cultivators which holds considerably more land than the average size of holdings in India; but other sources, too, indicate that the rate of saving even among destitute farmers should not be belittled. If the area of potential savings is enlarged so as to include other voluntary saving activities, the picture becomes even more positive. An Indian family budgets' inquiry of 1943–5 arrived at an average surplus over expenditure of more than 25% for all brackets above Rs.2,400.[3] Another

[1] Jathar and Beri, op. cit., pp. 131–2.
[2] B. Datta, The Economics of Industrialisation, Calcutta, 1952, p. 226.
[3] Report of an Inquiry into Family Budgets of Industrial Workers, Bombay, 1946, p. 26, quoted by Datta, op. cit., p. 227.

result reported in this inquiry was that the savings of Indian industrial earners were positive during 1943–4 for income brackets starting at Rs.720 to Rs.960 per year, and that about two-thirds of the family units were above the zero saving line. The weighted savings average for 21 centres in the Indian Union amounted to about 9·6% of income. These results should not be generalised, since they relate to conditions in specific income groups only. Yet they are not irrelevant even when compared to the more massive saving processes characteristic for middle- and upper-class strata in some underdeveloped countries.

Students of living conditions in backward economies are often surprised to find that many lower-middle-class people maintain an extremely modest standard of life, although they could easily afford more amenities.[1] Indeed for many, such a frugal standard is still one of the time-honoured patterns of life. Since the development of certain modern forms of investment which serve as absorbing agents of local savings, data on savings have become more abundant and show an impressive rise. The life funds of Indian insurance companies increased from Rs.5·83 crores in 1913 to Rs.56·33 crores in 1939, and to Rs.116·70 crores in 1946. Premium incomes show corresponding trends: from Rs.7·96 crores in 1930 to Rs.14·26 crores in 1939, and to Rs.33·27 crores in 1948.[2] Even taking fully into account depreciation of local currency, the rise in these figures is remarkable and reveals the considerable investment operations which have been going on in the expanding Indian economy. Datta emphasises the difficulties in obtaining exact figures for the increase in domestic savings owing to overlapping of data. His figures on the annual average growth of these savings are impressive even if we have to take into account the statistical deficiencies,[3] as shown on p. 202.

[1] The interesting fact that in certain rural areas of Brazil the local inhabitants are not only going to have to be taught to spend much more of the money they have—they are also going to have to be taught to *want* and *need* more goods and services, turns up in a report received by the Food and Agriculture Organisation. Its author, Dr. W. J. Timmer, of Wageningen, Holland, is a technical assistance expert who advised the Brazilian Government in its programme for rural welfare improvement.

Dr. Timmer came across the problem north of Colatina, in the northern part of Brazil's Espirito Santo. Here, according to his report: 'We visited a farmer and talked with him about his work and his life, sitting in his poorish and miserable house that was more like a mere shelter against climatic conditions than a home. He had ten children of whom the elder ones were nearly adult girls, but all were illiterate. So we had to put on record a living standard on a rather low level. When, after our departure, I asked Dr. Bemvindo de Novaes, who was accompanying me, how much money he thought that this farmer had behind him, he answered that he estimated this as being 600,000 cruzeiros (U.S. $30,000). I was very amazed to hear such a high figure and at first I could not bring this into focus with the extremely low living standard we had just seen. Later on I made more observations of this kind.' From F.A.O. Press Release No. 77, June 1952.

[2] Datta, *op. cit.*, p. 230.   [3] *Op. cit.*, p. 233.

THE MOVE TOWARDS ADJUSTMENT

Annual Average Increase in Deposits, Savings and Premia
(in Rs. crores)

	1920–1 to 1924–5	1925–6 to 1929–30	1930–1 to 1934–5	1935–6 to 1939–40
Increment in small savings	+ 3·1	+ 6·4	+ 10·6	+ 2·2
Insurance premia	4·2	7·3	10·8	15·1

Rates of annual increment in co-operative deposits, bank deposits, small savings and insurance premia have been positive in almost all cases. Certainly this trend continued during the war and post-war period, under the influence of inflationary phenomena.

Yet in spite of the existence of domestic capital accumulation among large groups of the population, we should not overrate its importance for the following reasons: first, total financial requirements will in any case vastly exceed the potential of voluntary domestic saving. Second, there exists today a considerable inducement to reduce savings in order to improve standards of living. The urge to imitate consumption patterns of advanced social groups may have operated before as a fringe phenomenon in many underdeveloped economies, but at no time was there such a well-supported movement from without to raise higher consumption standards of the population as a whole.

The 'exogenous' urge to raise levels of living is supported by propensities towards higher consumption growing from within. They have been found to exist in Western societies with a much higher level of satisfaction of consumer needs than in underdeveloped countries. These trends towards higher spending have in recent years frequently been discussed as the 'demonstration effect', a concept developed by J. S. Duesenberry.[1] This is defined as the effect of the spending habits of high income classes on the consumption habits of lower income classes which come into contact with them. In investigations of consumer behaviour in the United States it was found that the spending of lower income classes, which is usually closely dependent on the scope of saving, is not directly related to the absolute level of real income, but strongly influenced by the pattern of spending practised by the high income classes. This influence leads the lower income classes to higher spending, with detrimental results for savings and capital formation. The low income classes easily maintain the new consumption habits, and if they have access to loan funds spend even more than they can afford out of their incomes.

There have indeed been concrete indications of the spread of

[1] See also above, p. 57.

higher spending habits in Middle Eastern countries and India. Increased spending for non-essentials has in several countries affected the use of income surpluses for productive purposes.[1] So far only few exact data are available to prove the operation of the demonstration effect in underdeveloped countries. It is thus difficult to show to what extent this phenomenon has absorbed all the surplus income which would otherwise be available as saving and for capital formation. The few indications point rather to a 'co-incidence' of increased spending on non-essentials and a degree of saving in the form of hoarding or bank deposits in economies where farm output is rising —except for those countries where inflation has strongly reduced the saving propensity.

Yet whatever the residuum is, it would be unjustified to rely on the continuation or development of a high rate of voluntary saving in the immediate future. We have to regard the potentialities of compulsory saving as more promising avenues to the financing of econmic development. The following section gives an outline of these potentialities without analysing in each case the conditions and prospects of application of the compulsory devices.

(b) Compulsory Savings

The most reliable means towards securing an optimum amount of domestic saving without disturbing the generation of national income is progressive taxation. Newly established administrations today are in a better position than Western governments were when they introduced modern forms of direct and indirect taxation. The vast experience in public finance available nowadays benefits newcomers to fiscal thought and practice. Many of the financial achievements in newly established states are due to this possibility of utilising knowledge accumulated during recent decades. This knowledge will also help to avoid exaggerated hopes for a rapid development of tax revenue.

The first and basic conclusion the development economist will arrive at in this context is that the proportion of national income which has been collected in taxes in underdeveloped countries is much lower than in advanced economies. Industrialised countries such as the United States, Belgium, England, Germany, have years ago reached a tax ratio amounting to from 20 to 40% and more of national income.[2] During the same period underdeveloped countries hardly succeeded in attaining a tax–income ratio of 10 to 15%.

[1] Cp. the author's 'Recent Changes in Levels of Living in the Middle East', *Middle Eastern Affairs*, October 1954.

[2] Cp. W. Heller, 'Fiscal Policies for Underdeveloped Economies', in *Papers and Proceedings of the Conference on Agricultural Taxation and Economic Development*, Cambridge, 1954, p. 67.

THE MOVE TOWARDS ADJUSTMENT

Taxes as a Percentage of National Income*

	1900	1924	1947	1950
Argentina				
(Central Government)	—	—	5·5	—
Canada	(1903)			
(Central Government)	3·9	7·6	23·0	18·7
France	(1903)			
(Central Government)	11·9	—	17·7	23·8
Total	16·2	—	22·3	30·0
Guatemala				
(Central Government)	—	—	9·3	—
Japan				
(Central Government)	—	8·7	20·7	17·4
Total	—	13·9	22·9	23·2
Mexico				
(Central Government)	—	—	8·6	—
Sweden				
(Central Government)	5·9	7·1	13·1	14·3
United Kingdom				
(Central Government)	7·1	17·6	36·5	37·0
Total	9·9	22·4	39·8	40·1
United States				
(Central Government)	3·3	4·5	22·1	21·1
Total	7·5	—	29·1	29·2

* From a paper by H. S. Bloch, 'The Relation of Tax Policy to Economic Growth', included in *Tax Institute Symposium Volume on the Limits of Taxable Capacity*, p. 174.

Of course it should not be assumed that this ratio is firmly fixed; in the latter countries, too, there are indications of an increase in the ratio of public revenue to national income, and thus for an improvement in the potential contribution of government to development purposes. This is a signal prospect, and it is indeed important to observe that recent experience in raising tax income in under-developed countries has been encouraging.

For a considerable time many underdeveloped countries were not concerned with the problem of raising their tax revenue; during the same period governments of economically advanced countries were already able successfully to apply refined concepts and devices of taxation. Thus the tax structure in both types of countries shows great differences for this period: in most underdeveloped countries land and property taxes provide a substantial part of direct revenue; yet customs duties are the largest single source of total government revenue, which altogether remains within a range of 10–15% of national income. In the thirties, income tax begins to occupy a more important position in the budgets of less advanced countries; even Oriental treasuries could not maintain the traditional consideration for high income classes for very long if they were to adopt modern concepts of development and their implications for domestic financing.

The first effects of new ideas in the field of economic development can indeed be seen in the remarkable increase in the share of direct taxes accompanied by a decline in that of land and indirect taxation. The composition of government receipts in Middle Eastern countries in more recent years shows countries with a more progressive fiscal policy, such as Israel and Turkey, obtaining between 20 and 30% of their revenue from taxes on income and wealth.

The Role of the Income Tax

In most Western countries income tax has long since been regarded as the most suitable device for collecting current surplus income from the individual and corporative earner. Neither the resentment of tax payers nor the original lack of refinement in assessment and collection have prevented income tax from becoming universally one of the most important sources of public revenue. When war conditions reduced revenue from custom receipts, income tax even became the pillar of governmental budgets.

The British approach to income tax became the pattern for the early introduction of this developed form of taxation in the outlying parts of the British Empire, particularly India, Pakistan and Burma. Iraq and Turkey introduced it in the inter-war period. During the Second World War income tax was introduced in Palestine, Egypt and Cyprus,[1] and after the war in Malaya and Hong Kong. Income tax thus already has a tradition even in underdeveloped Oriental countries. Yet these beginnings should not be overrated. Neither the rates nor the position of the tax in public revenue can be compared with its rates and position in developed economies. Among the main reasons for the great difference the following should be mentioned:

(*a*) In India, Pakistan and certain Middle Eastern countries, agricultural income is exempt from the scope of central government

[1] Cp. 'Income Tax in the Middle East', *Bulletin of the Economic Research Institute of the Jewish Agency for Palestine*, Vol. V, 1941, p. 75.

income tax because such income is supposed already to be covered by land taxes.[1]

(b) Income taxes in underdeveloped countries cover in general only a small segment of the population. At the conference on Agricultural Taxation and Economic Development held at Harvard University in 1954, under the auspices of the International Programme in Taxation, this problem was discussed at length. It was stated that the number of assessees in India does not exceed half a million people, which means that the tax covers only about 2·5 million people out of a total population of more than 360 million.[2] Only 5% of the incomes received are subject to income and super taxation. Even if the

National Income; Government Expenditure and Revenue, Development Expenditure and Direct Taxes on Income and Wealth as Percentages of National Income

Country and year	National income in millions of national currencies	Government expenditure as percentage of N.I.	Government revenue as percentage of N.I.	Development expenditure of government as percentage of N.I.	Direct taxes on income and wealth as percentage of N.I.
Egypt:					
1948	1,017	9·3	9·7	1·3	1·8
1950	860	19·0	18·5	3·8	2·1
1951	750	25·4	24·7	4·3	2·6
Israel:					
1950	337·6	26·4	11·3	10·6	2·8
1951	531·2	23·9	12·9	12·4	3·6
1952	765·0	24·1	14·0	10·8	4·1
1953	1,050·0	23·8	16·0	10·9	4·5
Lebanon:					
1950	830	10·2	10·0	2·4	1·6
Syria:					
1952	1,220	21·7	21·2	1·5	2·6
Turkey:					
1948	7,815	18·0	16·6	1·3	5·2
1950	6,951	22·9	21·8	2·5	6·8
1951	8,229	17·3	16·1	1·2	5·0
1952	9,607	16·5	14·0	1·3	3·3
1953	10,454	16·7	14·8	1·7	3·2

Sources: Absolute figures of Government Expenditure and Revenue, 'Review of Economic Conditions in the Middle East', U.N., 1951–2, p. 76. *Statistical Yearbook*, U.N., 1953, pp. 455–92.

[1] *Papers and Proceedings*, etc., p. 96.　　　　[2] *Op. cit.*, p. 96.

corporative tax should be added, total receipts from income taxation would be very much less than 2% of national income. Similarly, small percentages of national income are collected in income taxation in Burma, Ceylon, Malaya, the Philippines and Thailand, where the rates amount to between 0·6 to 3% of the national incomes. The corresponding data for Middle Eastern countries are somewhat higher, as the table opposite indicates; but here, too, income tax covers only a fringe at the top of the social pyramid, whilst the mass of income earners remains unaffected.

(c) The major reason for the small number of income tax payers is the high minimum set as tax-free income. Before a person in India has to pay any tax on income he has to earn more than 17 times the national per capita income, and this high figure may be even higher if allowance is made for married couples with children. Against this considerate approach, incomes in advanced countries are taxable even if they are lower than the national per capita income average! As the following table shows, the ratio of earned income to national per capita income up to which no income tax is payable by a married man with three children was 1·9 in the United States (1950), 2·3 in Canada and 2·2 in Australia.[1]

Ratios of Earned Income to National Per Capita Income up to which no Income Tax is Payable by a Married Man with Wife and Three Children

Australia	1950	2·2
Canada	1950	2·3
France: from labour	1950	2·6
other income		0·4
Japan: from labour	1951	2·0
other income		1·7
United Kingdom	1950	2·1
United States	1950	1·9
Argentina: from labour	1949	7·3
commercial income		6·2
Egypt	1951	3·6
Mexico	1950	1·5
Burma	1950	21·4
Ceylon	1952	15·0
India	1953	16·8
Philippines	1950	15·3

Another way of showing this difference is to compare the rate of income tax which will be applied to the identical multiple of the national per capita income in various countries. Thus, for instance,

[1] Vide *Papers and Proceedings*, etc., p. 98.

THE MOVE TOWARDS ADJUSTMENT

an Australian has to pay as income tax 57% of his income if it reaches a level of 50 times the national per capita income. The corresponding rates of income tax for Canada, France, Japan, the United Kingdom and the United States are (in per cent) 41·4, 31·1, 48·3, 64·9 and 53·7 respectively, for an income 50 times the per capita national income. Against these high rates the Egyptian who earns 50 times the national per capita income pays only 9·6% of his income as income tax; the Mexican, 4·2%, the Indian, 5·7% and the Burmese, 6·3%. All income referred to is income from labour.[1]

All available figures for underdeveloped countries point to the conclusion that the absolute and relative scope of direct taxation for current as well as capital expenditure can still be enlarged. To what extent the additional collection of income tax should be driven in each case is a matter of individual exploration. No general answer which would hold good for all situations is possible; yet experience hitherto points to the feasibility of raising rates of taxation towards gradual approximation to the tax : national income ratio in more advanced countries. The major problem will consist in finding the optimum level which will ensure a maximum amount of tax revenue without affecting the no less important incentives for private investment.

Indirect Taxation

Indirect taxation is an instrument easily adaptable to requirements of development finance. The administrative simplicity which marks the collection of numerous indirect taxes is a considerable advantage over direct taxes in underdeveloped countries. Another advantage lies in the fact that indirect taxes have as a rule hardly any effect on the incentives to work.

The field of indirect taxation covers a wide range of devices. Apart from numerous forms of customs duties which have long yielded considerable revenue, recent trends towards introduction of luxury taxes, turn-over taxes and high duties on specific categories of commodities such as alcoholic beverages have achieved good results.

Royalties

A most important source of income has developed in countries possessing abundant valuable natural resources—particularly oil— in the form of royalties and taxes paid by foreign companies exploiting these resources. In certain countries the rise in oil production has been so phenomenal that the amount of royalties paid by the concessionary companies has reached a staggering size. In the cases of Saudi Arabia, Iraq, Kuwait, Iran and Bahrein these oil revenues now

[1] *Papers and Proceedings*, etc., p. 100.

form a very substantial share of government income, and enable the financing of most important development projects.

Inflation as Means of Financing

Another method of securing considerable means through deliberate state policy is inflation, either direct or through deliberate decision not to combat inflation. Its harmful effects on income distribution and social stability are obvious; but though everyone denounces inflation, it has become to a greater or lesser degree a tolerated means of supplying funds for current and one-time financial requirements. Inflation is, to use the explanation given in the U.N. Report quoted, 'a non-voluntary method of financing economic development through attempting, in the absence of deliberate policies of a non-inflationary nature, to reduce effective demand to the volume of available real resources'.[1] The Report emphasises the difference between inflation and inflationary pressure. Inflationary pressure, according to the Report, is an inevitable result of a development programme based on accelerated investment financed from domestic resources. Fiscal measures, direct controls or import surplus can prevent the emergence of inflation in the orbit of inflationary pressures. Yet as a rule inflationary pressure itself cannot be avoided, since it would mean the abandonment of development itself; although it is possible to supress severe forms of inflation through proper means. The prevention of inflation as a self-defeating and disastrous development is a primary issue of development policies.

It goes without saying that most financial authorities responsible for the conduct of budgetary policies are aware of the dangers of inflation. If nevertheless inflation has so frequently been unavoidable, the reasons must be quite forceful. They lie, as a rule, as much in the field of administrative deficiencies as in ignorance of the mechanics and dangers of inflation. In periods of large spending for development, only countries with an efficient and loyal government machinery are able to operate anti-inflationary devices with a fair measure of success. Inefficient controls of exchange operations, foreign currency and capital movements, and leakages of impending measures in financial legislation which are quite common in inexperienced administrations, can entirely offset the attainment of anti-inflationary objectives.

Another point of importance is that the effects of inflationary expenditure on production are different in underdeveloped countries as compared with industrialised economies. The latter show a con-

[1] 'Methods of Financing Economic Development in Underdeveloped Countries,' U.N., 1949, p. 19.

siderable elasticity of output levels in response to injected effective demand, and react rapidly to incentives towards increase or reduction of output. Increases in output at considerable rates have been registered within short periods following an increase in effective demand, and have thus led to stoppage of the inflationary process in its first stages.[1] In underdeveloped countries, with their rudimentary productive apparatus, production rises only slowly after similar inducements, and would thus not quickly repair the negative effects of inflation. Also the different effects of changed income distribution have to be considered in an appraisal of inflationary processes. Inflation frequently results in an increased polarisation of income distribution, which in highly developed countries increases saving and private investments. This effect cannot easily be achieved in underdeveloped countries: in an underdeveloped economy incentives and preferences as to how to invest savings and inflation profits operate very differently from their operation in economically advanced countries. In normal times wealthy people in Oriental countries, as the Clapp Report found for Syria, showed 'little disposition to lend their money for long-range economic projects yielding a relatively small return. So long as interest can be obtained on private loans ranging as high as 30%, the lower rate of return to be anticipated from public development investments will not be attractive. Another deterrent to resident private investors is their apparent unwillingness to regard their governments as stable and prudent custodians of public enterprise.'[2] Similar traits characterise the investment mentality of wealthy classes in other Oriental lands, and limit prospects for the inauguration of broad locally financed development projects until a socio-political change paves the way for them.

Compulsory Saving by Manipulating Prices
A potential source of development finance attaining considerable importance is price determination through authority for the purpose of collecting the difference between the price paid to the producer and that paid by the buyer. However, price manipulation policies require strong governmental power in order to use or replace the market mechanism successfully for obtaining profits—either directly, from purchasing and selling operations '*en regie*', or by creating a gap between producer and consumer prices and collection of difference through government agencies.

The most comprehensive system of utilising an artificial price difference has been built up by the Soviet government; it has in this way succeeded in collecting very considerable amounts from the

[1] H. W. Singer stressed his aspect in his (mimeogr.) Brazilian lectures.
[2] Clapp Report, Part I, p. 3.

public. In the thirties, receipts from the turnover tax exceeded more than two-thirds of the total Soviet budget, and were vital for financing the constant expansion of the Soviet economy.[1]

In Oriental countries the system was already tested on an impressive scale during the first half of the nineteenth century, when the then ruler of Egypt, Mohammed Ali, attempted to force industrialisation on that country. The enormous means required for the implementation of this scheme were obtained by the establishment of state enterprises and trade monopolies, the profits from which had to furnish funds for the industrialisation programme. In this case, too, the main pre-condition for the experiment's success was of a socio-political kind. Only an authoritarian or totalitarian government can in this way intervene in economic life. A free economy would not tolerate the operation of such government business for any length of time; the use of government powers in times of emergency or for occasional trade operations is a very different matter.

Improvement of Terms of Trade

A special case of price policies intended to secure substantial revenue through government channels is the manipulated improvement of terms of trade. Terms of trade (or the ratio between the index of export and import prices) have a great impact on the economic situation of underdeveloped countries. These countries are dependent for their supplies of vital foreign goods on the proceeds from their exports, which consist mainly of agricultural products and industrial raw materials. An unsatisfactory ratio of trade terms and the absence of stability in the prices of these commodities have a detrimental effect on the economic situation of the exporting country. As long as the determination of prices for these commodities was in the hands of, or influenced by, strong buyer organisations controlled from abroad, the large profits resulting from this price fixation were drawn to the processing countries.

With the emergence of national governments in most of the territories which in the past supplied primary products to industrialised countries on the terms of the latter, the interests of the country producing primary products became safeguarded on a different level. The new sovereign governments have the means to apply modern devices for promoting local produce and its adequate marketing, thereby retaining a much higher share of the international price for the home economy. The power to shape terms of trade

---

[1] According to M. Dobb, *Soviet Economic Development since 1917*, London, 1948, p. 364, a fairly close correlation can be traced between the mounting curve of expenditure on investment and defence throughout the decade and the mounting revenue from the turnover tax.

entirely at will is certainly limited; yet there are several methods of influencing such terms of trade in favour of the exporting countries:[1]

  a Establishment of government agencies which conduct negotiations with foreign buyers on equal terms on behalf of local producers;
  b Improvement of the value of exporting goods by encouraging processing in the producing country, and by introducing measures to raise the quality standards of the export products;
  c Establishment of services which have in the past been performed by the buying countries for the producing countries. The substantial costs of transportation on land and sea, insurance and banking, formerly payable mostly in foreign currency, can, at least in part, accrue as revenue to the native economy through local enterprise.

The change in the political position of countries producing primary products and the improvement of the terms of trade which has occurred since the war have already brought with them a remarkable improvement in the balance of trade of numerous producing countries.

Collective or Corporative Saving
Interesting new forms of financing economic projects have emerged in countries where development functions have been assumed by collective or corporative entrepreneurs. Trade unions and other professional organisations have often used their considerable moral and economic standing to accumulate funds and invest them in new economic and socio-economic ventures. This method of carrying out development projects has considerable chances of success, because it is based on the unity and loyalty of the members, who frequently respond wholeheartedly to the appeal. More important, it utilises the saving potential of a large, well-organised association, and directs it into specific channels of investment. Experience with this type of finance has so far been remarkable. Impressive housing developments, rural settlement projects, industrial enterprises and even health and educational institutions have been created and financed within the framework of such organisations. In certain countries with a high level of socio-economic organisation, such as Great Britain and Israel, these activities have become an outstanding contribution to the general progress and welfare of society.

Unused Labour as Capital Substitute in Economic Development
In analyses of the potential capital resources of an underdeveloped

[1] Cp. also the listing of such methods in the U.N. Report on Financing Economic Development, New York, 1949, p. 20.

area, primary consideration is usually given to resources of a monetary or commodity nature. One important source, the potential of unused labour, had been dealt with hardly at all or regarded rather as a burden, because it involves outlay for workers' consumption. Yet more recently a change in approach has set in, in particular under the influence of Nurkse whose starting point is that labour counts among those resources which are abundantly available in many underdeveloped economies. Certain aspects of the problem have been discussed before under the head of disguised unemployment, usually resulting in a pessimistic appraisal of development prospects in the areas affected by such unemployment.

Yet this treatment of diguised unemployment has given way to a more balanced consideration of the positive results deriving from a more efficient utilisation of those already employed, or from a shifting of practically unemployed manpower to the employed sector of the population. These additions to the labour force can be used in building houses, for public works, afforestation, protective measures in flood areas, and certainly for industrial employment as well; yet changing attitudes towards spending, work and community values must precede such a departure from established behaviour. Interesting examples of constructive enterprise performed by such additional labour have been noted in recent years, particularly in India and in resettlement areas of the Middle East.[1]

Our outline of the saving potential, voluntary and compulsory, has shown the considerable scope of financial resources which does exist in underdeveloped countries. With the increasing improvement in administrative services and the expected rise in real income, these resources may cover part of the financial requirements which is not negligible at all. However, as we have seen, the scope of the available domestic means will not be sufficient to satisfy those requirements which are needed to cause a substantial rise of national income. Underdeveloped countries will have to turn to foreign sources in order to obtain from them additional financial help. The following survey of former experience in the field of foreign investment will assist us in appraising the potential of lending from foreign sources.

[1] A report in the London *Observer* mentions the case of the building of the new township of Faridabad, near Delhi, on the initiative of a young Benghali disciple of Ghandi. Sudhir Ghosh, a former employee of the Ministry of Rehabilitation, and according to the report of the correspondent dismayed by the money wasted there, went to a camp containing 30,000 Hindu refugees from the North-west Frontier Province and urged them to construct a new, self-supporting township. His men started by levelling the ground and making bricks—they had to create from nothing. 'Ghosh sweated, cursed and praised his often disgruntled refugees, scrounged and pulled every string he knew in order to carry out the housing project.' See Rawle Knox, 'Nehru and the Peasants,' in the *Observer* of July 29, 1951, and Chester Bowles, *Ambassador's Report*, New York, 1954, p. 201.

THE MOVE TOWARDS ADJUSTMENT

THE POTENTIAL OF LENDING FROM FOREIGN SOURCES

a. CHIEF SOURCES OF FOREIGN CAPITAL INVESTMENT BEFORE WORLD WAR I BY AREAS

The principal lending countries had in 1913–14 invested approximately $44,000 million in foreign countries. Three-fourths of this amount was lent by the United Kingdom, France and Germany as long-term investments, which had grown over a period of forty years, from 1874 to 1914, from $6,000 million to $33,000 million.[1] The annual growth in investment of the three countries, according to the same source, was steady though not uniform, and appears to have been close to the yield (interests, dividends and profits) of the investment. Over the entire period the total of the estimated capital exports from the three countries practically equalled their aggregate income from the investments; the growth appears to have been financed from the investment yields.

These observations of the U.N. Report point to three remarkable facts: (a) The four decades up to the First World War saw an outflow of European capital which was without precedent before that period and without recurrence thereafter; (b) the United States did not figure conspicuously in these activities; (c) aggregate investments of the three first named countries proved so rewarding that they tended to double every twelve to thirteen years out of yields.

Long-term Foreign Investments by Major Lending Countries in 1913–14

Investing countries	Millions of U.S. dollars
United Kingdom	18,000
France	9,000
Germany	5,800
United States*	3,500
Belgium, Netherlands, Switzerland	5,500
Other countries	2,200†
Total	44,000

* Foreign investments in the United States amounted to some $6,800 million; on balance, therefore, the United States was a debtor country.

† Rough estimate; includes the investments of Japan and Russia (e.g. in China), of Portugal (e.g. in Brazil) and of Sweden (e.g. in Russia).

---

[1] The data and tables of this section, when not otherwise stated, are taken from *International Capital Movements during the Inter-War Period*, U.N. Department of Economic Affairs, 1949, pp. 1 ff.

THE FINANCE OF ECONOMIC DEVELOPMENT

Approximate Distribution of Investments by Continental Areas

Foreign long-term investments in	Millions of U.S. dollars
Africa	4,700
Asia	6,000*
Europe	12,000
North America (north of Mexico)	10,500†
Latin America	8,500
Oceania	2,300
Total	44,000

* Of which China, $1,600 million.
† Of which the United States, $6,800 million.

The first table shows clearly the predominating position of the United Kingdom among capital exporting countries. It has lent 41% of the total investment and five times more than the United States. It is likewise noteworthy that in 1913–14 more than half of the total amount was invested in Europe and North America—including the United States, which received much more capital than it exported—whereas Asia had not received more than $6,000 million, or approximately 14% of the total.

In per capita figures the data would work out at $25 for Europe, $119 for America and less than $7 for Asia. Yet throughout the whole period there was an interesting movement of British capital investments from European to non-European countries. The U.N. report quotes sources according to which British investors held in 1875 in Europe and Egypt no less than £500 million, out of a total of £1,200 million; against this the corresponding distribution of British investment in 1913 was £240 million in Europe and Egypt, of a total of £3,715 million. According to another source nearly 60% of British foreign investments in 1854 were placed in Europe; this share fell to 6% in 1913.[1] The United Kingdom thus provided much earlier than other countries considerable funds for semi- and underdeveloped countries, a development largely connected with the rising production of cheap steel and the improvement in means of transportation which this production made possible. The British investments were directed primarily to railways, which account for 40% of the total. Loans to governments, central and local, account for 30%, whereas all the other groups—raw materials, banks and finance, industry, commerce and public utilities other than railways —account for the remaining 30%.[2]

[1] Report on International Investment, O.E.E.C., 1950, p. 14.
[2] Sir Arthur Salter, 'Foreign Investment', *Essays in International Finance*, Princeton, 1951.

THE MOVE TOWARDS ADJUSTMENT

The character of the investment was largely *direct*, i.e. the means were placed directly in the enterprises by the investors as risk capital. In this case the investors could also operate through agents, branch factories or corporations. Part of the capital was lent as portfolio capital. In this case the funds were channelled through a public body, offering, as a rule, the facilities which appeal most to a rentier-type investor who prefers a stable revenue along the lines of investment in bonds. The original source of the funds could in both cases be private; yet there is a difference in the degree of risk which the distinction expresses. Direct or venture capital goes out for profit openly facing loss; whereas portfolio capital, although subscribed, too, by private investors, wants a degree of security which is obtainable only through public guarantee. There were, of course, numerous variations in arrangements and conditions for the lending of capital to foreign countries.

TRENDS IN THE INTER-WAR PERIOD

The scope of foreign investment during the inter-war period never achieved the peak level of 1913. Lending operations towards the end of the twenties showed a drastic decrease after the 1929 crisis. The annual average of capital issues for foreign accounts in the chief creditor countries—the United States and the United Kingdom—point to this effect.

Capital Issues for Foreign Account
(excluding refunding operations)
Annual averages in Millions of $

	1919–23	1924–8	1929–31	1932–8
United States	531	1,142	595	28
United Kingdom	416	587	399	143

At the same time a more rapid pace in respect of American capital issues became evident. Securities floated for foreign accounts assumed, in the main, the form of bonds and debentures. The loans placed were largely for the account of central or local governments; but even industrial investments, generally for railways and other public utilities, had to a large extent been guaranteed by government. Of the total par value of foreign dollar bonds floated in the United States government-issued and government-guaranteed bonds have constituted no less than four-fifths. The scope of portfolio invest-

216

ments was actually not too different from that of direct investments in 1929, as is shown by the following table:

	United Kingdom	United States
	(millions of U.S. dollars)	
Portfolio investments (par value), 1929	8,900	7,100
Direct investments, 1929	7,900	7,500

It appears that, in general, direct investments showed a downward tendency, whilst portfolio investments, although not growing conspicuously, became the main channel of foreign lending until the present time. Only one type of direct investment showed an upward trend after the 1930's, and even accelerated after the Second World War: namely, private foreign investment in oil. If we deduct the outflow for this specific purpose from the total of foreign lending, we obtain much lower sums indeed. Capital-poor underdeveloped countries received less capital throughout the period under consideration than those which had already made substantial progress in their economic development. There was also a marked difference in the investment direction of the two principal lending countries: whereas the United Kingdom was supplying nearly all undeveloped and underdeveloped countries, the United States did not take part in the floating of capital issues for the account of either China or India during that period.

United States: Outstanding Direct Investments at end of 1929, by Countries

(*book values in millions of U.S. dollars*)

	Amount	%
A. Creditor countries (Belgium, France, Netherlands, Sweden, Switzerland, United Kingdom, Ireland, Luxembourg and Portugal)	787	10·4
B. Developed and semi-developed debtor countries (Argentina, Australia, New Zealand, Canada, Newfoundland, Union of South Africa, Denmark, Germany, Italy, Japan, Norway, Austria, Czechoslovakia, Finland, the Saar, Spain and the Baltic States)	3,072	40·8
C. Underdeveloped debtor countries (Latin-American countries, except Argentina, European underdeveloped countries, China, India, Netherlands Indies, other Asian countries, British Africa, except the Union of South Africa, other African countries)	3,669	48·8
Total, all countries	7,528	100·0

THE MOVE TOWARDS ADJUSTMENT

United Kingdom: Outstanding Direct Investments at end of 1929

(*nominal values in millions of U.S. dollars*)

Area	Amount
'British' countries:	
Australia and New Zealand	231
Canada	895
Union of South Africa	372
India and Ceylon	630
Other countries	905
'Foreign' countries:	
United States	248
Europe	552
Latin America	2,661
Rest of world	624
Total	7,118
Total	14,644

The main area of interest for the United States was Latin America. The United Kingdom supplied a relatively large share of the loans raised by members of the British Commonwealth, and figured prominently in issues for Asian and African countries, and for Australia and New Zealand. Thus India and China, which together represent about 40% of the world's population, each received an amount of foreign capital similar to or less than that received by Argentina and Australia, with only one per cent of the world's population. Asia altogether, representing over half the world's population, received only 4½% of the investments.

If we add the portfolio investment of $8,900 million for the United Kingdom and $7,100 million for the United States we receive a total amount of approximately $30,600 million. This amount, though nominally larger than the total investment of both countries in 1913, was not higher, considering its purchasing power, than the total investment of $21,500 million in 1913.

The third aspect, the classification of investments by purpose, shows that direct investments tended to be absorbed by public utilities and transportation. Manufacturing came in for only a fraction of the total amount; even to that extent the largest part—in the case of the United States, 84%—was invested in developed or semi-developed countries. A more detailed analysis of British direct investments would show that the great bulk was made in railways, public utilities, finance, mining, metal smelting, oil production, plantations, etc. The explanation of the U.N. Report for the relatively small proportion of foreign investments in manufacturing for the domestic market refers to the manner in which the trade of these countries developed, and in particular to the small scale for foreign operations. This seems, however, to explain only one aspect of the problem. We have to consider also the specific nature of manufacturing, implying as it does a much higher degree of risk than other capital uses.

b. GRANTS-IN-AID AND INTERNATIONAL CAPITAL IN
THE POST-WAR PERIOD

Considering the shock to international investment produced by the First World War the destruction and dislocation on a nearly universal scale caused by the Second World War would have justified denying any prospect for the renewal of international capital transfer for many years. The wiping out of industrial centres in Europe and East Asia, renowned as sources and objectives of international investment; the decline and dismemberment of colonial empires; the slaughter and displacement of peoples numbering many millions— all this could not fail profoundly to affect traditional sources of saving and capital formation. Yet the ensuing situation turned out very differently from that which could be expected. War-torn continents were provided with a flow of means which exceeded by far the pre-war magnitudes. The flow of means from the United States alone jumped on the average to more than $5 billion p.a. during the years 1946–50, exceeding $26 billion for this period.

The explanation of this unexpected development is the emergence after the war of the United States as the foremost lending and aid-giving country of the world. The change is indeed profound: American investments during 1945–50 equal the estimated aggregate value of all international investments throughout the world in 1944. United States total portfolio and direct long-term investments in 1939 amounted to only about 40% of the total for the post-war period.

The development of American capital transfer after the war is surprising also in the light of the experience in the inter-war period described above. Yet it is evident that the resumption of international capital transfer was not due to an improvement of economic prospects for American capital export.

Its main reason was the acceptance of a non-economic motivation for the new international capital flow since 1945. The nature of the post-war outflow of capital from the United States is indeed very different from capital transfers in the former periods. Immediately after the Second World War there was an urgent need for relief and rehabilitation expenditure; it was organised and operated by U.N.R.R.A. and other regional aid centres. When it became clear that the restoration of stable and efficient economies did not proceed quickly enough, large-scale loans and grants under various schemes followed. They developed into a system, formulated in the Foreign Economic Assistance Act in April 1948, which was an entirely new approach. Orthodox economic criteria were not regarded as decisive considerations, and it became recognised that political ends could be promoted or achieved through economic means. The new approach was, perhaps more than it seemed at the time, a conspicuous departure from former rules guiding international financial support. Although the new policies were primarily destined to meet the needs of war-devastated Europe, they actually had much deeper implications. They showed two things: (*a*) during the preceding decade the American economy had become so amazingly resourceful that an outflow of many billions of dollars over a short period, very largely not for self-liquidating purposes, did not affect its strength at all; (*b*) recognition had come about of certain new aspects in the distribution and placing of American capital.

The phenomenal rise of the American national income gross and net revealed a potential of capital export which threw the former outflow of capital from the United Kingdom entirely in the shadow. Even generous calculations of annual requirements in underdeveloped countries would not exceed the potential of capital export from the United States based on recent levels of United States national income and the needs of domestic investment in the American economy. On the economic plane it would not be difficult to prove the ability of the United States to provide the world at large with the necessary development funds out of its real income.

The following tables show a great variety of purposes and conditions in the targets for which American funds were spent. Allocations for aid and recovery, summarised under the head 'Unilateral Payments', are one main line. Investments and loans increasingly administrated by specific institutions present the other main field of capital supplied to foreign countries. Two institutions, in particular, specialise in foreign lending to underdeveloped countries: namely the Export-Import Bank of the United States and the International Bank for Reconstruction and Development, an agency of the United Nations. An interesting prelude to the present phase of activities of the Export-Import Bank can be seen in the removal of the prohibition on loans for foreign governments which were in default on their debts to the United States. On June 30, 1950, the Bank had actually disbursed $2·6 billion out of a new credit authorisation of $3·5 billion. Credits for economic development went to Latin America, China, Turkey, Israel and Indonesia, primarily for the purchase of capital goods, material, services, etc.

THE FINANCE OF ECONOMIC DEVELOPMENT

United States Government Grants, other Unilateral Transfers, and
Loans to Foreign Countries, 1946–50

(*millions of dollars*)

Type of Aid	1946	1947	1948	1949	1950
A. Unilateral payments					
Total	2,454	2,250	4,362	5,585	4,295
Less: Unilateral receipts	166	303	205	264	175
Equals: Net unilateral payments	2,288	1,947	4,157	5,321	4,120
B. Long-term loans and investments					
Total	3,348	7,143	1,416	679	414
Less: Repayment	86	294	443	205	287
Equals: Net long-term loans and investments, including to International Bank and International Monetary Fund	3,262	6,849	973	474	127
Less: Subscriptions to International Bank and International Monetary Fund	323	3,062	—	—	—
Equals: Net long-term loans and investments, excluding to International Bank and International Monetary Fund	2,939	3,787	973	474	127
C. Outflow of short-term capital (net)	− 250	108	− 87	173	− 10
Total net unilateral payments and total capital movement, excluding to International Bank and International Monetary Fund (A+B+C)	4,977	5,842	5,043	5,968	4,237

THE MOVE TOWARDS ADJUSTMENT

TABLE 2

Net Outflow of United States Private Direct-investment Capital by Area, 1946–9

(*millions of dollars*)

Year and Industry	Total	Canada	Latin-American Republics	E.R.P. countries	E.R.P. dependencies	Other Europe	All other countries
1946: Total	182·4	37·9	58·5	18·0	6·1	0·8	61·1
Petroleum industry	170·0	12·0	103·0	7·0	4·0	*	44·0
Other industries	12·4	25·9	− 44·5	11·0	2·1	0·8	17·1
1947: Total	723·5	13·0	441·7	47·4	53·0	1·1	167·3
Petroleum industry	487·0	37·0	257·0	20·0	50·0	1·0	122·0
Other industries	236·5	− 24·0	184·7	27·4	3·0	0·1	45·3
1948: Total	645·1	37·8	321·0	48·2	68·5	5·2	164·4
Petroleum industry	486·0	44·0	205·0	38·0	61·0	2·0	136·0
Other industries	159·1	− 6·2	116·0	10·2	7·5	3·2	28·4
1949: Total	834·4	103·2	480·4	33·8	38·3	13·3	165·4
Petroleum industry	677·0	54·0	397·0	10·0	34·0	13·0	169·0
Other industries	157·4	49·2	83·4	23·8	4·3	0·3	− 3·6

* Less than 50 thousand dollars.

The International Bank had until the end of March 1954 issued loans for somewhat more than $1,866 billion. The United States provided most of the investment capital. The particular attitude of the International Bank towards the problems of lending to under-developed countries has already been mentioned before. This stand can be generally characterised as a rather conservative attitude regarding the pre-conditions for foreign lending—an attitude which did not please the more aggressive sponsors of economic development. The individual criticisms were directed against the specific project approach, the preference for lending for elaborate projects only, as against granting funds for general development. Another point encountering opposition was the demand on the part of the Bank that the major portion of the capital requirements of an underdeveloped country must come from within the country itself; and that foreign financial assistance should originate in the main from private sources. This was and is contested by the financial spokesmen of under-developed countries, who demand a more generous and imaginative approach. They do not ignore the importance of sound business principles in bank policies in general. Their emphasis, however, is on the entirely new requirements which have come up on the international scene in close connection with the grave and urgent problems of underdeveloped countries. Since many of the difficulties to foreign lending encountered by the applicants cannot be removed by traditional approaches, attention is drawn to the entirely novel character and the comprehensive nature of most development programmes which aim at a transformation of agriculture and at industrialisation and thus require the provision of means on a very much larger scale than the present policies of the International Bank and the Export-Import Bank allow.

The International Bank itself has recognised the significance of this problem, which is in its view primarily an issue concerning the provision of funds by private enterprise. As a result of the discussions of this problem in various international agencies, the proposal was made to establish a new institution, the International Finance Corporation. The International Bank was invited to submit a report as to whether such a corporation could make significant contributions to economic development over and above those that can be met by existing organisations. In an instructive memorandum of April 1952, the International Bank submitted its views on the subject. The report of the Bank mentions former attempts to supplement the flow of private capital by means of national financing institutions of a public or semi-public character. The sponsorship of government has provided these banking institutions with public funds, and has given them safeguards not available to the private investor.

The most important institution in the field is the United States Export-Import Bank, which is outstanding for the scope of its lending activities and for the absence of geographical restrictions, which allow it to offer its loan funds to governments and government-sponsored undertakings practically everywhere. Yet the report observes that national institutions of this type are in general inadequately equipped to meet the problem which gave rise to the proposal for the corporation.

The International Bank itself cannot contribute directly to the growth of private investment, since there are two restrictions by statutory requirements: the first is that all loans made by the Bank must be guaranteed by a government, or by the Central Bank or its equivalent in the country in which the private enterprises to be financed are located. This discourages private borrowers, who are afraid of government interference connected with such a guarantee. The second limitation is the fact that the Bank does not engage in any equity financing. The Bank has attempted to overcome these difficulties by operating through the medium of a development bank or a banking consortium, but this technique of providing credits through such an agency is only a partial answer to the problem.

For all these reasons the most immediate contribution of the Corporation would be seen in the provision of funds to private investors, both domestic and foreign, which would enable them to carry out promising projects now held back by lack of adequate capital. The amount of capital, on which the Bank did not wish to make any detailed comment, has been suggested to be equivalent to $400,000,000, of which a third would be paid in initially, the balance being subject to call to be subscribed by members of the Bank.

LESSONS OF THE PERIOD

EFFECT OF POLITICAL CHANGES

The main factors responsible for the relatively large flow of private foreign investments to underdeveloped countries up to the Second World War were: (1) the legal and economic privileges enjoyed by foreign capital interests; (2) the necessity of securing key raw materials for the metropolitan countries' expanding industries; (3) the promise of attractive profits to be gained from pioneer projects and exploitation of unknown countries in an age of discovery, prospects nourished by the lucrative experience of pioneering enterprises in the past.

The attainment of political freedom by most of the formerly dependent areas during or after the First World War deeply affected the position of foreign capital, which had come to be regarded as the spearhead of foreign domination. But political independence did not automatically bring with it economic independence. All of the resentment against past developments could not invalidate the fundamental fact that without a considerable increase in economic strength, i.e. without the development of natural resources, farming, manufacturing and service, all of which required capital investment, the newly-won freedom would be meaningless. In recognition of this fact the hostile attitude of governments and populations in underdeveloped countries towards foreign capital has become modified.[1] Instead of

---

[1] A case in point is the changed attitude of Turkey towards participation of foreign capital in the search for and exploitation of oil. The new law, No. 792

the former outspoken opposition to any future investment of foreign capital, different policies have emerged which reflect the outcome of the following considerations:

(a) domestic savings are definitely insufficient to bring about the desired all-round economic and social development; (b) foreign private capital, which in the past created much resentment against its activities because of its imposition of unfair terms, has abandoned such practices; (c) owing to their new-won sovereign status, governments of underdeveloped countries are now able to prevent abuses of rules and concessions by foreign investors; (d) an increasing part of the flow of capital which is now available and being directed into underdeveloped countries has 'international' character, i.e. is collected and allocated by international agencies.

As a result, the new terms of international lending are quite different from those which determined its operation in the past—particularly in the sphere of industrial development.

The League of Nations Report of 1945, 'Conditions of Private Foreign Investments', enumerated the following risks as significant obstacles to investment in foreign countries: (a) lack of equality in access to law and fear of arbitrary behaviour by the administrative authorities; (b) double taxation; (c) fear of discriminatory taxation; (d) compulsory reinvestment of profits; (e) compulsory participation with domestic capital; (f) inflexible provisions regarding employment of foreign personnel; (g) restrictions on ownership of land, mineral deposits, etc.; (h) restrictions on the transfer abroad of profits; and (i) lack of assurances of appropriate compensation in case of nationalisation or expropriation.[1] These difficulties had been reported in 1945; the experience of foreign investors in more recent years has certainly not been more encouraging. It has reduced the scope of investment-ready private capital for foreign areas to an insignificant level as compared to the requirements.

Following the stagnation in international private capital flow and its effects on the pace of economic development, international agencies have taken up the problems of investing private and public capital in foreign countries, and have published relevant data and conclusions. Most reports demand a significant increase in the flow of private investments to underdeveloped countries, yet at the same time admit that substantially greater incentives than those which

of December 1952, authorises the government to co-operate with foreign persons, firms and capital in exploring for and working oil wells, after a nationalisation law had failed to produce satisfactory results. See *News from Turkey* (Turkish Information Office, New York), Vol. 5, No. 50, December 1952.

In Egypt, the Permanent Council for the Development of National Resources has approved new rules in order to encourage the investment of foreign capital. See International Financial News Survey No. 36, 1953, p. 287.

[1] 'Conditions of Private Foreign Investments', League of Nations, 1945, p. 97.

exist at present are required to increase the flow of such investments. Among those incentives, non-discriminatory treatment of investments, guarantees of the transfer of income and capital by governments of capital importing or exporting countries, and convertibility of transfer payments are mentioned, and their merits and disadvantages discussed.

Since then it has become clear that these measures have not been sufficient to release a capital flow of the magnitude required at present.

First the considerable premium earned in former times by foreign investment no longer exists, and thus domestic capital uses have much increased their attraction. In 1948, American investors obtained from investments in the United States about 14% interest, as against 17% abroad.[1] The difference was thus quite small. Furthermore, most of the other conditions which produce a proper investment climate are more favourable at home, in particular the degree of security. This aspect has in fact become the overriding consideration for the private investor.

Most reports suggest that investors now prefer safe domestic investments, and increasingly place their funds in domestic savings banks, real estate and insurance companies, which have proved more reliable media of investment than the risky lending of capital to underdeveloped countries.

Some of the obstacles mentioned in the League of Nations Report of 1945 have in the meantime been removed or smoothed down in many underdeveloped countries. Yet, for the reasons discussed, even the removal of all those obstacles would not have paved the way for a recurrence of that flow of private investment which once fertilised these regions. This does not mean, however, that the flow of capital had altogether ceased. Rather it changed its origin, course and nature.

THE NEW TRENDS IN DEVELOPMENT FINANCE

When we compare the various development schemes and projections of development phases prepared by national governments, international agencies or private researchers, with the approaches to national development problems in the past, we observe one striking feature in the new presentations: they are marked by an entirely different order of magnitude of the requirements. In many statements and calculations of total development needs, figures are quoted which would have been regarded as fantastic twenty-five years ago.

[1] 'Measures for the Economic Development of Underdeveloped Countries', U.N., 1951, p. 81.

The statements which contain such data are no utopian projections into the remote future, but sober expositions of a possible course of development, granted certain assumptions which can likewise be regarded as feasible.

The changes which have occurred in the approach to problems of development finance during the last generation or so can be summed up as follows:

1 The new order of magnitude. Against the very modest average level of investment per earner of a few hundred dollars characteristic of development projects in preceding phases, an investment level of many times the erstwhile amount is today regarded as necessary to warrant a minimum rate of economic progress. This increase corresponds to recent experience of the effect of such increases in capital on the level of per capita national income, the raising of which is the primary target of economic development. To assure the availability of the required funds, new and more exacting financing methods are elaborated, proposed and applied today. Among these, pride of place is taken by measures substantially to increase and properly guide domestic savings, and to obtain the flow of foreign capital at a scale exceeding all preceding measures.

2 In the approach to development, all-out programmes replace the former single-purpose project with its limited effect on the national economy. A multi-purpose programme aims, in the nature of things, at lifting the whole network of production, consumption and services to a higher level, thus also taking care of those sectors of the economy which are either repaying investments only slowly or not repaying them at all in terms of money. The immediate consequences of these new policies have been twofold:

a A 'spraying' of investment over a wide range of development targets, comprising every field of primary production, secondary industries, communication and transportation facilities, social services, etc., in order to make possible a process of balanced growth.

b Large allocations of 'social capital', the absence of which is largely responsible in underdeveloped countries for the inability of their populations to achieve levels of production reached in Western countries. This social capital, which has a cardinal function in the reclamation of wasteland and swamps, the provision of health and education facilities and the development of communications, as a rule never attracts private capital, since it promises no direct returns. Yet it can be said without exaggeration that the investment of social capital is very frequently a prerequisite of any rewarding activity of private capital. The results of large-scale investment of social capital in a number of semi-developed countries are convincing proof of its significance as a pioneering agent in the development of economically uninviting areas. Where the large funds required for this type of fundamental needs cannot be obtained from within, foreign capital sources have been sought for the purpose, and have in fact frequently been obtained.

3 Another important innovation is the habit of co-ordinating and organising all necessary measures in the field of mobilising and spending funds for purposes of economic development within a broadly conceived national planning scheme. Development planning, which has replaced former *ad hoc* activities of entrepreneurs and public authorities, includes not only the elaboration of new income-producing activities but also planning techniques for the collection, allocation and spending of funds, usually for a number of years in advance. Such planning offers the public a clearer notion of the connection between various branches of economic life, and thus stimulates co-operation and support. On the other hand, it forces those in charge of development activities to keep in line with the scope of available resources and the provisions laid out for their expenditure.

In general, it appears that under the conditions of many under-developed countries a well-conceived development plan, linked to an investment plan, offers better prospects for the attainment of de-velopment goals than unco-ordinated development ventures. Con-siderations of prices and costs during the less promising stages of planned investment would not be the only criteria to determine the fate of projects, as they often did in the sphere of exclusive private enterprise. Planning authorities must not continuously examine the success and progress of their programme from the viewpoint of commercially adequate returns to their investment.

At the same time, the existence of a plan commits the authorities to determine an order of priorities for the various investment ex-penditures, and to keep an eye on them with a view to modifying this order in accordance with changing conditions.

4 Another important new feature in the practice of development planning and execution is the increasing share of international institu-tions. The acceptance of financial support from foreign sources under conditions imposed by the creditors has often left an un-fortunate memory, which was exploited in order to induce and strengthen nationalist policies against foreign enterprises. Quite frequently, however, the conditions stipulated by foreign financial interests had nothing to do with the fact that the lending agencies were of foreign origin. If certain conditions of rendering financial assistance are stipulated by international organisations, much resent-ment and opposition will be avoided.

5 One of the less popular aspects of the new methods of financing development in underdeveloped countries is the need for a certain form of control of expenditure and, most frequently, for restriction of consumption. It goes without saying, in the light of the difficulties in obtaining minimum funds for new all-round development programmes, that only by the supreme saving efforts of the populations concerned can substantial amounts be spared for domestic financing. This rule holds good also for those poverty-stricken areas particularly in need of capital investment. Without preparedness, at least for a certain period of time, to sacrifice part of even very moderate amenities just above the bare necessities of life, local capital formation cannot come into being. Hardships to the population caused by such rigorous austerity can be softened by the subsidised provision of essential consumer goods at low prices. Yet it should not be overlooked that it is precisely here that a genuine conflict is present between the austerity demand, on the one hand, and the necessity to take care of the new requirements of a population awakened towards such requirements and conscious of the possibility of satisfying them.

CHAPTER XI

PROBLEMS OF APPRAISING PROSPECTS OF ECONOMIC DEVELOPMENT

IT has become by now sufficiently clear that the reliance on the profit incentive and the price mechanism would not in itself be sufficient to induce and keep in motion important processes of economic development in less advanced countries.

TEMPORARY STIMULI VERSUS ESTABLISHED INCENTIVES

Because of the necessity to accelerate the formation of conditions towards a state of spontaneous economic growth, i.e. towards a state in which the motive power of profit performs its function, devices are increasingly applied in order to shorten the period of growth towards maturity. Let us mention a few such devices: pioneering efforts in the field of vocational instruction at a cost which exceeds what local financial resources would permit, in particular a level of payment for foreign experts and skilled foremen, which is far above local rates and certainly not borne out by the productivity of the local economic process; allocations or premia in various forms to reduce prices of local produce which are relatively high when compared to the same product on the international market. There are other forms of incentives aiming at the launching and maintaining of production activities for which normal profit prospects do not exist but which are nevertheless regarded as crucially important. The common feature of such promotion efforts is their temporary character; their main purpose is the generation of skills, levels of productivity and preferences which it is assumed will lead to the development of an economically sound production. Appraisals of the soundness, or of the sound prospects of development programmes in less advanced economies have thus to take this element of temporary suspension of the profit criterion into account. This consideration raises immediately the question of the length of the suspension and of the nature of the financial efforts which are needed in order to bring about a satisfactory working of the profit incentive at some later date. We have thus to face the problem of how to determine the time span regarded as necessary for the generation of the normal conditions of a profit-yielding production and also the problem of the cost of the devices to be applied in order to realise a production potential which today is economically not feasible. In the consideration of this issue numerous factors will have to be weighed. Against the 'excessive' cost in terms of financial outlay for the promotion of development on the one hand the huge losses to an underdeveloped economy and society which are implied in an acquiescence with the present state of destitution and distress, physical and other, must be fully taken into account. These are questions which are not always sufficiently treated in the context of discussions of the soundness of development schemes.

Somewhat related to this issue is the position of another central tool in economic reasoning, the price mechanism and its function as regulator of the economic process; it certainly needs re-examination and adjustment when applied to problems of development in underdeveloped areas. In theory the price mechanism ensures that resources are used in the most advantageous manner for society under the assumption of perfect competition and proper distribution of purchasing power. But numerous deviations disturb the working of this ideal mechanism. In underdeveloped countries economic power is frequently concentrated in monopolistic hands or groups; the masses are unable to improve their share and acquiesce in the resulting extreme reduction of their purchasing power; in such conditions it would be senseless to expect even an approximation to the price and output relationship postulated in theory. Another aggravating factor already dealt with before is the deficient knowledge of consumers as to how to improve their choice of commodities; this deficiency prevents them from acting as theory wishes them to. Consumers must be responsive to prices even before they obtain full knowledge of market conditions. They must be able and disposed to change their demand reaction in accordance with the changes in commodity prices. If they do not yet react to such influences, as for instance in economies consisting largely of subsistence farms, conclusions based on the normal functioning of the price mechanism in the market will not be applicable. This, too, means that we cannot content ourselves with the application of the tools developed under conditions of mature economies to the examination of the 'soundness' of a new programme of economic activities in underdeveloped countries.

THE MOVE TOWARDS ADJUSTMENT

A different issue constitutes the problem how to judge long-term prospects of economic development as a process of per capita increase in physical production and per capita consumption in view of the effect of the enormous growth of population in the under-developed countries. On this general plane the ratio of population growth to economic growth becomes one of the yardsticks for the judgment of prospects of economic development.

To this day many observers view the population growth in under-developed countries with a strong Malthusian bias and apply their findings in particular to the capital problem.

Not a few of the gloomy appraisals of the effects of population growth in underdeveloped countries are the result of calculations of the capital requirements for economic development in such countries. These calculations indicate that the rates of capital formation re- quired for raising output per capita are much higher than the present rates of saving in these countries. Furthermore, numerous authors hold that there is no prospect whatever for future improvement of these rates towards a level which will provide for a substantial rise in levels of consumption. The reason lies in the very depressed level of income. The proportion of the national product which can be ploughed back into production through savings seldom exceeds 4% or 5% in underdeveloped countries; this percentage may, perhaps, suffice to maintain the population increase at the existing level of consumption, assuming a capital–output ratio of 4 : 1, but it will certainly not lead to higher productivity or to a rise in levels of living.

It is evident that in these reasonings the potential trend and level of per capita output are primarily, if not exclusively, viewed in relation to the rate of increase of the population, thus giving this rate determinating weight.[1] The more refined production functions also rely entirely on assumptions of given rates of growth of the labour force under very specific conditions—primarily in highly developed countries. But it should be made very clear that only for such countries can the results be meaningful. An attempt to express in exact data and equations the relationship of population growth and economic performance of an underdeveloped society will of necessity encounter great difficulties—and not only because of the very limited applicability of the production functions, which are

---

[1] It is one of the many merits of the recent United Nations publication *The Determinants and Consequences of Population Trends*, New York, 1953, that it gives full consideration to the connection between population growth and per capita output as mutually interdependent relationship.

based on conditions in modern industrialised economies, i.e. on a very special combination of the agents of production, to other areas. The main reason, as every student of development in underdeveloped countries discovers, is that the level of per capita output is a very complex phenomenon which is dependent on a series of variables, of which only one is capital formation. If in an underdeveloped country only the population and labour force were to grow while other conditions and factors of production remain constant, the conclusion that per capita income must decline would be correct. But the assumption of such one-sided dynamics is erroneous, and therefore deductions and equations based on it must fail to produce useful results.

Because demographic changes can be expressed in quantitative terms, projections of population growth predominate among the attempts to predict trends of societal changes. This, however, cannot and should not conceal the effect of dynamic conditions in other fields as, for instance, in the scope and quality of the economic organisation, in the amount and levels of skill, in the attitudes of the agents and powers which are in control of economic processes, in the attitudes of labour, and in the range and depth of knowledge relating to the availability and usefulness of resources. There are probably many more variables which have not hitherto been fully considered in this context. Some of these variables are more accessible to quantitative measurement, others less.

Let us discuss for a moment the place of natural resources in this reasoning. The traditional approach to this datum is to appraise the resources currently in use and perhaps to add some allocation for estimated reserves. This might be a quite feasible procedure in the case of a preliminary exploration of the effect of population growth on per capita output, assuming a given set-up of natural resources. But it certainly does not suffice to regard the rate of population growth as the focal datum for a long-term appraisal without taking into account the potential change in resources utilisation. Experience nearly everywhere points to the great possibilities in the extent, degree of utility and range of uses of resources over a given period. It is true that in certain countries exploitation of resources was disappointing after a certain lapse of time. But against these there are many other cases where amazing and unexpected results were produced in the course of exploitation.[1]

1 Natural resources share the criterion of being unpredictable and at the same time of high potential significance in economic development with another factor: new knowledge. Its dynamic character and importance was not always recognised in the past; now it has advanced to a high position in the evaluation of the causes of economic progress, as the following statement shows:
'It is probably safe to say that only the discovery and exploitation of new

The dynamics in resources utilisation is only one of several major variables which evade exact quantitative determination, but which must be closely considered in the appraisal of our basic problem: the relationship of population growth to economic growth.[1]

It is only natural that differences in the appraisal of variables recognised as important to economic growth must vitally affect conclusions concerning the real development potential. There is hardly a discussion of the prospects of given areas which does not reveal the effect of such differences in approach, part of which may perhaps be due to a lack of understanding of the specific character of the development process.

The extent to which changes in approach and new knowledge have influenced our thinking in this field in the course of a few years becomes clear from a re-reading of comments made not too long ago on the same issues. The present writer may be permitted to refer to his personal experience because it seems to him to be relevant to the issue. In 1946, in a review of my *Economic Development of the Middle East*, F. J. Fisher in *Economica*, censured me for undue optimism which in 1945 seemed to the reviewer out of place in view of actual conditions both in the Middle East and elsewhere. 'Dr. Bonné realises clearly enough that reconstruction must be financed and that capital shortages can be made good only by the investment of new capital. For that new capital he looks partly to internal loans to be floated by the governments of the various Middle East territories and partly to funds to be obtained from some American or international organisation for the development of backward countries.'[2] Dr. Fisher regarded such prospects as very doubtful, because of the unpopularity of state-loans in the Middle East, the absence of external organisations likely to finance Middle East development with a certain disregard of normal economic criteria, and the political backwardness of the region, all of which form major obstacles for the execution of a planned policy of economic development. Hardly ten years later even a very sceptical observer would have to note far-reaching changes in the conditions for intergovernmental and international capital flow which deeply affect prospects of development.[3]

knowledge rivals capital formation as a cause of economic progress.' From 'Economics of Growth' by M. Abramowitz in *A Survey of Contemporary Economics*, ed. B. F. Haley, 1952, p. 146.

[1] A comprehensive list of factors which have a bearing on the level of capital output is given by J. J. Spengler, in his searching study *Economic Factors in the Development of Densely Populated Areas*, Proceed. American Philos. Society, February 1951, pp. 21–5.

[2] Cp. *Economica*, 1946, pp. 315 ff.

[3] I could, of course, also refer to the order of magnitude of the calculations which I made at the time in an attempt to give an idea of the financial requirements implied if certain targets were to be reached. It was then certainly not my

APPRAISING PROSPECTS OF DEVELOPMENT

The appraisal just referred to was not isolated. Over a considerable period observers of standing approached the subject of Middle Eastern development with great scepticism and let their analysis of economic prospects or their judgment of the problems of the area frequently be influenced by a certain bias. An illustrative case is the attitude taken by Doreen Warriner in her *Land and Poverty in the Middle East*.[1] To start with, Miss Warriner omitted, in an otherwise remarkable survey intended to cover conditions of land tenure and land resources in the whole Middle Eastern region, Turkey, a country with very large land resources. The result was a substantial diminution of the potential of the thus reduced region when compared with the potential obtained by me for the region which included Turkey. Ignoring this essential difference she compared the potential obtained by me with her data and ascribed the different result to the use of inadequate measuring rods by me.

The potentialities of the region were further reduced by the author's limitation of her comparisons of crop yields to *grain* crops, which were seen by her as representative indices of soil fertility in an area where high yielding commercial crops such as cotton, citrus and dates have gained a predominant position in the agricultural economy. Miss Warriner's conclusions thus unavoidably became extremely gloomy. On the other hand, that aspect which would allow for a more hopeful appraisal, namely, the appearance of new factors such as revenue from oil resources in the Middle East, and progress in large-scale irrigation works, was whittled down. Miss Warriner thought the expansion of oil production unlikely to stimulate general development, since the companies are foreign and will presumably be investing their profits outside the Middle East. It may be well to remember at this point that the total direct payments made in 1954 in the area in forms of royalties, taxes and dead rents amounted to approx. $600 million, or more than a quarter of the national income of the countries concerned. It has to be mentioned that Iraq, Kuwait and Saudi Arabia together are receiving the bulk of these direct payments, yet even so the position of the area altogether was changed by the oil discoveries.[2]

It is difficult to say to what extent more recent reports on Middle

intention to *predict*, yet it is perhaps not without interest to observe that my figures, regarded as extravagant, remained in fact below the size of the capital resources which became available to the region.

[1] Published by Chatham House in London, 1948.

[2] The availability of oil revenues of immense size means great temptations to careless spending in the countries endowed with these resources. The use made of these revenues is indeed not even. There are regions where the windfall has been well utilised. In places which were until yesterday the domain of time-honoured yet stagnant institutions and patterns, a remarkable pace of economic and social development has been inaugurated. Kuwait is a case in point. At the same time

East prospects have been influenced by the preceding climate of appraisal. In 1949 the United Nations Economic Survey Mission to the Middle East was so impressed by unsolved political financial and demographic problems in Middle Eastern countries that while recognising certain favourable basic factors, they were hardly able to raise themselves above the maze of their reservations and concluded rather melancholily: 'At the beginning of its task the Economic Survey Mission cherished a hope—a faint hope to be sure—that several large development projects, devised on the basis of the numerous surveys and reports already made by government missions, private engineers and other experts, could be recommended for immediate exploitation by large capital outlays. The Mission's hope has not been realised. The region is not ready, the projects are not ready, the people and governments are not ready for large-scale development of the region's basic river systems or major undeveloped land areas. To press forward on such a course is to pursue folly and frustration and thereby delay sound economic growth.'[1]

Already at the time the Report appeared it was difficult to read these views without concern. Was it not the very function of the Economic Survey Mission to give advice as how to overcome obstacles, to expose them and to spur the spirit of enterprise in the region, and to devise means and procedures to attain these objectives? Nobody had in fact denied the existence of the obstacles; numerous underdeveloped regions can compete with the Middle East as far as obstacles to economic development are concerned. Had conditions in India or Latin America been examined with similar yardsticks and conclusions, very important projects, sometimes of utmost significance for the fate of the countries concerned, would hardly have been tackled and successfully implemented.

Not all the discrepancies in the judgment of development prospects are due to a dissension in the evaluation of basic pre-conditions. Not infrequently errors in the appraisal of factual data creep in. A good case in point is the Report of the International Bank on Turkey which appeared in 1950. The Bank's report is marked by an extremely sceptical appraisal of the prospects, a tenor which at the

an incredible degree of squandering can be found among the royal entourage of Saudia rulers where the new fabulous riches have given life to habits of luxurious life rarely met elsewhere today. Cp. H. S. Philby, *Arabian Jubilee*, London, 1952, p. 232.

[1] Final Report of the U.N. Economic Survey Mission to the Middle East, Part I, New York, 1949, p. 3. I had at the same time readily acknowledged the positive contribution of this Report, and the many important data and information on the countries of the region included in it. (Cp. *American Economic Review*, 1951, pp. 208 ff.). But these merits are one thing; the disinclination or lack in belief on the part of the Commission that it is possible to tackle the problems is another.

time also roused misgivings among Turkish economists, who expected a different approach from an international team of economists sent by an institute for the promotion of development. The Turkish government in fact did not identify itself with the Bank's recommendations, and proceeded to execute its own farm development policy, which was crowned with considerable success. This success was partly due without doubt to favourable price trends connected with the Korean situation, and continuous good weather during the following years. But this is only part of the explanation, and it is important to clarify why the prognosis of the report was so far off the reality. Professor W. Nicholls, one of the members of the Bank team, frankly admits, as the following statement shows, the failure of the mission in this respect, attributing it to several shortcomings for which, however, the mission was not entirely responsible. '. . . In view of this success, the recommendations of our Bank mission report respecting Turkish agricultural development undoubtedly appear, with the benefit of hindsight, to have been overly cautious and pessimistic. It is clear that we underestimated the opportunities for expanding rapidly Turkey's total area under cultivation. We recognised in 1950 that Turkey faced considerable difficulty in even maintaining its modest level of per capita food consumption. We further recognised Turkey's heavy dependence upon raw agricultural land (in 1951 purchased inputs and depreciation amounted to only 19% of Turkey's gross farm income) in expanding its food supply but failed fully to appreciate the possibilities of increasing the inputs of cultivated land.'[1]

The relevant point in this and other cases is the inadequacy of a static analysis for the evaluation of development prospects. Estimates of productivity levels, the suitability of a piece of land for higher crop yields, the cost and effect of external economies, etc., are subject to considerable changes even over short periods; to insert them as rigid data in a calculation invites the risk of failure. Yet this is only one aspect of the problem of appraisal of future, i.e. uncertain prospects within a framework of given or constant assumptions.

Another aspect which might be called the 'releasing' effect of development processes lies somewhat outside the economic plane, and is important for the economist primarily because of its influence on other pre-conditions of economic development. Professor Bernard Lewis, who is not an economist himself, brought this point out very clearly when he pointed to the, perhaps unexpected, effects of economic development projects on the dynamics of Turkish society. The economic projects carried through by Kemal Ataturk and his successors were in purely economic terms frequently undefendable.

[1] *American Economic Review*, Vol. XIV, May 1955, No. 2, p. 67.

'Nevertheless, in the light of subsequent events, it must be agreed that these reforms, however much open to criticism on economic grounds, have wholly justified themselves in terms of their social consequences. I refer especially to the emergence of a new middle class of business men, managers, technicians, and the like, self-confident and self-assertive, increasingly intolerant of the other ruling groups of civil servants, landowners, and military men, and increasingly assertive of their own rights.'[1]

This statement demonstrates well the dilemma of the economist who has to appraise the prospects of development schemes. He cannot afford to ignore major considerations which are not within the limits of economic reasoning though he exposes himself thereby to the blame of transgressing into areas beyond his province.

One of these considerations is the effect of the economic policies themselves on the formation of the non-economic prerequisites for economic development; these prerequisites are frequently produced only through a process of trial and error which evades a close calculation of cost and return in advance. The experience in Turkey is a case in point.

Another consideration is the measure of imagination needed and permissible for economic development. The process of planning is essentially anticipation of the future, certain assumptions being given. The larger the gap is between existing and envisaged magnitudes the greater is the measure of uncertainty in drawing the lines of the objectives to be attained.

Judgment of the prospects of a development scheme will thus depend to a considerable extent on the capacity of anticipation, i.e. will of necessity include an element of subjective evaluation.

The following examples will exemplify the problem.

POTENTIAL IMPORTANCE OF OIL

It is obvious that the availability and utilisation of oil resources in a given region are major factors in its development. Yet their scope is not a fixed datum. Experience in the Middle East is illuminating in this respect. Twenty years ago oil production in the region did not go beyond a moderate volume and was a relatively small factor in the economy of the then major oil-producing countries, Iran and Iraq. As mentioned above, the picture has now changed completely.

The estimated proved reserves of crude petroleum in the Middle East which were less than half of total world reserves after the Second World War—even then no small part—were evaluated in

[1] B. Lewis, 'Democracy in the Middle East, its State and Prospects', *Middle Eastern Affairs*, April 1955, p. 107.

1953 at no less than 53·3%, or 8,307 million tons of the world's total oil resources. In the light of the most recent oil discoveries in the area, probable reserves of petroleum in the Middle East are believed to be much greater; so far only part of the area has been surveyed. An appraisal of oil resources as potential sources of capital thus leads to staggering figures. The potential addition to the capital assets of the region from this single item of natural wealth may be estimated at no less than $1,000 per head of population, or $4,000 to $5,000 per family living in the region; this estimate, of course, represents a very rough calculation and is subject to numerous qualifications. It is meant primarily to illustrate the size of the amounts involved. It should also be borne in mind that oil reserves do not benefit the whole region but only the countries producing oil.

There are reservations, too, as to whether the price of oil will remain at its present level and whether conditions of production will as hitherto favour the utilisation of Middle Eastern reserves. Yet if these conditions are met our appraisal would lead to a potential which is apt entirely to change the present order of magnitude of capital supply to the countries of the region. Moreover, it should be taken into account that this revolutionary prospect is connected with the utilisation of a product which occupies a key position in modern industrial development.

A different aspect, though related to our general problem of appraisal of the effects of development, is the question of the social cost. In his paper in the *American Economic Review*, Professor W. Nicholls frequently draws attention to the social problem of displacing agricultural workers by introducing mechanised techniques of cultivation. But does this particular case in Turkey represent a unique case of raising the productivity level of an economic sector at a certain price? Has not economic progress during the last two hundred years generally been accompanied by a high degree of temporary displacement and even waste of human resources? It seems to this writer that the waste and loss accompanying mechanisation in present-day Oriental economics remain in relative terms much beneath the scope of similar phenomena in European countries following the introduction of machine production.

Another example of an overcautious approach which may defeat the generally accepted aim, is the exclusion of large-scale irrigation and flood control schemes from the recommendations of the International Bank Report on Turkey. The reasons given by the authors of the Report are that the peasants in the region involved are not yet ready for the changes in production methods necessitated by irrigation. Furthermore, the capacity of the power plant included in the multi-purpose scheme will for some years be in excess of demand.

In his answer to these arguments, Professor Omer Celâl Sarc rightly points out that the peasant can hardly be prepared for irrigation before there is a possibility to irrigate; since the completion of the project would need several years, there would be sufficient time for preparation and adjustment.[1] As to the excess capacity of the power plant, this could partly be avoided by building it in stages.

The above examples as well as the experience elsewhere again confirm our previous conclusions: important as the economic analysis of the development specialist is for any decision on the execution of a given development project, it will form only part of the job. A degree of imagination for the elaboration of larger development schemes is indispensable; in those countries where traditional habits and motivations in economic life are still powerful, means to overcome institutional deficiencies must form part of the development scheme, even if their direct economic relevance is doubtful.

At the same time, the development planner must well bear in mind that economic processes cannot be conceived of as a series of phenomena connected by the simple relationship of cause and effect working along a logically deduced formula. Professor Frankel, in one of his essays in 'The Economic Impact on Underdeveloped Societies' has wisely drawn the attention of the social scientists to the fallacy of neatly constructed '*final*' solutions. Economic development has no use for the concept of finality.

Limitation of space prevents an elaboration of these reflections on potential and reality. Still, we feel that the experience, even in such a limited area, supports the belief in the capacity of man to adjust, through proper action, the supply of goods to the needs of world population. In the course of the development which performs this adjustment function—an increasingly universal phenomenon—the problem of carrying the process from the advanced to the less developed regions becomes crucial.

The following chapter starts from a criticism of representative historical-theoretical views of this process and defines it as a process of implanted development against the phenomena of economic growth which occur without such a drive and mode of causation.

[1] O. C. Sarc, 'International Bank Report on Turkey', *The Middle East Journal*, Summer 1952, pp. 339–40.

CHAPTER XII

IMPLANTED ECONOMIC DEVELOPMENT IN UNDERDEVELOPED COUNTRIES

MODERN efforts to promote, by means of international co-operation and organisation, 'higher standards of living, full employment and conditions of economic and social progress' have, as yet, only a short history. First vaguely formulated in 1941, in the Atlantic Charter, and then set forth in greater detail in 1945, in the Charter of the United Nations, these objectives have become an established part of major national and international economic policies, aiming in particular at the improvement of conditions in those countries which are economically less advanced.

A universal policy now affecting nearly two-thirds of the world's population, and still gathering momentum, offers every inducement to social scientists, and above all to economists, to bring the immense amount of descriptive and analytical material, suggested theorems and mutually independent trains of relevant thought into a coherent theoretical structure. This would not only meet a vital need for the explanation of past and present phenomena of great consequence; it would also make it easier to indicate probable trends of development in the future, given the continuance of existing or similar conditions; moreover, it would help to explain the difference in developments when the original conditions change. It should be obvious, however, that, since there is as yet no comprehensive general theory of economic growth which would account for the unique phenomenon of Western economic development, we can hardly expect a complete and satisfactory theory of economic development for underdeveloped countries. Still, this should not prevent us from attempting to construct such a theory with the aid of the building stones at present available or at least making whatever contribution we can towards the laying of a foundation for it. It would be unwise to embark upon

241

this attempt without taking into account existing theories and individual elements of economic thought which have a close bearing on our subject. Needless to say, our present treatment of the question can be no more than extremely brief; a more detailed discussion must be reserved for a later occasion. On the same grounds we shall limit the scope of our reasoning by certain qualifications:

a The points to be made will, at this stage, be more in the nature of historical generalisations than that of pure economic theory. The triad of motivation, mechanism and aims of economic development will serve as basis for the analysis.

b The term economic development, as used here, means a process of increasing productivity resulting in a larger volume of production for the national economy as a whole and in a higher level of performance by the individual. Hence, the task of the theory will be to explain how this process of change is initiated and maintained.

Our first step will be to review some of the previous attempts to construct a theory of economic development, and to see how far these propositions fit the economic process in underdeveloped countries.

PREVIOUS THEORIES OF ECONOMIC DEVELOPMENT
CONFRONTED WITH CONDITIONS IN UNDERDEVELOPED COUNTRIES

The Classicists

In Schumpeter's posthumous *History of Economic Analysis* a short chapter is devoted to the classical conception of economic development.[1] Three theories of economic development (or 'visions of the economic future of mankind') were formulated by the classical economists between 1790 and 1870. The sub-division made by Schumpeter can conveniently be used in our present discussion since it considers the factor of population pressure on limited resources as an important element in the classification. The first type of theorist is the 'pessimist', exemplified by Malthus, West, Ricardo and James Mill; the second type, the 'optimist', is represented by Carey and List; and the sole exponent of the third theory is Marx. Considerations determining the 'pessimist' approach are: pressure of population; nature's decreasing response to human efforts to increase the supply of food; hence falling net returns to industry, more or less constant real wages and ever-increasing rents of land.[2]

[1] Joseph A. Schumpeter, *History of Economic Analysis*, London/New York, 1954, pp. 570–4.
[2] Though the influence of Adam Smith is clearly recognisable in the work of the writers mentioned, they do not accept his belief in the beneficent, self-regulating force of the process of development. His concept of economic development

IMPLANTED ECONOMIC DEVELOPMENT

Schumpeter was struck by the complete lack of imagination which this view of the economic future of mankind reveals. In spite of the immense development possibilities which had come to fruition before the eyes of these writers, they saw nothing but cramped economies struggling more and more desperately for their daily bread.[1] According to them, the law of decreasing returns would finally counteract and nullify the effect of technological improvements. The fundamentally pessimistic attitude of this school, caused by a strange determinism with regard to all consequences of population growth, has received fresh impetus in recent times from the current demographic trends in underdeveloped countries.

The second, or 'optimistic', type of economic theory of development can, according to Schumpeter, best be illustrated by such writers as Carey and List. This group of writers gave full recognition to the power of capitalism to create productive capacity. Over and over again, in his famous polemics with Adam Smith, List, a widely travelled man who had been particularly impressed by his American experience, points out that an independent theory of productive forces is necessary to supplement Smith's theory of value which cannot alone explain the growth and decay of a non-stationary economy.[2] In List's writings we also find an early expression of the need for an explanation of the specific problem of the differential of development, which was, at the time, clearly recognised by the more thoughtful authors. List himself, who wrote his *Nationale System* more than a century ago, expressly referred to the lag between

hinges on his view of technical progress—a view remarkable for its optimism with regard to the effects of the introduction of improved machinery, which is supposed to facilitate and curtail labour but not to displace the worker who performs it. Technology, according to Adam Smith, has a labour-attracting effect and thus ensures the steady expansion of the market. His assumptions as to the effect of mechanisation and of the machine as a complement to labour rather than a substitute for it—assumptions on which Professor Lowe dwells in his penetrating study of 'The Classical Theory of Economic Growth' (*Social Research*, Summer 1954, pp. 132 ff., in particular p. 136)—could hardly maintain themselves in face of the progress of industrialisation on a broad front. In Ricardo's opinion, the labour-displacing effects of industrial technology, which were ignored by Smith, are of great import, and they account for his pessimistic outlook. Furthermore, Smith's assumption of constant returns is superseded by the law of diminishing returns on land the operation of which will have an injurious effect upon economic development.

[1] Cp. *History of Economic Analysis*, p. 571.

[2] 'The capacity to create wealth is thus infinitely more important than wealth itself; it not only provides security of possession and increase of acquired wealth, but also replacement of losses. This holds good even more for nations than for individuals. Germany was devastated in every century by pestilence, famine or internal and external wars; yet each time it saved a great deal of its creative power and thus rapidly attained prosperity again—whilst rich and powerful Spain, in full possession of internal peace, yet despot- and cleric-ridden, sank lower and lower in poverty and destitution.' Translated from List's *Das nationale System der politischen Ökonomie*, Jena, 1904, pp. 220 f.

243

European and Asian countries in this respect and showed great insight into the underlying causes of this phenomenon. His emphatic and repeated assertion that individuals draw most of their creative strength from the institutions and conditions of society may usefully be borne in mind in similar discussions today.

Another classical writer who had a grasp of the problems of a growing industrial economy, J. S. Mill, occupied an interesting intermediate position owing to his refusal to share the gloomy conclusions of the sceptics, on the one hand, and the enthusiasm of the believers in economic progress, on the other. He beheld the unrestrained release of the forces of an acquisitive industrial society and became increasingly worried by its possible consequences. Though fully aware of the tremendous differences in levels of production and living between fully developed and backward economies, and the necessity of bridging the gap, he tended to regard a stationary society as a preferable state of affairs.[1] Yet this was only an expression of a reflective state of mind and not a result of his analysis. Like many classical writers he attached the greatest importance to the process of saving and physical investment as a pre-condition for further expansion.

It might have been expected that Schumpeter, who raised the entrepreneur to the rank of a supreme creative force, would censure J. S. Mill for his underestimation of the element of personal initiative, which is a cardinal theme in Schumpeter's writings. But it would seem that the span of the analytical interests of both Mill and Schumpeter—in spite of the latter's encyclopedic command of modern social science—was spatially defined by the limits of modern industrial society.

Marx

In considering Marx, it would be well to remember that his analysis is described by Schumpeter as the only genuine evolutionary economic theory that the period produced. No other social scientist has, according to Schumpeter, so deeply understood the impact of the capitalist machine and shown in so grand a vision its immense power

---

[1] J. S. Mill, *Principles of Political Economy*, New York, 1893 (5th ed.), Vol. II, p. 336: 'I cannot, therefore, regard the stationary state of capital and wealth with the unaffected aversion so generally manifested towards it by political economists of the old school. I am inclined to believe that it would be, on the whole, a very considerable improvement on our present condition. I confess I am not charmed with the ideal of life held out by those who think that the normal state of human beings is that of struggling to get on; that the trampling, crushing, elbowing, and treading on each other's heels, which form the existing type of social life, are the most desirable lot of human kind, or anything but the disagreeable symptoms of one of the phases of industrial progress.'

to transform human civilisation in the process of technological and social change.

What would be the Marxist answer to our question regarding the three cornerstones of economic development? It seems permissible, for the purpose of this discussion, to summarise it in the following way: The motive power of this process is the investing capitalist who, impelled by the profit incentive ensures technological advance and produces more surplus funds, which will be re-invested, thus keeping the machine going. The process continues in a self-propelling manner; more technical progress and a higher production potential (productivity) are continuously achieved. Owing to the structure of property, this increased productivity, which could easily support a general rise in consumption, is not utilised; the market glut generates tension and crises, which undermine the foundations of capitalistic society.

In the light of such an appraisal, it would be only natural to expect to find in the writings of Marx some specific thought on the problems of economic and technological progress in those countries which are referred to today as 'underdeveloped'. But, apart from a few allusions remarkable for their determinist note with regard to the obtaining prospects for economic development in regions like Western Asia or India, no special attention is given to the problems of change in underdeveloped countries.[1]

The reason is one which applies equally to the first two types of theory and to the views expounded by Marx, in spite of the great difference between them in vision, scope and level of analysis: they all deal with the capitalist system. Development in colonial or dependent areas formed a special case of capitalist expansion. The indifference to, or inability to see, the problems of independent underdeveloped areas as we see them today will become particularly clear when we examine the meaning of some of the concepts which occupy a major position in theories relating to capitalist development and in present-day thought on underdeveloped countries. We shall begin with the concept of underconsumption.

At first sight the concept of *underconsumption* in the Marxist sense appears to fit the situation in the destitute underdeveloped countries

---

[1] 'Not all nations have the same ability for capitalist production. Some primeval peoples ("Urvölker") like the Turks have neither the temperament nor the disposition for it. But these are exceptions.' Translated from K. Marx, *Theorien über den Mehrwert*, Stuttgart, 1921, Vol. III, p. 519.

Neo-marxist writers have, of course, dealt in detail with the problems of economic development and 'liberation' of underdeveloped countries. Yet their view of the economic potential of the underdeveloped areas was and is largely affected by their basic belief that the regimes in these regions are instruments of monopoly capitalism and cannot thus act as 'neutral' trustees for the economic promotion of the masses.

quite well. The central economic phenomenon in the state of under-development in these countries is the low per capita level of consumption as compared with corresponding data for economically advanced countries. Yet this state of underconsumption has only a superficial similarity to its counterpart in Marxian thought, as becomes immediately apparent when the relevant passages in Marxian writings are consulted.

In the *Communist Manifest* the recurrent commercial and industrial crises, which bring society to the verge of complete collapse, are closely and causally related to the phenomenon of overproduction. Business and industry are threatened with ruin because there is 'too much civilisation, too much food, too much industry, too much commerce'.[1] Similarly, in the third volume of *Capital*, we read: 'The last cause of all real crises always remains the poverty and restricted consumption of the masses as compared to the tendency of capitalist production to develop the productive forces in such a way that only the absolute power of consumption of the entire society would be their limit.'[2] Sweezy has dwelt at length on this issue in his *Theory of Capitalist Development*, whilst attempting to lend weight to a theory of underconsumption as one of the important principles of Marxian economics.[3]

For our present purpose, there is no need to discuss the interpretation of Marx's views on the connection between crises and underconsumption. What is important is the manifest difference in the meaning given to the concept itself. Underconsumption, in the Marxian as well as in the classical models, exists only as measured against the swollen forces of production which operate in an economic system marked *by a high* production potential and periodical eruptions into an unmarketable abundance. In contrast to this, the meaning of underconsumption in underdeveloped countries has a physiological ring; it is measured against a subsistence minimum, or a norm of consumption below which it should not fall. Its roots lie in exceedingly low levels of output which are, as a rule, due to a very low production potential. Even if, through some supra-natural event, an entirely different system of distribution came to replace the existing one, it would hardly be possible—given the low capacity of existing productive equipment—for more goods to be allotted to the average consumer. On the other hand, if the system of distribution remained unchanged but production was greatly increased, the impact on per capita consumption would be considerable.

[1] 18th authorised German edition, Berlin, 1918, p. 31.
[2] *Capital*, Chicago, 1933, Vol. III, p. 568.
[3] Cp. Paul M. Sweezy, *The Theory of Capitalist Development*, London, 1946, p. 180. Sweezy's position is relevant to the discussion of the extent to which in Marxian literature the underconsumption theory has a *central* place in the system.

IMPLANTED ECONOMIC DEVELOPMENT

Another important point of difference, despite an apparent common element, is the position of the surplus population in the Marxian system as compared with the present-day notion of surplus population in underdeveloped countries. In the Marxian system the concept of a relative surplus population is identical with that of the 'industrial reserve army'. Its origin is either technological unemployment consequent upon the introduction of labour-saving machinery or the slowing-down of the rate of accumulation, which produces employment crises. The existence of this labour reserve is an important factor in the inherent logic of the system. It means that industrial growth will not be arrested by a shortage of labour, since labour is, at slightly changing wages, always available and willing to serve the employer.[1] In underdeveloped countries the origin and character of the 'labour reserve'—if this expression can be used at all—are quite different. It is primarily a demographic phenomenon deriving from a decrease in the death rate, and it appears in the first instance as concealed rural unemployment, though it can be regarded, too, as a kind of reserve army for industrial expansion. It is not, however, an uprooted class of workers who are forced to accept the decisions of industrial entrepreneurs. These workers frequently resist the incentives offered them, and can afford to do this at least as long as they form part of the rural society and derive from it the means of supporting themselves—though on a level, it is true, which is often far below that offered by industrial employment.

Another aspect of Marx's view of the process of development is the role attributed to changes in social organisation as well as in methods of production within the global process of evolution. Economic development in a capitalist society is marked not only by the process of ceaseless accumulation but by continuous changes in production methods. There is no need to point out that these two main criteria did not apply to the situation in the stagnating underdeveloped countries of yesterday. Marx was fully aware of this stagnation. For him it was another case of the process of simple reproduction in self-sufficient societies, which reproduce themselves continually in the

[1] The whole concept which classical writers made use of in order to develop the law governing the supply of labour has a strange ring when applied to conditions in most underdeveloped societies. Cp., for instance, the formulation used by Adam Smith: 'The demand for men like that for any other commodity necessarily regulates the production of men.' Accordingly, to quote from Professor Lowe's paper, two balancing forces, the propensity to procreate and the available wage-fund, dominate the volume of labour supply. The funds which govern variations in labour supply are the result of saving, which itself arises from another alleged human propensity of the social mechanism: the desire to better our conditions.—Between these assumptions and the reality in underdeveloped countries there is a world of difference. It would be difficult to find a description more remote from reality in underdeveloped countries than this passage from Adam Smith.

same form.[1] The principle of simple reproduction on which these economies function means that the flow of production and consumption goods repeats itself without accumulation or changes in techniques; it follows the same patterns and keeps to the same scale as during previous generations.

In earlier papers dealing with specific issues in underdeveloped countries, the present writer dwelt on major points of difference between the two types of economies which make it necessary to apply different devices and methods for the solution of the various economic and social problems confronting the governments of underdeveloped countries.[2] Amongst these problems were traditional resistance to change, the scarcity of entrepreneurs, the absence of a skilled and acquisitive-minded working-class and, in general, the difficulty of finding quick solutions for problems resulting from the tensions and contradictions in underdeveloped countries now exposed after centuries of quiet and secluded existence, to the impact of modern world conditions.

We are thus driven to conclude that, although the immediate purpose of economic development, namely expansion of production, may be the same everywhere, there must be more than one type of process by which this purpose is achieved. Occasionally, distinct types of economic development may be found at the same time even in the same country, since only rarely is there complete homogeneity throughout a single country. Terms like 'mixed economies' or 'plural economies' point to the existence of several economic systems within one country's boundaries. Yet, if we attribute to each system a set of principles of its own, then we shall have to find several hypotheses to explain them, and we cannot be satisfied with a single theory.

Schumpeter

It has been stated above that almost the only time the capitalist process of production occasioned an important advance in the theory of economic development was when it came into full swing. Of more recent theories in this field, the major contribution is that of Schumpeter. Because of its unified view of the whole economic process, Schumpeter's concept of economic development seems to offer a promising basis for the attempt to build up a comprehensive theory of development. In recent literature much attention has, indeed,

---

[1] *Das Kapital,* Volksausgabe, 2nd ed., Vol. I, Stuttgart, 1919, p. 305.
[2] Cp. 'Aspects of Economic Reconstruction in East and West', *International Affairs,* 1946, pp. 521 ff.; 'Incentives for Economic Development in Asia', *Annals of the American Academy of Political and Social Science,* Vol. 276, July 1951, pp. 12 f.; see also *Proceedings of the 27th Institute,* Norman Wait Harris Memorial Foundation, Chicago, 1951, pp. 182 f. (mimeogr.).

IMPLANTED ECONOMIC DEVELOPMENT

been given to the applicability, or otherwise, of Schumpeter's theory of the economic process to the phenomena of economically backward countries. Our first question then, is, to what extent this theory, which was developed in order to explain the unique course of Western capitalism, will serve our purpose. Should it appear that the principles of this theory do not fit the conditions of under-developed countries, and should it be possible to find an adequate explanation of their failure to do so, this should help us to arrive at a satisfactory set of conclusions applicable to retarded economies won entering upon a new phase of their development.[1]

If economic development means a process of increasing produc-tivity, it is impossible to overlook the fact that Schumpeter's theory dismissed important cases of economic development as lying outside his province, although they constitute cases of genuine development in both mature and underdeveloped economies. There are, in ad-dition, inconsistencies in his theory which reduce the applicability of such a suggestive, though over-simplified, analogy.

These difficulties are caused by a fundamental limitation in Schum-peter's definition of economic development. Schumpeter insists that his concept of development comprises only such changes in economic life 'as are not forced upon it from without but arise by its own

[1] An important comment on Schumpeter's theory of economic development from the standpoint of its applicability to underdeveloped countries has been made by Professor H. C. Wallich in a (mimeographed) paper presented to the Third Meeting of Central Bank Technicians in Havana in 1952. In this paper, the main premises of Schumpeter's theory are examined in regard to their bearing on the phenomena of less-developed countries. Professor Wallich's line of thought is as follows: the generating force in Schumpeter's model is provided by the entrepreneur; the economic process is largely kept in motion by innovation and the goal is the establishment of a position of wealth and power for the entre-preneur. The situation in underdeveloped countries is found to be very different. To begin with the role of the entrepreneur, there is ample evidence that it is not he who is the main driving force in new development, but rather that this is the function of semi-public and public bodies. Mechanised production is not based on endogenous innovation but on transferred technology. The dominant goal of economic development is not personal enrichment for capitalists but a rise in the standard of living of the masses. Professor Wallich's consequent conclusion is, of course, that Schumpeter's model does not fit conditions in underdeveloped countries. As the discussion in the text shows, there are additional reasons for this lack of congruity.

Dr. H. W. Singer has dealt at some length with Professor Wallich's essay in his article 'Obstacles to Economic Development' (*Social Research*, Vol. XX, Spring 1953, pp. 19 f.). Dr. Singer analyses Professor Wallich's findings in order to explain the obstacles to economic development characteristic of underdeveloped countries.

Schumpeter's theory of economic development has been widely commented upon in many recent discussions of problems of economic development. Only a few writers who have recently dealt with this subject can be mentioned here: W. W. Rostow, *The Process of Economic Growth*, New York, 1952; R. Nurkse, *Aspects of Capital Formation in Underdeveloped Countries*, Oxford, 1953; Norman S. Buchanan and Howard S. Ellis, *Approaches to Economic Development*, New York, 1955.

initiative from within'.[1] But can we accept such an interpretation and all the implications of a concept of development based only on changes 'from within'? Let us take the case of a factory established in an underdeveloped Middle Eastern country by European capital at the height of its flow towards the East half a century ago. Is the establishment of a plant under the regime of the *capitulations* a case of economic development in the Schumpeterian sense? Looked at from the 'mother country', the establishment of the plant may perhaps be regarded as part of a genuine process of development fitting Schumpeter's theory; it is fed by the initiative and the capital of entrepreneurs of the metropolitan country and not by factors operating from without. But from the viewpoint of the capital-receiving country, the activities of these same founders would have to be classified differently, because the plant has been 'forced' upon it from without and thus lies outside the range of Schumpeter's idea of development; yet this exclusion from Schumpeter's definition would not make the new plant cease to be a case of genuine development, having in view precisely those goals which are the essential objectives of development activities in economically backward countries.

An even greater difficulty in accepting the implications of Schumpeter's model is its limitation to activities which are *not* caused by the 'mere growth of the economy as shown by the growth of population and wealth'.[2] According to Schumpeter, the effects of these factors of growth are currently absorbed and do not lead to the discontinuous changes essential to his concept.

The object of Schumpeter's limitation is, of course, to enable him to concentrate on one aspect of his conception of the development process—an aspect to which he devotes detailed reasoning. But, whatever his reasons may have been, it is impossible to bring the complex of vigorous development activities caused by trends of population growth and wealth into line with Schumpeter's restricted concept. Numerous recent reports on spectacular processes of economic expansion point to their close relationship to the growth of population and of new knowledge in the use of natural resources, etc. Schumpeter's definition of economic development would, indeed, leave out many crucial development phenomena in underdeveloped countries. His two 'negative' criteria can be applied to nearly all development activities in such countries. These are, indeed, caused by the fact of changes in data concerning real trends of growth and are based upon such data and upon an initiative which is exercised 'exogenously', i.e. from without, and frequently maintained from

---

[1] *The Theory of Economic Development*, Cambridge, Mass., 1949, p. 63.
[2] *Ibid.*

without for a considerable period. This is a major characteristic of the development process in underdeveloped countries. This finding does not dispute the existence of certain development processes in underdeveloped countries to which the criteria of Schumpeter's theory do apply. But what we have to determine here is the dominant trends and features, and these are not covered by him. The difficulties do not, however, end there; in Schumpeter's model the element of innovation is cardinal, whereas in 'derived' development in underdeveloped countries no novel technique is required. Yet the transfer of ready-made and proved techniques of production from elsewhere does not affect the possibility of a basic change in the economy concerned. This transfer may even have a positive content, since it saves the time and effort required to produce the change. New branches of industry in underdeveloped countries often have more modern technical equipment than the corresponding branches in the country from which this machinery comes.

Moreover, numerous processes and methods of production which have grown up locally, in order to meet the requirements of a region deriving from its specific geographical conditions, have also exhibited striking features of innovation. The necessity of expanding production in a densely populated underdeveloped area has, time and again, caused revolutionary changes in local agricultural techniques, and, in particular, in irrigation. Innovation is frequently the result of population pressure, a nexus not adequately allowed for in Schumpeter's model.

In general, the effects of growth and change in external conditions have been underrated by Schumpeter. Attention has already been drawn to the enormous potential and the basically unpredictable character of natural resources in an age of breathtaking technical progress. When the *Theory of Economic Development* was written this was already a familiar experience, and it has since become axiomatic. It is all the more surprising that Schumpeter did hardly take into account the tremendous impact that physical environment, including population trends and developments in technology and in the utilisation of resources, would have on economic systems in general and on the situation in underdeveloped countries in particular.[1] Yet he shared this lack of recognition with the man whose socio-economic analysis he admired, Marx; and both their theories remained

---

[1] The unwillingness of Schumpeter to concede this influence, though he felt its existence, is clearly brought out in the following sentence: 'Increase in productive resources might at first sight appear to be the obvious prime mover in the process of internal change. Physical environment *being taken as a constant* [the italics are mine, A.B.], . . . that increase resolves itself into increase of population and increase in the stock of producers' goods.' *Business Cycles*, Vol. I, New York and London, 1939, p. 74.

unsatisfactory as regards the present process of economic growth in 'post-capitalist' underdeveloped countries.

The main reason for the inability of these two outstanding thinkers to envisage a new status and potential of underdeveloped countries is, perhaps, their fundamental belief in the uniqueness of the development in the Western World. They were Occidentalists in their socio-economic credo and were not aware of the potential of growth existing in underdeveloped countries and destined to emerge from its latent state thanks to the increasing transferability of major factors of economic development.

SUGGESTIONS FOR A NEW THEORY

This phenomenon of transferability of major factors of production will form the focal point of the following reflections. The point of departure is replacement of the spontaneity of the economic process by an implanted mechanism. The implications of this approach for the construction of a theory of economic development in under-developed areas are obviously far-reaching. We shall start with a re-statement of the meaning of economic development and its goals in underdeveloped countries, and then go on to an appraisal of the factors, conditions and phases (and their interconnection) in the process of development itself.

Definition of Economic Development

1 Economic development in underdeveloped countries consists of a series of economic activities causing an increase in the productivity of the economy as a whole and of the individual earner, and also an increase in the ratio of earners to total population. The various phases of increasing productivity and of the structural changes in the economy, which constitute the process of development, may be concerned with such fields as utilisation of resources, production techniques, capital formation, labour efficiency and the acquisition of skill and knowledge. Many of the changes can be measured by comparing the volume and types of production of goods and services; their range extends from slight modifications to the 'creative destruction' of the existing system, to use a term coined by Schumpeter for the capitalist process. From this definition it becomes evident that the limitations discussed above as being part of Schumpeter's view of the process of economic development have been dropped from our concept.

2 The second definition to be given concerns the *goals* towards which economic development in underdeveloped areas progresses and which it aims to attain. These goals can be narrowed down to a

general rise in per capita consumption of physical as well as of immaterial goods.[1]

3 Improvement of income distribution is frequently included among the goals of economic development, although in many cases it is also one of the means of attaining it. This improvement may entail the removal of a stratified income distribution which runs parallel with the prevailing distribution of property, in particular landed property. In this context, income distribution and the change in it will also include the allotment of salaried positions in central and local governments.

Main Factors Reponsible for Western Economic Development and for Conditions in Underdeveloped Countries

The starting-point for any attempt to construct a theory of development in underdeveloped countries must be an analysis of the major factors and conditions responsible for economic growth in Western countries. Inadequate as such a condensed analysis must necessarily be, it nevertheless serves to establish the following factors as having played a major role in Western economic growth: (1) Capital formation of an impressive magnitude, as a continuous process increasing in scale and intensity, and including the formation of intellectual capital. The introduction of mechanical means of production was of paramount importance in this process, because it radically changed the rate of progress; (2) Operation of effective incentives either in the form of material rewards (profits) or spiritual inducements, or both; (3) Availability of an expanding market to absorb the rising flow of goods; (4) Tendency for a balanced ratio to be maintained between population growth and economic growth; (5) A succession of scientific discoveries and a readiness on the part of entrepreneurs and technicians to utilise them for the continual improvement of techniques of production; (6) A political regime and a social order conducive to economic development.

Since several of these factors either do not obtain at all in underdeveloped countries or obtain only partially, a theory of economic development built on the cornerstones of economic growth in Western countries would not fit conditions in underdeveloped countries. The situation there, however, is far from being clear-cut. It is marked by the presence, simultaneously, of factors characteristic of developed and of underdeveloped countries, with a consequent co-existence of advanced and retarded economic systems. For the

---

[1] Physical goods, as understood here, are consumer goods, such as food and other non-durable, as well as durable, consumer goods, whereas immaterial goods are primarily services in the fields of education and health, and governmental benefits such as security afforded by laws, public order, communications, etc.

purpose of this discussion, it is necessary to limit the analysis to those underdeveloped countries where, so far, none of the major factors responsible for capitalist development is in operation. Our next question, then, is to what extent the factors mentioned can be reproduced in underdeveloped regions. In attempting to answer this, the order of enumeration used in the preceding section will be maintained.

(1) *Capital formation:* It will be a considerable time before there is any possibility of achieving a rate of capital formation approaching the level attained in Western countries. Left to themselves, the local economies would in the majority of cases be incapable of maintaining a rapidly increasing population out of domestic savings—much less of supporting a rise in standards of living.

But, as soon as we abandon the determinist outlook in our approach to this problem in backward economies, the prospects change. If we transfer concepts, techniques and means of economic development from without and implant them in local conditions, we shall be able to change the process of 'simple reproduction', which has marked these economies for generations, into a process of expansion. We shall then discover that the potential for the mobilisation of capital resources is not negligible, and that funds in the form of voluntary and compulsory domestic savings and new types of international capital may generate a modest degree of economic growth. We may find that the unused potential of resources in the form of disguised unemployment and insufficiently explored natural resources will become an important reserve in the inventory of such areas. We shall find that, in spite of the considerable differences in the equipment of the various underdeveloped areas with resources, one aspect of the potential of capital formation has, in all of them, the same bearing on the pace and scope of economic growth: this common factor is the effect of the introduction of machinery, which has begun to transform the economic scene in underdeveloped regions all over the world.

(2) The *incentives* of a material and spiritual nature which worked with such success in the Western world have, in the past, not made themselves felt in underdeveloped countries. It is doubtful whether they can now be brought into action to the extent required to stimulate a comprehensive process of development in the immediate future. But if there is no profit incentive, substitute incentives can be implanted on a different level and may operate in a similar direction. Modern nationalism is one of these motive forces of economic development, and is apt to impel individuals as well as public and semi-public bodies towards new economic activities. On the same plane lies the acceptance of entrepreneurial functions by government agencies. The new programmes of economic and social

betterment may themselves become a driving power and strengthen the general trends towards a change in the economic climate.

(3) The absence of a steadily *expanding market* is a major obstacle to the development of a backward economy with a low level of consumption; without generation of purchasing power by the creation of employment on a broad front, the successful expansion of production will be impossible.

This is a concept which has been elaborated by R. Nurkse under the name of 'balanced growth'.[1] The creation of a state of 'balanced growth' is, again, not a spontaneous action. It demands not only the power to plan and carry out economic development, but also great knowledge of its laws and techniques. Some information is available on the attempts made hitherto in this field, with varying degrees of success, by governments in underdeveloped countries; in the light of this experience a policy of balanced growth may well become an important device of economic planning in underdeveloped countries.

(4) The attainment of a *'balanced ratio' of population increase to economic growth* is, at present, one of the least tractable problems in underdeveloped countries. The successful practice of birth control requires a considerable level of education and behavioural discipline. Among the masses in underdeveloped countries these qualities are rare. The *task* of producing a state of receptiveness for birth control is largely a matter for the government. It has to impart to the population the best available devices and techniques in an extremely delicate field.

(5) Obstacles to a rapid spreading of *scientific discoveries* and *modern techniques of production* beyond the advanced countries were for generations so formidable as to justify a classification of the regions of the world according to their degree of scientific enlightenment and economic progress. Within limited areas the former barriers to such progress have been surmounted. Modern techniques have been transferred to underdeveloped areas and the mobility of applied science may become the factor of outstanding importance in the transformation of less advanced economies.

There has been a remarkable local increase in scientific work in regions remote from the world centres of learning, and ground has been gained by the spirit of rationality, which is so important for the advance of economic progress. Whilst the lag between the advanced and underdeveloped countries is still considerable, the implantation of off-shoots of scientific progress in less advanced regions has become an established process.

(6) For the greater part of the period since the beginning of the

[1] R. Nurkse, *Problems of Capital Formation in Underdeveloped Countries*, Oxford, 1953.

industrial revolution, underdeveloped countries have not had the advantage of *political and social regimes conducive to economic development*. This problem continues to be a major issue even now, in spite of advances made in other fields and improvement in public administration in many countries. The character of the socio-political regime is of such crucial importance for our main theme that it would be justifiable to treat the problem of development in a retarded economy largely as a problem of political science. In no other branch of economics does the political element exert such an influence on motivation and the formulation of economic programmes as in the field under review here.

It is a common experience in underdeveloped countries that obstacles to economic development are primarily those presented by the continued existence of old-established political and socio-economic institutions in these countries. The traditional distribution of property, the control of real power by a political and social élite of landowners, and in particular the existing hierarchy of moral values and, associated therewith, many religious traditions, are either indifferent or hostile to the measures required for the transformation of an underdeveloped economy into a highly productive, expanding and progressive one.

To sum up: In underdeveloped countries major factors in economic development which were and are present in advanced countries are wholly or largely absent. Some of them, such as capital formation and labour skill, are indispensable, but they are, in principle at least, capable of developing in the course of time to a much higher level than that prevailing today. There are, however, other factors essential to economic progress, such as profit incentives, birth control and a growing effective demand which cannot be expected to operate in the immediate future. Here other expedients must be found. But this is not exclusively a question of available substitutes. The difference between the process of economic development in economically advanced and economically retarded countries lies also in a difference in the mechanism by which various elements of the socio-economic process are geared together and kept in motion.

The Mechanism of Economic Development
Capitalist development could rely for its mechanism on the operation of the profit incentive, setting in motion an automatic process by which the flow of goods continually increases as the re-investment of surplus funds feeds the further expansion of production. In the development of the economically advanced countries this is a spontaneous and unceasing process; as soon as it is set in motion it is hardly possible to single out any one phase which can be regarded

as particularly significant for the continuance of the process. In underdeveloped countries where this self-propelling force does not operate, everything hinges on the proper starting-up of the driving force and its efficient release of the other elements vital to the economic process.

In order of sequence it is reasonable to distinguish between three consecutive phases through which the development process will have to pass. The *first* phase is the phase of conception in which various lines of motivation and stress tend toward policy decisions; the *second* phase, the period of decision, is of crucial importance also because it often proves to be the first real test of the correctness of the assumptions and calculations of the development planner. It is in this phase that the lack of spontaneous capitalist activity has to be overcome by the application of suitable incentives and principles of economic organisation. They have to be implanted in an environment which is frequently unresponsive. The successful initiation of economic development therefore depends primarily on the success of a series of engrafting activities, i.e. the careful implantation of incentives, techniques and patterns of production. The *third* phase is a process of nursing and guidance, consisting mainly in directing the flow of available means into such external economies and such lines of goods production as are recognised as having priority by the agencies responsible for the direction of the process.

In a number of ways these phases are closely inter-connected, though the connection is not always evident. We shall consider some of their main characteristics.

The first phase may best be described as a situation of challenge, in which phenomena of tension, friction and pressure coincide with the formation and self-assertion of new ideas and objectives for the future economic and social development of the community. One of the most important sources of decisions to initiate processes of development is the growth and consolidation of nationalist movements in the young independent states which have sprung up in former colonial and dependent areas. In the action programmes of nationalist movements, a preponderant role is played by measures for economic 'liberation' by means of drastic changes in political and institutional patterns and of expansionist production policies. In the twentieth century the effect of the removal of an old-established regime by revolution is, from the economic viewpoint, another case of 'creative destruction'. Such a removal may give a major impetus to intensified economic growth. But there are numerous, less drastic changes on the economic plane which do not derive from economic causes. Thus defence requirements and the slogan of self-sufficiency in supplies account for the development of important industrial sectors in an underdeveloped economy, and add their weight to that of the other motive forces operating towards economic expansion.

Since development in underdeveloped countries is not a self-induced process generated from within, it needs a strong hand to guide and protect it—a function which, at least for a transitional period, will have to be performed by the authorities. This brings us, however, to problems characteristic of the next phases of the process of development, i.e. those pertinent to the executive functions of government.

Four functions can be listed here as cardinal government functions: (1) The function of deciding on acceptance and execution of development plans; (2) The nursing function, i.e. provision of a steady flow of means; (3) The pruning and clearing function, i.e. the removal of obstacles; (4) The controlling and guiding function.

In the nature of things, these activities in underdeveloped countries are largely governmental activities and all aim to generate, direct and maintain a process of induced economic development. For the reasons mentioned, an appropriate term for this kind of development would be 'implanted development'. This term brings out more clearly than any other the delicate and peculiar character of this series of activities, and in particular it suggests the very considerable skill required to guide and control the new development. It also draws attention to the need for suitable conditions of environment, which are vital to the successful growth of the implanted process.

The Control of the Economic Process
The question of the direction and control of the economic process is a central issue in underdeveloped countries. In working out a theory, consideration has to be given to this problem of responsibility for the development process—i.e. the question of who should carry out and control the course of economic development, and to what extent it can be directed by gearing the individual movements—in view of the frequent lack of agreement between those in charge of development and those who are affected by these activities and their results. But, apart from this aspect of the degree of identity of interest, the control function itself needs to be defined. It comprises, *inter alia*, (*a*) the adequate timing of the various steps to be taken in the course of the economic development and (*b*) the proper selection of the individual economic areas to be developed, with a view to directing the production of goods towards such areas, which will ensure their smooth absorption by consumers.

The judgment of the prospects of this direction 'from above' depends, of course, on the nature of the relationship between government and the '*volonté générale*', the general will of the people.

IMPLANTED ECONOMIC DEVELOPMENT

Modern schools in the field of political science and theory of government do not accept the view that those in power are unable or unwilling to devise a policy against their own group interest. They assume, indeed, that a government can work on an essentially neutral plane and promote the interests of the community at large, irrespective of changing political situations. Experience in Western countries supports such an assessment of the ability of modern administrations to carry out programmes of economic development which are devised with a view to promoting the welfare of the whole population and ensuring that the benefits aimed at reach the proper quarters.

A different situation confronts us when we come to deal with conditions of public administration and government in underdeveloped countries. Here an approach which contents itself with examining the formal criteria of a modern adminstration would be insufficient. In the majority of underdeveloped countries, governmental activities, even if they have adjusted themselves to the administrative patterns of more advanced countries, still adhere to customs and traditions in the field of public administration which prevailed in the countries concerned many generations ago. Real power has not yet been divorced from the classes which occupy the highest rank in the community by their wealth and social standing, and which because of this standing were able to appropriate to themselves the lion's share of political, economic and social influence. It must then be asked, whether governments with such a structure can be regarded as faithful and reliable executors of a development policy whose main objectives will, if attained, of necessity bring about the removal, or at least the reduction, of overpowerful class and partisan interests.

To the question thus formulated, the answer must obviously be negative. Yet the implication that there are virtually only two types of government policy—for and against development—is felt to be a misleading simplification. There are few underdeveloped countries today which are ruled by a class-dominated government for the benefit of a limited section of the population only. The existence of a streamlined pattern of class-interests culminating in direction of government actions by these same interests has to be proved. In particular, in the sphere of economic development policies, experience does not bear out such an assumption. There is a wide range of variation between the attitudes of different governments towards economic development, the majority of them gravitating towards an active policy of broad economic expansion. In a sense, it could be contended that one of the few features common to left and right regimes alike consists in their positive interest in the growth of

259

production. The benefits of this expansion spread far beyond the narrow limits of the class represented by the initiators of such development activities.

The fact that the benefits deriving from an expanding production are distributed among a much larger section of the population is due in part to the close affinity of development schemes to the ideologies underlying modern nationalist movements. The field of economic development is one of the more important outlets for the satisfaction of nationalist urges; and it is for this reason that development programmes in the more advanced underdeveloped countries have met with such a remarkable degree of response.

Another aspect of the changing scene of political and social institutions which influences the pace and scope of economic progress in underdeveloped countries is the emergence of new forms of entrepreneurship based on a combination of public agencies with private capital and labour or tenant groups. In some cases the record of their practical achievements is so impressive that it calls for careful consideration in every attempt of appraising the effects and expediency of governmental planning in an economically underdeveloped society.

In other cases the value of the new entrepreneurial forms lies clearly in their pilot character and in their effect on the acceleration of the pace of development.

It would seem that here, as well as in many other fields of economic development, the economist needs to pay more attention to one of the far-reaching implications of the mechanism of modern economic growth: the more a process of development becomes impersonalised and 'automatised', the easier it will be to transplant it to other areas and to find, or train, substitutes for the once indispensable entrepreneur. The underdeveloped areas are only just starting out on this route. Yet the belief is there that this route leads to the goals they have set themselves, even if the road signs and vehicles are quite different from those which served economic development in other regions.

APPENDIX I
INSTITUTIONAL RESISTANCES TO ECONOMIC CHANGE

THE power of persistence of social and political institutions in a changing world was always a fascinating subject for independent social research; yet rarely before have there been more abundant opportunities for studying their bearing on the pace and direction of economic advance than at the present time. In fact the contemporary scene in many underdeveloped countries is primarily the story of increasing contradictions and conflicts between new ideas and forces and the established political and socio-economic structure. This treatise is not a sociological study, yet the importance of these problems in our context makes it necessary to summarily appraise the significance of social and political institutions and patterns from the viewpoint of their bearing on economic development.

ESTABLISHED ORDER AND ECONOMIC PROGRESS

Frequently, the main reason for the continued existence of social institutions is the perpetuation of economic privileges afforded by them to specific groups and individuals. These privileges are recognised and rationalised in spite of the inequality they create and maintain, and they can exist as long as the institutions and relationships supporting them have a powerful and respected position in society. Modern notions of an economically progressive society deny the legitimacy of such privileges and insist that each member of society has the same clearly defined rights and obligations.

This is a relatively new situation and one grown out of specific conditions in the Western world. Countries which have not yet experienced the development of the individual from a princely subject or feudal tenant to a modern citizen still have to pass through phases in which traditional institutions fight for their existence. In this struggle the defenders of the established order discourage, or even prevent, economic progress if such progress means a limitation or abolition of privileges accorded to those associated with these institutions. Why should landowners who occupy, either by law or through custom, key positions in a legislative body be helpful in the introduction of land reform? They prefer the maintenance of existing conditions, not only for the immediate benefit they enjoy, but also because every drastic change exposes them and even their tenants to unknown experiences and risks. The conflict between security and progress is particularly characteristic of present conditions in under-developed countries, where it may appear in many situations. For the purpose of our discussion, the following institutionalised patterns and relationships should be considered:

1 The large family unit or joint family.
2 Tribal structure and discipline.
3 Authoritarian relationships within the same economic sector based on the property rights such as:
   a The landowner-tenant relationship.
   b The employer-worker relationship.
4 Glorification of ascetic and contemplative attitudes.
5 Vested political power and economic change.
6 Impact of illiteracy.
7 Dependence of colonial areas on the metropolitan country.

This is not an exhaustive list. There are numerous other established structures and attitudes in underdeveloped societies which can likewise form obstacles to economic progress. Yet their discussion would not reveal essentially new features for the clarification of our fundamental issue: the resistance of social and political institutions to economic change and progress.

1 THE LARGE FAMILY UNIT OR THE JOINT FAMILY

A cornerstone of traditional Asian societies, in particular of the Indian and Chinese, is the 'joint family'—a family association comprising three or even four generations living under the same roof. A somewhat loose division of labour regulates the relations between the various members of the joint family. Economically, the system works by a pooling of income in money or in kind, and a common household. Socially, a most important aspect is the affinity of the members to the family unit as a spiritual and physical centre. As long as the ties of membership are strong, the mobility of the individual members is very limited. They tend to cling together and to remain

rooted in their common living place, thus offering considerable resistance to the demands of a progressive and expanding economy for
mobile labour. New economic developments following the discovery
of natural resources, or the opening of railways, ports and other new
communications, have to face the obstacles implied in the joint family
system. At the same time the same new developments tend to create
or increase the degree of mobility of labour which is necessary to
maintain a steady production. But it is not only a question of family
mobility. In a remarkable article on 'The Root of the Social Problem
in India' (in *Associations*, 1954, No. 12), Fr. J. D'souza, a member of
the Jesuit Order, arrives at far-reaching conclusions as to the necessity
of a complete change in the psychological and family mentality in
India. The people of India must 'realise that the virtues of devotion
to the family and the caste and the community understood in the
old sense—which was the Indian type of altruism—has become a
danger in the new context; that the older loyalties are, under new
conditions, not loyalty but treason to the State. That is the root of
the social problem in India. To achieve this psychological change
it is necessary that the currents of ideas from the democracies of the
West from which we have received our new inspirations should
continue to flow as before.'

2 TRIBAL STRUCTURE AND DISCIPLINE

A unique feature of many old-established societies in Asia and Africa
is the nomadic way of life to which even now millions of people
adhere. A line of demarcation divides the settled population from the
nomads, who as a rule are organised in tribal associations. Their life
follows patterns which are widely different from those of the settled
population. The loyalty of the members of the tribal organisation
resembles the bond which ties a member of the joint family to his
little unit.

Yet instead of the lack of mobility which is so characteristic of the
joint family, we face in the case of nomadic society an excessive
mobility of the social unit as a whole, a feature which is no less disturbing to economic progress than excessive immobility. Both forms
are extremes and now increasingly exposed to the impact of modern
economic development. But the question of mobility is only one
aspect of the attitude of a primitive tribal society towards economic
and social progress. The very notion of a planned, regular activity
for the purpose of solving the livelihood problem would have been
abhorrent to the mentality of the genuine Beduin until a few decades
ago. Forethought, systematic preparation for what is to come, is
absent from the rules of conduct which regulated the life of the

Beduin. Thus, he, too, needs drastic adjustment of his mind before he will be able to perform economic standard functions in a modern society.

3 AUTHORITARIAN RELATIONSHIPS WITHIN THE SAME ECONOMIC SECTORS

Another set of obstacles to economic advance in Oriental societies can be seen in the unique position of economic interests which were at one time regulated entirely, and now still quite frequently, by the power and prestige vested in property.

We refer primarily to the following relationships:

a Landowner-tenant farmer.

b Employer-employed.

No rigid and uniform pattern exists for these relationships. Numerous variants can be found in each category, but all of them frequently show an ingenious mechanism to secure the preservation of power and wealth for those already in possession of them. Since Oriental societies are predominantly agrarian, the predominant form of wealth is land, and efforts to secure wealth are directed to the maintenance and expansion of landed property in the hands of landowners. The combination of political power, land-ownership and frequently other forms of wealth was for generations practically indestructible.

Often the possession of knowledge, too, was monopolised by the same group and helped to perpetuate the existing distribution of power. It has remained in force in many underdeveloped areas up to the present day, except in cases where violent changes have broken the alliance.

Though there were phases in the history of land tenure conditions where the interests of tenants were considered with a certain benevolence, the factual regulation of the mutual relations always aimed at the strengthening, or at least the preservation, of the superior position of privileged landowner groups with respect to the allocation of wealth and power. Against this, considerations of genuine economic advance, the need for improvement of soil, crops, cattle, etc., receded into the background, notwithstanding the potential beneficial effect they would have had on the situation of the landowners themselves.

Early relations between employers and workers in pre-capitalist stages showed a similar pattern of authoritarian relationship. It could not produce the results obtained through the new approach to the problem of labour as developed in Western countries; an approach which aims at the transformation of the worker into an interested and important partner in the process of production by giving him equal status as a contracting party and a rising share in the yield of his work.

4 THE GLORIFICATION OF ASCETIC AND CONTEMPLATIVE ATTITUDES OF MIND (INCLUDING ECONOMICALLY WASTEFUL RELIGIOUS TENETS)

In order to ensure that a socially and economically dispossessed population acquiesced in its situation, change itself was deprecated. In certain religious systems of the Orient, such as early Islam and Judaism, living in conformity with tradition was sanctioned as an ultimate value and supported by premiums and promises of spiritual rewards. In other Oriental religions the defamation of material enjoyment was extended to a deprecation of worldly life as a whole, and redemption through emancipation from worldly needs or even worldly forms of existence became a supreme goal. Where such evaluations struck root, the underprivileged masses could acquiesce with the idea that fate had imposed suffering and hardship on them as transitory conditions, and that it was not up to them to change them.

This issue has an eminently practical significance. The indifference of certain underdeveloped societies to conditions of squalor and utter destitution and to the possibilities for economic and social betterment presents a fundamental obstacle to the realisation of this progress. Numerous observers have dealt with this problem and explained many of the present-day phenomena in the social sphere by the impact of religious teachings. More recently, Professor F. S. C. Northrop has given considerable thought to the questions involved.[1]

The gist of these Asian teachings is that the nature of things in this world of here is transitory; 'these things do not deserve an unswerving attachment on the part of man, himself in part a transitory phenomenon. The Hindu blandly accepts the ugliness of the world around him and aims merely to attain spiritual equanimity within it. If everything runs in a circle coming back at some later date to precisely where it is now, what is the point in trying to change the present state of affairs? One merely hastens, if this be possible, the time when tomorrow becomes today.

'The good is to dedicate one's self to the indeterminate, all-embracing immediacy which is Brahman and to give up determinate desires and actions, treating them as the worldly and transitory things which they are.'[2] Although there are considerable differences

[1] The text quotations concerning Hindu attitudes refer in particular to his book *The Taming of the Nations*, A Study of the Cultural Bases of International Policy, New York, 1952, pp. 74, 78.
[2] The contrast reveals itself in particular around the value of action. In the

between the various philosophies of Asian religious systems, the Chinese mind—according to Northrop—in common with other Far Eastern mentalities, is basically 'fatalistic'. 'Confucianism shares with Hinduism, Buddhism and Taoism a non-aggressive, non-militant attitude in contradistinction to the religions of the West.'

Though from the viewpoint of certain militant traits Islam can compare with the West, it, too, has a contemplative outlook towards many social phenomena. In particular, Sufism became responsible for an attitude of surrender and submission to Providence and fate belittling even the necessity of gaining a regular livelihood.

In the present writer's *State and Economics in the Middle East*, the social ethics of Moslem Society were briefly confronted with doctrines and teachings to be found in the works of leading Protestant and Calvinist authors. Whereas Protestant and Calvinist ethics expressly place a very high value on work and vocation—'Work is first and foremost the one and only divine purpose of life'—Islamic social doctrines lack, though certainly not as decidedly as the Hindu and East Asian religions, the incentive to enter vigorously into worldly affairs.[1]

Against such complacency and not seldom denial of the value of worldly efforts, the tenets and inducements of Western religious and mundane philosophies form a stark contrast.

These tenets were conducive to the deployment of enterprise and economic activities which needed a disposition of mind towards new ventures in production and distribution; they implied, as Marx expressed it, a constant 'revolutionising of the means of production'. Such a constant alertness and disposition of mind for the possibilities of change in the world of goods production is indeed the complete extreme of the 'Oriental' state of mind referred to above.

It stands to reason that such a different approach to issues of 'ultimate' values has analogies also in other spheres of thought and intellectual life. Rationality, i.e. the detached scientific observation and analysis of nearly all phenomena of life, is a feature of Western spiritual development since the Renaissance; it has contributed

Bhagavad Gita the story is told of Arjuna who finds himself on the field of battle about to kill members of his own clan on his enemy's side. Arjuna faces a dilemma in his desire to avoid killing of his relatives and not lose his prestige as a warrior. He submits his problem to God Krishna who encourages him to act as warrior. In the course of the dialogue Arjuna asks whether knowledge is not superior to action and Krishna answers that there is a twofold path in this world. Action will be good only if performed with non-attachment and indifference.

[1] An attitude characteristic for the Western mind is that of a Puritan like Bunyan who stressed in *Pilgrim's Progress*: 'At the day of Doom men shall be judged according to their fruits. It will not be said then: "Did you believe?", but "Were you doers or talkers only?" Quoted in Bonné, *State and Economics in the Middle East*, 1955, 2nd ed., p. 355.

enormously to the spread of modern economic development because it makes possible the calculability of many economic reactions and events along the lines of economically and legally rational behaviour. Economic interests in the modern sense strive everywhere towards a prior calculation of prospects and towards the removal of all those hindrances—legal, psychological and others—which hamper a free disposal of goods and services. This rationality has been achieved in most Western economic societies. The situation is still very different in Oriental countries.

A report by an academic teacher who spent fourteen years in Egypt is revealing in its discussion of the contradictory and unexpected attitudes of students which he witnessed. These attitudes cannot be explained by the usual references to an Oriental enigma or unconcern, but need a deeper, more penetrating understanding. The teacher referred to explains these phenomena by pointing to a discrepancy in fundamental psychological and intellectual disposition:

'. . . It is because they do not really live in a universe governed by the principle of causality, one where hard work will be followed by good marks "as the night the day", but in a universe of religious bounty. In the same way, I once heard a person ask a railway guard a specific simple question—something like, "Will the train be stopped at such and such a station?"—and the answer was, in all sincerity: "That, Madam, is as God wills!" '[1]

A great deal of discussion has been going on for some time on the question of the practical impact of such attitudes and outlooks. It was certainly a tremendous influence in the past, and though the effect of the traditional doctrines and teachings is waning everywhere, they are still a potent factor.

Modern India shows many examples of how even moderate programmes of economic advancement can be frustrated by such attitudes. The significance of overcoming the mentality of the masses educated towards indifference to conditions of material life, has been forcefully pointed out by Mr. Nehru time and again before the Indian Parliament.

Mr. Nehru, it is true, disapproved of compulsory measures to be used for the speeding up of reforms, but acknowledged that to some extent such a programme might be envisaged and beneficial here. He stressed the necessity of shaking India out of the 'mental rut' encouraged by an ancient social system, which in the traditional Hindu caste structure compels vast numbers to remain in overcrowded occupations and to stay for unnumbered generations in overpopulated areas, while other occupations and immense

[1] Owen Holloway, 'University Students of the Middle East', *Journal of the Royal Central Asian Society*, January 1951.

areas of unutilised but potential farm lands cry out for development. '. . . as a people we in this country are proud to be too philosophical, indeed to be too metaphysical, all of us in a greater or lesser degree.'[1]

Rehabilitation projects in India, which are such an urgent necessity, had not worked fully, because large numbers 'preferred living in hovels in one place than living in a good house with land to work on 200 or 500 miles away'. Mr. Nehru added that some peoples who had been transferred to better sites had preferred to return to old squalid conditions in their overcrowded ancestral home sites and hinted that in such cases compulsory settlement might have to be considered in the national interest.

'I suppose the reason for our living and following a rather definite, set and precise way of life is that our social system has been rigid. . . . Our professions, our castes, etc., have rather petrified it. Our social life has to undergo a change to fit in modern economic conditions. . . . The old National Planning Committee recommended that every graduate or every person getting a diploma or degree should not be given the diploma until he had put in a year's labour in a field or factory or somewhere.'

Mr. Nehru rejected any attempt to solve India's economic problems on the Russian pattern, though 'there is much in the Russian example that is very helpful to us and from which we can learn'. He urged Parliament to 'remember the high price that Russia paid for it, the price of tighening the belt not for a month or a year, but for a generation'. . . . 'We cannot do it, at least not under democratic processes dear to Indians.'[2]

5 VESTED POLITICAL POWER AND ECONOMIC CHANGE

Societies in many underdeveloped countries, and in particular in Oriental countries, show a rigidity of government structure and of government institutions which tends, as a rule, to arrest modern economic progress. The traditional Oriental state is a class state, i.e. it is run by a dominating class composed primarily of landowners, by means of an efficient and developed technique to maintain its rule. New fields of economic activities are supported or promoted only in so far as they are in line with the interests or ideas of the ruling groups. If modern economic life in the West has grown largely owing to the conditions and opportunities Western state development has offered to a free citizen in a democratic society, then, we must conclude, the absence of such conditions has had a negative effect on economic and social progress in regions without

[1] See *New York Times*, October 24, 1951. [2] *Ibid.*

such Western heritage. The absence of a truly representative government, of an equitable taxation system, of personal and economic security for the citizen and his enterprise, of impartial application of the law, of a genuine sense of social justice, of vital public services in the fields of education, health, housing, etc.—all this means an immense handicap for the formation of a progressive economic society. Quite frequently, ingeniously conceived development programmes have failed because of these deficiencies. It is not that such backward state structures could not one future day achieve the economic and social goals of more advanced societies. But it has been found that the process cannot be telescoped. Where the attempt has been made by a premature use of imitated patterns, the results were not encouraging. The approximation of Eastern state life to that of Western democracies is a long and wearisome process. For it is easy to imitate Western patterns; but the new forms remain mere façades if they are not fitted into the local setting and if they do not become a constituent part of the particular social and political framework of the countries concerned.

The introduction of the franchise has frequently been turned into a tool of the various factions and cliques already in power, who, sometimes under the guise of democracy, continue their old autocratic rule. The adherence to the precepts and practices of modern statehood is quite frequently nothing but lip service, and, even worse, is being used to obstruct genuine progress. In these circumstances the small groups which are honestly concerned with the progress of democracy, regarded by them as vital for the welfare of their country, have an extremely difficult task. As against them, the new popular movements which appeal to the masses work without refined programmes. They are not interested in long-term programmes of political education nor in a carefully elaborated adjustment of old political and social patterns to new ones. Their programmes combine, in a language understandable to everybody, slogans of national, political and economic 'liberation,' sometimes with dramatic success.

The question may be asked as to why those classes who are at present in an overwhelming majority, the rural population, have today, as before, no weight in the representative bodies of many Eastern countries. Some of these countries have indeed long had Parliaments or representative bodies, either for the whole country or for special sections. Yet these representative bodies reflect primarily the interests of the ruling classes. There exist well-established techniques to deprive the underprivileged classes of their influence in public life. The majority of the peasants everywhere are poor, frequently extremely poor; a large percentage are tenants only. They are economically dependent on their landlords. Efforts to provide them with education are either stifled or only reluctantly carried out. There exist only modest beginnings for the organisation of the population on the basis of clear-cut economic associations or independent class interests. Only rarely have rural or urban working-classes come forward as coherent political groups sending their deputies to the Parliament and making effective demands there. The same is true also in respect of the small peasants.

6 THE IMPACT OF ILLITERACY

In contrast to conditions in Western countries, the majority of inhabitants in underdeveloped countries is still illiterate. The printed word, which has attained a significance for the making of modern society far beyond anything thought possible a few generations ago, does not reach these populations. Any educational programme to be carried out through reading and writing is thus severely limited in its application. Economic progress is today in a hundred ways dependent on the spread of written information as to the use of improved devices and methods of production, distribution, handling of goods, etc., and, on a general plane, on the co-operation of the enlightened citizen with the bodies responsible for the implementation of development plans. The degree of illiteracy still prevalent in underdeveloped societies slows down the pace of their adjustment to levels of modern progressive economies.

7 THE DEPENDENCE OF COLONIAL AREAS ON THE METROPOLITAN COUNTRY

Mention has already been made of the important issue presented by the political status of the underdeveloped colonial areas. In an age dominated by movements for economic betterment, the declared economic policy of the government could become the practical and concrete expression of these trends on a national plane. It is probable that a completely independent country will devise methods of economic policy and planning quite different from those which would be proposed were the country under a colonial administration. The policy goals of an independent state are determined by its own interests. Foreign claims or foreign intervention concerning the determination and safeguarding of these interests are not admitted. As against this, the government of an area with a dependent status is just not able to ignore the economic interests of the dominating power; it is the latter which guides production and distribution, and controls the economic and social system of the country. This has not always a negative effect on the indigenous economy but as a rule either goals or pace of the economic development in subject countries are considerably affected by foreign control.

The influence of foreign domination on dependent territories has made itself felt mainly in three directions:

a In the preservation of inherited forms of land tenure which secured the position of the landowners who accepted or supported the foreign rule;

b In the growth of the sector of primary production working for export, while other branches of the local economy remained neglected;

c In the lack of promotion of those general economic activities which would have benefited primarily the local population as against the forced development of specific areas advantageous to foreign interests.

APPENDIX II

TABLES

No. 1

Crude Birth Rates

	1935–9	1950	1951	1952	1953	1954
(a) Countries with low growth potential:						
France†	15·1	20·6	19·6	19·3	18·8	18·8*
Belgium	15·5	16·9	16·4	16·7	16·6	16·7
Sweden	14·5	16·4	15·6	15·5	15·4	14·6
Czechoslovakia‡	17·1	23·3	22·8	22·2	21·2	20·5
Canada	20·3	27·1	27·2	27·9	28·2	28·7
U.S.A.	17·1	23·5	24·5	24·7	24·6	24·9
Australia	17·2	23·3	23·0	23·3	22·9	22·5
U.K.§	15·3	16·3	15·8	15·7	15·9	15·6
(b) Countries with transitional growth potential:						
India‖	33·8	24·9	24·9	24·8	26·7	28·4
Chile	32·9	34·0	33·9	32·7	34·7	34·3*
Thailand	34·9	28·4	29·3	29·1	31·0	
Japan¶	29·2	28·2	25·4	23·5	21·5	20·1
(c) Countries with high growth potential:						
Egypt	42·8	44·4	44·8			
Puerto Rico	39·1	39·0	37·6	36·1	35·1	35·9*
Mexico	43·5	45·5	44·6	43·8	45·0	46·4
Ceylon	35·7	40·4	40·5	39·5	39·4	36·2
Venezuela**	32·7	42·6	43·8	43·7	46·1	46·8

Source: *Demographic Yearbook*, 1955, U.N., pp. 608–19.

* Provisional.
† France ex Saar.
‡ Data 1950 to 1954 not computed by the Statistical Office of the U.N.
§ 1949: Rates computed on population including armed forces outside country and merchant seamen at sea.
1950: Rates computed on population including merchant seamen at sea.
‖ Prior to 1947, registration area of former British Provinces, comprising approximately 75% of former India, not including Burma. Beginning 1947, registration area of Republic of India, not including French India which became a part of India November 1, 1954.
¶ Japanese nationals in Japan only. Prior to 1953 excluding Amami Islands.
** Excluding Indian jungle population, estimated at 56,700 in 1950.

TABLES

Crude Death Rates

	1935–9	1950	1951	1952	1953	1954
(a) Countries with low growth potential:						
France†	15·6	12·7	13·4	12·3	13·0	12·0*
Belgium	13·2	12·5	12·6	11·9	12·1	11·9
Sweden	11·7	10·0	9·9	9·6	9·7	9·6
Czechoslovakia	13·2	11·5	11·4	10·6	10·5	10·4
Canada‡	9·8	9·0	9·0	8·7	8·6	8·2
U.S.A.	11·0	9·6	9·7	9·6	9·6	9·2
Australia	9·6	9·6	9·7	9·4	9·1	9·1
U.K.§	12·2	11·7	12·6	11·4	11·4	11·4
(b) Countries with transitional growth potential:						
India‖	22·6	16·1	14·4	13·6	15	13·2
Chile	23·7	15·0	15·0	13·0	12·4	13·1*
Thailand	16·4	10·0	10·3	9·7	9·4	
Japan¶	17·4	10·9	10·0	8·9	8·9	8·2
(c) Countries with high growth potential:						
Egypt	26·9	19·1	19·3			
Puerto Rico	19·0	9·9	10·0*	9·2	8·1	7·6*
Mexico	23·3	16·2	17·3	15·0	15·9	13·1
Ceylon	24·5	12·6	12·9	12·0	10·9	10·4
Venezuela**	17·9	10·9	11·1	10·8	9·9	10·1

Source: *Demographic Yearbook*, 1955, U.N., pp. 650–9.

* Provisional.
† France ex Saar.
‡ Ex Yukon and Northwest Territories.
§ 1949: Rates computed on population including armed forces outside country and merchant seamen at sea.
1950: Rates computed on population including merchant seamen at sea.
‖ Prior to 1947, registration area of former British Provinces, comprising approximately 75% of former India, not including Burma. Beginning 1947, registration area of Republic of India, not including French India which became a part of India November 1, 1954.
¶ Japanese nationals in Japan only. Prior to 1953 excluding Amami Islands.
** Excluding Indian jungle population, estimated at 56,700 in 1950.

APPENDIX II

Natural Increase

	1935–9	1952	1953	1954
(a) Countries with low growth potential:				
France	0·5	7·0	5·8	6·8
Belgium	2·3	4·8	4·5	4·8
Sweden	2·8	5·9	4·9	4·2
Czechoslovakia	3·9	11·6	10·7	10·1
Canada	10·5	19·2	19·6	20·5
U.S.A.	6·1	15·1	15·0	15·7
Australia	7·6	13·9	13·8	13·4
U.K.	3·1	4·3	4·5	4·2
(b) Countries with transitional growth potential:				
India	11·2	11·2	11·7	15·2
Chile	9·2	19·7	22·3	21·2*
Thailand	18·5	19·4	21·6	
Japan	11·8	14·6	12·5	11·9
(c) Countries with a high growth potential:				
Egypt	15·9			
Puerto Rico	20·1	26·9	27·0	27·4
Mexico	20·2	28·8	29·1	33·3
Ceylon	11·2	27·5	28·5	25·8
Venezuela	14·8	32·9	36·2	36·7

Based on data from the two preceding tables.

  * Provisional.

Income Increases and Birth Rates within 33 Nations

Income per Capita* 1925–34 dollars	Trend of birth rates† per 1,000 1935–9	Income per Capita* 1925–34 dollars	Trend of birth rates† per 1,000 1935–9
525	15·07	300	20·66
500	15·56	275	21·30
475	16·20	250	21·94
450	16·84	225	22·57
425	17·47	200	23·21
400	18·11	175	23·85
375	18·75	150	24·49
350	19·39	125	25·13
325	20·02	100	25·76

Source: S. Raushenbush, *People, Food, Machines*, Washington, 1950, Appendix 7.

  * See notes to following table.

TABLES

Per Capita Income (1925–34 Dollars) and Birth Rates (1935–9)
per 1,000—33 Nations

	Income			
	1925–34 dollars*	1948 dollars	Birth rates†	Trend‡
U.S.A.	525	792	17·1	13·7
Canada	521	787	20·2	13·8
New Zealand	457	690	18·8	15·7
United Kingdom	425	642	15·0	16·7
Switzerland	424	640	15·4	16·7
Argentina	430	649	24·3	16·5
Australia	392	592	17·3	17·7
Netherlands	358	540	20·3	18·7
Eire	308	465	19·4	20·2
France	287	433	14·9	20·8
Denmark	279	421	17·9	20·1
Sweden	287	433	14·5	20·8
Germany	290	438	19·3	20·7
Spain	257	388	22·2	21·7
Belgium	240	362	15·3	22·3
Chile	248	374	34·2	22·0
Norway	237	358	15·1	22·3
Austria	230	347	14·8	22·6
Czechoslovakia	214	323	17·9	23·0
Greece	180	272	28·3	24·0
Finland	171	258	20·0	24·3
Hungary	165	249	20·2	24·5
Japan	159	240	29·7	24·7
Poland	165	249	25·4	24·5
Portugal	144	217	28·2	25·2
Latvia	161	243	17·6	24·6
Italy	154	232	23·2	24·8
Estonia	160	242	15·9	24·7
U.S.S.R.	152	229	44·2	24·9
Bulgaria	119	180	24·2	25·9
Rumania	112	169	30·2	26·1
Lithuania	97	146	23·3	26·6
India	90	136	34·7	26·8

* Data from Louis H. Bean, quoted in Raushenbush, *loc. cit.*
† The trend of birth rates was developed from figures given by W. S. Thompson and from League of Nations figures. The equation is $y_e = 28·31 - ·0255_x$ for 1925–34 dollars.
‡ In 1948 dollars for the same period, the trend of the equation is $y_e = 29·48 - ·02_x$.

APPENDIX II

Expectation of Life

		At birth		At the age of 20 years	
		Males	Females	Males	Females

(a) Countries with low growth potential:

		Males	Females	Males	Females
France	1950–1	63·6	69·3	68·4	53·4
Belgium	1946–9	62·0	67·3	48·0	52·3
Sweden	1946–50	69·04	71·6	52·1	54·0
Canada	1950–2	66·3	70·8	50·8	54·4
U.S.A.	1952	68·6		51·6	
Australia	1946–8	66·1	70·6	49·6	53·5
U.K.	1953	67·3	72·4	50·2	54·9

(b) Countries with transitional growth potential:

		Males	Females	Males	Females
India	1941–50	32·5	31·7	33·0	32·9
Chile	1952	49·8	53·9	42·7	47·1
Thailand	1947–8	48·7	51·9	39·8	42·7
Japan	1953	61·9	65·7	48·0	51·4

(c) Countries with high growth potential:

		Males	Females	Males	Females
Egypt	1936–8	35·6	41·5	39·8	46·1
Mexico	1940	37·9	39·8	37·6	40·0
Ceylon	1952	57·6	55·5	49·5	47·2
Israel	1954	67·5	70·5	51·7	54·0

Source: *Demographic Yearbook*, 1955, U.N.

TABLES

No. 7

Percentage Distribution of the Gainfully Occupied Population in
Certain Underdeveloped and High Income Countries

Country	Year	Primary industries	Secondary industries	Tertiary industries
Oriental Countries:				
Egypt	1919*	69	8	22
,,	1938*	71	8	21
,,	1949*	66	11	24
India	1919*	72	11	16
,,	1931*	67	10	22
,,	1951‖	71·1	16·4	12·5
Japan	1931*	51	19	30
,,	1950†	49	36	15
,,	1954‖	45·9	40·1	14
Malaya	1947†	67	19	14
Philippines	1939‡	74	18	8
,,	1948†	66	14	20
Thailand	1937‡	89	7	4
,,	1947†	85	11	4
Turkey	1938*	82	8	10
,,	1950†	85	10	5
Israel	1954§	18	50	32
Cyprus	1946‖	37·4	32·9	29·7
Pakistan	1951‖	76·5	13·8	9·7
High Income Countries:				
Australia	1947†	17	58	25
Canada	1951†	21	57	22
Netherlands	1947†	21	52	27
Switzerland	1941†	21	57	22
United Kingdom	1951†	9	67	24
U.S.A.	1950†	14	60	26

Sources: * *Processes and Problems of Industrialization in Underdeveloped Countries*, 1955, U.N., p. 104.

Computed from absolute numbers:
† *I.L.O. Year Book of Labour Statistics*, 1954, pp. 10–35.
‡ *Demographic Yearbook*, 1949–50, U.N., p. 262.
‖ *I.L.O. Year Book of Labour Statistics*, 1955, pp. 20–2.
§ Israel Central Bureau of Statistics: Survey of Manpower, June 1954.

Definition of industries:
Primary   = Agriculture, Forestry, Hunting, Fishing and Mining.
Secondary = Manufacturing and Construction.
Tertiary = Electricity, Gas, Water and Sanitary Services, Commerce, Transport and Storage, Communication, Hotels, Domestic Service, Public Services, Activities not adequately described, etc.

277

National Income

Net Geographical Product by Industrial Origin at Current Prices

Country and currency unit	Year	Total value	Percentage distribution					
			Agriculture	Manufacturing and construction	Trade	Transport and communication	Government	All others
High Income Countries:			%	%	%	%	%	%
United Kingdom (million £)	1948	10,349	6	46	13	10	7	18
	1949	10,945	6	46	14	10	6	18
	1950	11,847	6	46	14	10	6	18
	1951	13,227	5	47	13	11	6	18
	1952	13,575	6	46	12	11	7	18
United States (1,000 million dollars)	1938	67·1	9	27	17	10	13	24
	1948	223	10	37	19	8	9	17
	1950	238·6	7	38	18	9	10	18
	1951	276·9	7	39	17	8	11	18
	1952	289·7	7	38	18	8	12	17
Canada (million dollars)	1938	4,259	13	34	13	11	10	19
	1948	12,185	16	39	15	10	7	13
	1950	14,934	14	39	14	10	8	15
	1951	17,463	16	38	14	10	8	14
	1952	18,402	14	38	14	10	9	15
Denmark (million kronen)	1938	14,900	22	33	16	9	7	13
	1948	18,476	21	35	15	9	8	12
	1950	22,041	21	36	15	9	8	11
	1951	24,128	20	36	15	10	8	11
	1952	25,374	22	34	15	10	8	11

TABLES

Country	Year									
Israel (million £I.)	1950	337·6	10	36		15	6	15		18
	1953	1,130	12	29·1		12	8	23		16
	1954	1,461	14	28		13	8	21		16
Low Income Countries:										
Turkey (million £T.)	1938	1,620	49	16		10	5	10		10
	1950	8,964	50	16		11	5	10		8
	1953	14,696	49	17		11	6	9		8
	1954	14,273	42	20		11	7	10		10
India (1,000 million rupees)	1948	87·3	48	17		19		5		11
	1950	95·5	51·2	16		17		4·5		11·3
	1951	100·1	49·9	17·3		17·1		4·5		11·2
	1952	98·7	48·5	17·8		17·3		4·7		11·7
	1953	106·1	50·9	17		16·2		4·6		11·3
Pakistan (million rupees)	1949	16,814	61·2	6·5		—	2·6	4·8		24·9
	1950	17,088	60·5	6·6		—	2·9	5		25
	1951	18,347	61	6·3		—	2·8	5·7		24·2
	1952	18,082	60	6·7		—	2·9	5·7		24·7
Egypt (million £E.)	1950	873	40	11		15	6	22		6
	1952	836	32	11		14	7	27		9
	1953	857	32	11		15	7	27		8
Syria (million £S.)	1950*	1,250	44·2	10		13·2	9	7·5		16·1
	1953	1,360	64		13		4		19	
	1954	1,650	65		12		7		16	
Lebanon (million £L.)	1950	1,045	20	17		29	4	7		23
	1953	1,155	19	16		30	5	6		24
	1954	1,185	19	15		30	4	6		26

Sources: *Statistical Yearbook*, 1955; * *Economic Development in the Middle East*, 1954–5, U.N., 1956; Data for 1950 computed from *Bulletin Economique de la Chambre de Commerce Alep*, 1953.

APPENDIX II

Real Per Capita Income at Constant Prices

Year	India‡	Israel‡	Turkey‡	Burma*	United Kingdom*	U.S.A.†	Canada†§
1938			87			58	56
1939						63	59
1946					87	86	87
1947				81	86	84	86
1948	93		89	94	88	87	87
1949	94		79	84	91	84	88
1950	93	94	90	79	93	91	91
1951	94	106	100	89	96	95	95
1952	97	92	—	92	96	97	98
1953	100	100		100	100	100	100
1954				104	104	96	94

Source: *Statistical Yearbook*, 1955, U.N.

    * Per capita gross domestic product at market prices.
    † Per capita gross national product at market prices.
    ‡ Per capita national income.
    § Beginning 1949, including Newfoundland.

Percentage of Net Domestic Product contributed by Manufacturing, 1938, 1939 and 1949–52

Country	1938	1939	1949	1950	1951	1952
Low Income Countries :						
Egypt	—	8·0	—	11·0	—	—
India*	—	—	15·9	15·3	—	—
Israel†	—	—	—	24·3	—	—
Japan	24·1	—	26·9	25·7	25·6	22·8
Philippines	—	—	11·6	12·0	13·5	13·5
Thailand	9·9	—	11·5	12·7	—	—
Turkey	11·6	—	11·2	10·0	—	—
High Income Countries :						
Canada	24·0	—	29·2	29·9	29·4	29·2
United Kingdom‡	—	—	35·7	36·2	36·9	35·8
U.S.A.§	22·4	24·8	29·3	31·2	32·0	31·1

Source: *Processes and Problems of Industrialization in Underdeveloped Countries*, 1955, U.N., p. 105.

    * Including construction.
    † Including mining and public utilities.
    ‡ Before stock valuation adjustment.
    § The figures on which the percentages are based do not include profits on public enterprises.

TABLES

Index Numbers of Volume of Total and Per Capita Food Production
(*pre-war average = 100*)

Region	Total food production Average 1948–9 to 1952–3	1953–4	1954–5	1955–6 (prelim- inary)
Western Europe	107	123	124	125
North America	141	152	150	158
Latin America	125	135	141	142
Oceania	112	121	121	127
Far East (excluding China)	104	115	116	119
Near East	120	144	141	139
Africa	125	141	143	140
All above regions	118	132	132	135
WORLD*	110	122	123	126

Region	Per capita food production Average 1948–9 to 1952–3	1953–4	1954–5	1955–6 (prelim- inary)
Western Europe	97	109	109	109
North America	118	120	117	121
Latin America	93	93	95	94
Oceania	93	93	91	93
Far East (excluding China)	86	91	91	92
Near East	99	113	109	106
Africa	103	110	110	106
All above regions	99	105	104	105
WORLD*	96	103	102	104

Source: F.A.O., *The State of Food and Agriculture*, Rome, 1956, p. 10.

* Including estimates for the U.S.S.R., Eastern Europe and China.

APPENDIX II

Coefficient of Industrial Absorption of the Population

Country and Period	Annual Increment* in		Ratio of industrial employment increment to population increment
	Population (thousands)	Industrial employment (thousands)	
			%
Egypt:			
1927–37	161	4·9	3·0
1937–48	324	30·0	9·3
India:			
1911–21	1,200	40·0	3·3
1921–39	3,302	25·0	0·8
1939–45	3,365	150·0	4·5
1945–48	3,072	22·8	0·7
Mexico:			
1930–45	314	8·0	2·5
Philippines:			
1918–48	294	3·5	1·2
Turkey:			
1927–48	358	5·7	1·6
New Zealand:			
1915–28	29	2·3	8·1
1928–38	15	2·1	13·8
1938–49	25	3·7	14·7
Australia:			
1913–28	93	7·6	8·2
1928–38	67	11·4	17·1
1938–50	105	33·0	31·5

Source: *Processes and Problems of Industrialization in Underdeveloped Countries*, 1955, U.N., p. 139.

* Approximate arithmetic averages.

TABLES

No. 13
Estimated Consumption of Major Sources of Energy Expressed in Terms of Coal Per Capita

Country	In metric tons				Index numbers			
	1929	1937	1952	1954	1929	1937	1952	1954
Canada	5·21	4·91	6·86	6·88	100	94	132	132
U.S.A.	6·57	5·89	7·78	7·62	100	90	118	116
United Kingdom	4·11	4·28	4·57	4·78	100	104	111	116
Ceylon	0·09	0·08	0·11	0·09	100	89	122	100
Cyprus	0·07	0·12	0·31	0·43	100	171	443	614
India	0·07	0·09	0·11	0·11	100	129	157	157
Iraq	0·02	0·04	0·21	0·27	100	200	1,050	1,350
Israel	—	—	0·82	0·90	—	—	—	—
Japan	0·74	0·93	0·96	0·97	100	126	130	131
Pakistan	—	—	0·05	0·05*	—	—	—	—
Syria†	0·05	0·08	0·21	0·24	100	160	420	480
Turkey	0·09	0·13	0·28	0·34	100	144	311	378
Egypt	0·14	0·13	0·22	0·24	100	93	157	171

Source: *Statistical Yearbook*, 1955, U.N.

  * 1953.
  † Including Lebanon.

No. 14
Estimated Consumption of Steel Per Capita

Country	In kilograms			Index numbers		
	1936–8	1952	1954	1936–8	1952	1954
Canada	151	358	274	100	237	181
U.S.A.	318	518	478	100	163	150
United Kingdom	227	317	324	100	140	143
U.S.S.R.	—	35	41	—	—	—
Ceylon	4·1	5·7	5·6	100	139	137
India*	3·8*	5·1	6·0	100	134	158
Iraq	10	21	18	100	210	180
Israel†	42†	114	185	100	271	440
Japan	80	58	72	100	73	90
Lebanon‡	—	42	79	—	—	—
Pakistan*	—	4·7	2·9	—	—	—
Syria‡	9	8	21	100	89	233
Turkey	10	18	16	100	180	160
Egypt	11·9	7·6	10·6	100	64	89

Source: *Statistical Yearbook*, 1955, U.N., p. 308.

  * 1936–8: Pakistan together with India.
  † 1936–8: Palestine.
  ‡ 1936–8: Lebanon and Syria together.

Electric Power: Installed Capacity and Production in Selected Countries

Country	Year	Installed capacity thousand kw.	Installed capacity kw. per capita	Production million kw.h.	Per capita production kw.h.
Underdeveloped Countries:					
Egypt	1946	249	13		
	1951			576	28
India	1952	2,772	8	6,120	17
	1953	3,097	8	6,697	18
	1954	3,221	9	7,522	20
Iraq	1951			169	33
Israel*	1949	109	93	(1948) 217	301
	1950	109	80	(1952) 557	342
	1951	139	88	(1953) 633	379
				(1954) 746	434
Japan†	1937	6,978	100	30,391	434
	1952	11,148	130	51,647	604
	1953	11,889	137	55,698	642
	1954	13,015	148	59,605	677
Lebanon	1952			150	115
Pakistan*	1950	105	1·4	188	2·5
	1952	144	2	305	4
	1953	152	2	410	5
Syria	1950			81	25
	1952			99	29
	1954			129	35
Turkey†	1937	167	10	190	11
	1952	438	20	1,020	46
	1953	505	22	1,183	53
	1954	538	23	1,387	60
World's Highest Income Countries:					
Australia*	1937	1,356	198	3,972	581
	1952	2,621	303	11,297	1,308
	1953	2,972	337	12,045	1,366
	1954	3,417	380	13,587	1,512
Canada*	1937	6,374	562	30,009	2,647
	1952	11,854	821	66,104	4,581
	1953	13,084	885	69,978	4,734
Netherlands†	1937	1,746	203	3,485	405
	1952	2,904	280	8,599	828
	1953	3,249	310	9,603	915
Switzerland†	1937	2,130	510	7,043	1,685
	1952	3,230	671	12,881	2,675
	1953	3,440	705	13,465	2,761
	1954	3,590	729	13,180	2,677
United Kingdom	1937	9,365	198	24,231	512
	1952	18,407	365	63,897	1,267
	1953	19,837	392	67,372	1,331
	1954	21,256	419	74,706	1,471
U.S.A.†	1937	44,370	341	146,476	1,136
	1952	97,312	620	463,055	2,949
	1953	107,354	672	514,169	3,221
	1954	118,878	732	544,645	3,354

Source: *Statistical Yearbook*, 1955, U.N., pp. 274–87.

   * Enterprises generating primarily for public use.
   † Total installed capacity.

TABLES

Per Capita Production of Basic Raw Material—Kilograms

Coal

	1909–13 avg.	1925–9 avg.	1935–9 avg.	1948	1950
India*	47	76	76	89	97
Japan	335	539	643	418	464
Turkey	41	73	145	206	208
U.S.A.	5,500	4,600	3,150	4,020	3,331
U.K.	6,800	5,000	5,150	4,300	4,342
France†	1,700	1,200	1,800	1,060	1,212

Iron

	1913				
India*	0·6	3	5	4·3	4·8
Japan	4·6	15·3	34·3	10·0	28
Turkey	§	§	§	5	5·3
U.S.A.	342	327	220	375	397
U.K.	261	132	160	188	193
France†	228	232	159	157	185

Steel

India*	0·2	1·6	2·7	3·5	4
Japan	4·5	29	76	21	58·3
Turkey	§	§	§	5·0	4·5
U.S.A.	346	417	325	540	579
U.K.	195	171	245	297	327
France†	179	212	164	173	206

Cement

		1929–39			
Egypt		8	22	39	50
Palestine-Israel‡		61	102	205	302
India*		1·4	3·3	4·6	7·3
Japan		52	79	24	53·8
Turkey		4·8	14	17	19
U.S.A.		243	142	232	255
U.K.		95	147	173	196
France		101	105	129	177

Calculated from U.N. *Monthly Bulletins of Statistics* and League of Nations *Statistical Yearbooks*.

* India and Pakistan up to August 1947.
† Excluding Saar production, which would increase the figures by ⅛ to ⅓.
‡ Figures for all Palestine before 1948. Israel figures for 1948, 1950.
§ Turkey's first iron and steel works was erected in 1939.

Percentage Average Annual Increase (+) or Decrease (−) in
Manufacturing and Population

(a) manufacturing.
(b) population.
(c) manufacturing per head of population.

		1871/5–1881/5	1881/5–1896/1900	1896/1900–1911/13	1911/13–1926/9	1926/9–1936/8
United States	(a)	+5·1	+4·2	+5·2	+3·8	+ 0·2
	(b)	+2·3	+2·1	+1·9	+1·5	+ 0·8
	(c)	+2·7	+2·1	+3·2	+2·3	− 0·6
Germany	(a)	+2·7	+5·1	+4·0	+0·9	+ 2·2
	(b)	+1·0	+1·1	+1·4	+0·5	+ 0·5
	(c)	+1·7	+3·9	+2·5	+0·4	+ 1·7
United Kingdom and	(a)	+1·6	+1·8	+1·6	−0·03	+ 2·9
Ireland	(b)	+1·0	+0·9	+0·9	+0·4	+ 0·4
	(c)	+0·6	+0·9	+0·7	−0·4	+ 2·5
France	(a)		+2·5	+3·5	+2·0	− 1·0
	(b)		+0·1	+0·2	−0·1	+ 0·2
	(c)		+2·4	+3·3	+2·1	− 1·1
Russia—U.S.S.R.	(a)		+6·6	+4·8	+2·3	+20·2
	(b)		+1·4	+1·8	+0·7	+ 1·3
	(c)		+5·1	+2·9	+1·6	+18·7
Japan	(a)			+9·0	+7·6	+ 6·6
	(b)			+1·2	+1·3	+ 1·6
	(c)			+7·7	+6·2	+ 4·9
India and Burma	(a)			+4·3	+2·7	+ 4·9
	(b)			+0·5	+0·5	+ 1·3
	(c)			+3·8	+2·1	+ 3·5
				1931–6	1941–5	
China	(a)			+7·5	11·0	
	(b)			—	0·2	
	(c)			+7·5	+10·8	

Source: F. Hilgerdt, *Industrialization and Foreign Trade*, 1945.

Major Components of Government Receipts in Selected Countries, 1939 and 1949 to 1953

(as percentage of total receipts)

Country and year	Taxes on income and wealth	Taxes on land, land produce and livestock	Customs receipts	Other taxes	Total tax receipts
Egypt:					
1939	1	16	42	10	69
1951	11	4	59		74
1952 E	15	8	55		78
1953	15	8	8	44	75
1954	14	11	9	46	80
1955	17	10	8	47	82
Iran:					
1939 E	11	—	31	39	81
1954 E	14	—	21	25	60
Iraq:					
1939	6	11	34	10	61
1950	11	15	31	13	70
1951	10	15	31	12	68
1952	11	12	33	11	67
1953	6	8	23	8	45
1954	6	7	31	8	52
Israel:					
1951	28	—	13	41	82
1952	29	—	12	40	81
1953	36	—	12	36	84
1954	37	—	13	36	86
1955	37	—	23	27	87
Jordan:					
1939	—	—	37	39	76
1951 E	—	—	44	22	66
1952 E	—	—	42	20	62
Lebanon:					
1939	17	—	60	—	77
1951 E	16	1	24	48	89
1952 E	15	1	24	48	88
1953 E	13	1	30	43	87
Syria:					
1939	10	30	1	36	77
1951 E	8	10	26	39	83
1952 E	12	18	22	34	86
1953	12	14	19	40	85
1954	12	15	19	40	86
Turkey:					
1939	25	9	18	30	82
1951	30	2	8	49	89
1952	22	—	12	59	93
1953	24	—	12	61	97
1954	24	—	9	62	95
1955	26	—	10	56	92

Source: Published Government Budgets and official statistical yearbooks. Figures represent closed accounts unless otherwise noted, E = Estimates.

APPENDIX II

National Income: Government Expenditure and Revenue, Development Expenditure and Direct Taxes on Income and Wealth as Percentages of National Income*

Country and year	National income in millions of national currencies	Government expenditure as percentage of N.I.	Government revenue as percentage of N.I.	Development expenditure of Government as percentage of N.I.	Direct taxes on income and wealth as percentage of N.I.
		%	%	%	%
Egypt:					
1948	1,017	9·3	9·7	1·3	1·8
1950	860	19·0	18·5	3·8	2·1
1951	750	25·4	24·7	4·3	2·6
1952	836	25·1	20·8	—	2·7
1953	857	21·7	20·7	—	2·7
India:					
1948–9	87,300	5·7	4·9	1·1	1·6
1951	99,900	6·0	5·5	—	1·3
1952	98,600	6·8	6·8	—	1·5
1953	106,000	6·6	5·5	—	1·3
Israel:					
1950	338	26·4	11·3	10·6	2·8
1951	531	23·9	12·9	12·4	3·6
1952	765	24·1	14·0	10·8	4·1
1953	1,050	23·8	16·0	10·9	4·5
1954	1,450*	24·6	15·2	12·1	5·7
Lebanon:					
1950	830	10·2	10·0	2·4	1·6
1952	1,085	8·2	11·5	1·8	1·6
1953	1,155	9·8	9·8	2·1	1·3
Syria:					
1952	1,220	21·7	21·2	1·5	2·6
1953	1,410	14·0	15·4	—	1·9
Turkey:					
1948	7,815	18·0	16·6	1·3	5·2
1950	6,951	22·9	21·8	2·5	6·8
1951	8,229	17·3	16·1	1·2	5·0
1952	9,607	16·5	14·0	1·3	3·3
1953	10,454	16·7	14·8	1·7	3·2
1954	14,273	14·8	13·7	6·0	3·3

Sources: Absolute figures of Government Expenditure and Revenue: *Review of Economic Conditions in the Middle East*, U.N., 1951–2, p. 76. *Statistical Yearbook*, 1953, U.N., pp. 455–92. *Statistics of National Income and Expenditure*, 1955, U.N.

* From *Israel's National Income 1950–54*, by Daniel Creamer and others, (Falk Project for Economic Research in Israel), Jerusalem, 1956.

SUBJECT INDEX

SUBJECT INDEX

290

SUBJECT INDEX

SUBJECT INDEX

SUBJECT INDEX

For Product Safety Concerns and Information please contact our EU
representative GPSR@taylorandfrancis.com
Taylor & Francis Verlag GmbH, Kaufingerstraße 24, 80331 München, Germany